WEST ACADEMIC PUBLISHING'S LAW SCHOOL ADVISORY BOARD

JESSE H. CHOPER
Professor of Law and Dean Emeritus,
University of California, Berkeley

JOSHUA DRESSLER
Distinguished University Professor, Frank R. Strong Chair in Law
Michael E. Moritz College of Law, The Ohio State University

YALE KAMISAR
Professor of Law Emeritus, University of San Diego
Professor of Law Emeritus, University of Michigan

MARY KAY KANE
Professor of Law, Chancellor and Dean Emeritus,
University of California, Hastings College of the Law

LARRY D. KRAMER
President, William and Flora Hewlett Foundation

JONATHAN R. MACEY
Professor of Law, Yale Law School

ARTHUR R. MILLER
University Professor, New York University
Formerly Bruce Bromley Professor of Law, Harvard University

GRANT S. NELSON
Professor of Law, Pepperdine University
Professor of Law Emeritus, University of California, Los Angeles

A. BENJAMIN SPENCER
Earle K. Shawe Professor of Law,
University of Virginia School of Law

JAMES J. WHITE
Robert A. Sullivan Professor of Law Emeritus,
University of Michigan

CRIMINAL PRETRIAL ADVOCACY

Second Edition

■ ■ ■

Peter J. Henning
Professor of Law
Wayne State University Law School

Leonid Feller
Partner, Kirkland and Ellis LLP
Lecturer, University of Michigan Law School

Karen McDonald Henning
Associate Professor of Law
University of Detroit Mercy School of Law

AMERICAN CASEBOOK SERIES®

The publisher is not engaged in rendering legal or other professional advice, and this publication is not a substitute for the advice of an attorney. If you require legal or other expert advice, you should seek the services of a competent attorney or other professional.

American Casebook Series is a trademark registered in the U.S. Patent and Trademark Office.

© 2013 LEG, Inc. d/b/a West Academic Publishing
© 2016 LEG, Inc. d/b/a West Academic
    444 Cedar Street, Suite 700
    St. Paul, MN 55101
    1–877–888–1330

West, West Academic Publishing, and West Academic are trademarks of West Publishing Corporation, used under license.

Printed in the United States of America

ISBN: 978-1-63460-257-0

To Alexandra, Grace, and Molly, you are the best by taking after your mother.

P.J.H.

To Lucas F., Logan E., Levi F., and Lucy G., whom I hope to have taught the only lesson that really matters: to never give up and never surrender.

L.F.

To Molly, Alexandra, and Grace, who fill our lives with joy, love, and laughter.

K.M.H.

PREFACE

We wrote this book and created the accompanying case files to fill a gap in the materials available for the skills curriculum at law schools. Most schools offer courses in pretrial advocacy, but the focus of these classes (and accompanying class materials) is on civil cases in which students undertake the steps in a typical torts or contracts action. This usually involves drafting a complaint, conducting the different steps in the discovery process—such as document requests, interrogatories, and depositions—and drafting and arguing a motion for summary disposition.

For those who have practiced criminal law, the pretrial process in a prosecution could not be more different from a civil case. Depositions are not allowed in many states, the government generally has gathered the physical evidence and documents before (or shortly after) the charges are filed, and issues related to searches and interrogations are of paramount importance. Many of the issues that arise in the pretrial phase of a criminal case require the development of knowledge and skills that is distinct from what is presented in the typical civil pretrial advocacy course.

The pretrial phase of a criminal case is crucial to the ultimate outcome of the proceeding. Estimates vary across jurisdictions and by type of case, but it is generally accepted that the vast majority of criminal prosecutions are resolved through a plea bargain without ever going to trial. That makes the pretrial process even more important. And here again, the difference from a civil case could not be more stark—issues related to negotiating a plea agreement and dealing with sentencing do not arise in the civil arena. Thus, we created these materials to help train students who will focus on criminal cases, a field that employs a large number of law graduates, including many who have just passed the bar exam and need training before they represent actual clients in prosecutions.

This book provides a framework for students to develop oral advocacy and writing skills in the context of the pretrial phase of a criminal case. The Chapters explain the various stages of a criminal case as the charges are formulated and the process of criminal adjudication more forward. In addition, instructors are provided with detailed case files through a website that allow students to address a range of issues as both prosecutors and defense counsel. Students have the opportunity to undertake a number of basic tasks in a criminal case: draft the foundational charging documents; consider issues related to appointment of counsel, pretrial detention, and discovery; and prepare preliminary motions on issues that frequently arise in criminal cases, including motions to dismiss counts of an indictment, to suppress evidence, and to quash subpoenas. Students simulate the pretrial process by presenting arguments to the court relating to these issues as well as conducting evidentiary hearings where appropriate. Finally, because most criminal prosecutions are resolved short of trial, the cases are constructed to allow students to negotiate a plea bargain and argue contested sentencing issues.

The case files are designed to give the students options in how to proceed, much like a practicing attorney will have to make decisions regarding the best course to pursue. For example, there are a range of charges that can be filed, facts that could lead to the pretrial detention of one or more defendants, and questions about the conduct of the police in the investigation that could support a motion to suppress evidence. The book furnishes students with the basic legal doctrines related to the different phases of a criminal case so that those who have not previously studied criminal procedure can master the basic principles. This material provides a basis to pursue more advanced legal research on a particular topic that arises in a case. Finally, the case files can lead to negotiations for a plea bargaining and issues related to the appropriate sentence.

We are hopeful that instructors will find these materials provide all that is necessary to conduct a successful course in criminal pretrial advocacy. It is possible to supplement the course with materials from a local jurisdiction, and the cases have not been placed in a specific location so that these materials can be easily integrated into the course.

In the course of drafting the book and putting together the case files, we received the generous assistance of a number of people. At Wayne State University, Ms. Olive A. Hyman was instrumental in helping to organize the case files. At the University of Detroit Mercy, Mr. Jeff Johnson provided administrative and technical support. And, finally, at both schools and the University of Michigan, the students who took our Criminal Pretrial Advocacy and Federal Prosecution and Defense classes provided us with valuable feedback on the content of both the casebook and the case files.

PETER J. HENNING
LEONID FELLER
KAREN MCDONALD HENNING

Janurary 4th, 2016
Detroit, Michigan

ABOUT THE AUTHORS

Peter J. Henning is a Professor of Law at Wayne State University Law School. He was a law clerk to Chief Judge Murray M. Schwartz of the United States District Court for the District of Delaware, a Senior Attorney in the Enforcement Division of the U.S. Securities & Exchange Commission, and a Trial Attorney in the Criminal Division of the U.S. Department of Justice, assigned to the Fraud Section.

Leonid Feller is a partner with Kirkland & Ellis LLP, and a Lecturer at the University of Michigan Law School. He was a law clerk to Judge David A. Nelson of the United States Court of Appeals for the Sixth Circuit and an Assistant United States Attorney for the Eastern District of Michigan.

Karen McDonald Henning is an Associate Professor of Law at the University of Detroit Mercy School of Law. She was a law clerk to Judge Collins J. Seitz of the United States Court of Appeals for the Third Circuit, an associate at Skadden, Arps, Slate, Meagher & Flom, and an Assistant Corporation Counsel in the Appellate Division of the District of Columbia Office of the Corporation Counsel (now the Office of the Attorney General).

Summary of Contents

Preface V
About the Authors VII
Table of Cases XVII

PART 1. PRELIMINARY PROCEEDINGS

Chapter 1. Complaint and Arrest 3
A. Contents of a Criminal Complaint 3
B. Arrest Warrants 4
C. The Decision to File Charges 6

Chapter 2. Initial Appearance and Appointment of Counsel 19
A. Initial Appearance 19
B. Appointment of Counsel 20

Chapter 3. Speedy Trial Act 27
A. Basic Requirements of the Speedy Trial Act 27
B. Delay Related to the Defendant 29
C. Other Delays 30

Chapter 4. Pretrial Detention and Bail 35
A. Pretrial Detention 35
B. Release on Bail 38

PART 2. PREPARING THE CASE FOR PROSECUTION

Chapter 5. Preliminary Hearing 43
A. Procedures 43
B. Benefits of a Preliminary Hearing 45
C. The Bindover Decision 46

Chapter 6. The Grand Jury Indictment 49
A. Historical Background 49
B. Investigatory Power 49
C. Challenging Grand Jury Subpoenas 52
D. The Charging Authority 55
E. Requirements for a Valid Indictment 56
F. Amending the Information or Indictment 60
G. Use of Grand Jury Subpoenas After Indictment 61
H. Arraignment 62

Chapter 7. Discovery and Notice of Defenses 75
A. The Scope of Criminal Discovery 75
B. Rule 16 Discovery 76

C. Rule 15 Depositions 78
E. Rule 17(c) Trial Subpoenas 79
E. *Brady* Material 80
F. Jencks Act (Rule 26.2) 83
G. Witness Immunity 85
H. Notice of Defenses 87

Chapter 8. The Pretrial Conference 91

PART 3. PRETRIAL MOTIONS

Chapter 9. Pretrial Motions and Rule 12 Procedures 99

Chapter 10. Challenging the Charges and Motions in Limine 103
A. Jurisdiction and Failure to State an Offense 103
B. Venue 104
C. Bill of Particulars 105
D. Joinder of Offenses and Defendants 107
E. Motions in Limine 113

Chapter 11. Motions to Suppress Evidence for Violations of the Fourth Amendment 117
A. Searches Pursuant to a Warrant 117
B. Warrantless Searches and Seizures 120
C. Limits on Claims for Fourth Amendment Violations 129

Chapter 12. Motions to Suppress Statements and Eyewitness Identifications 133
A. Fifth Amendment *Miranda* Requirements 133
B. The Sixth Amendment Requirements 138
C. Eyewitness Identifications 140

Chapter 13. Pretrial Motions, Memoranda of Law, Evidentiary Hearings, and Oral Arguments 143
A. Pretrial Motions 144
B. Drafting Memoranda of Law 146
C. Conducting an Evidentiary Hearing 154
D. Preparing for Oral Argument 164

PART 4. PLEA AGREEMENT AND SENTENCING

Chapter 14. Plea Agreements 181
A. Types of Guilty Pleas 182
B. Contents of Plea Agreements 183
C. Withdrawal of Guilty Pleas 186

Chapter 15. Sentencing **199**
A. Section 3553(a) Factors 199
B. The Sentencing Guidelines 201
C. Presentence Investigation Report and Sentencing Hearing 203
D. Probation and Supervised Release Violations 204

INDEX 207

TABLE OF CONTENTS

PREFACE V
ABOUT THE AUTHORS VII
TABLE OF CASES XVII

PART 1. PRELIMINARY PROCEEDINGS

Chapter 1. Complaint and Arrest 3
A. Contents of a Criminal Complaint 3
B. Arrest Warrants 4
    1. Probable Cause 4
    2. Content and Execution of a Warrant 5
C. The Decision to File Charges 6

Chapter 2. Initial Appearance and Appointment of Counsel 19
A. Initial Appearance 19
B. Appointment of Counsel 20

Chapter 3. Speedy Trial Act 27
A. Basic Requirements of the Speedy Trial Act 27
B. Delay Related to the Defendant 29
C. Other Delays 30

Chapter 4. Pretrial Detention and Bail 35
A. Pretrial Detention 35
B. Release on Bail 38

PART 2. PREPARING THE CASE FOR PROSECUTION

Chapter 5. Preliminary Hearing 43
A. Procedures 43
B. Benefits of a Preliminary Hearing 45
C. The Bindover Decision 46

Chapter 6. The Grand Jury Indictment 49
A. Historical Background 49
B. Investigatory Power 49
C. Challenging Grand Jury Subpoenas 52
D. The Charging Authority 55
E. Requirements for a Valid Indictment 56
    1. Duplicity and Multiplicity 57
    2. Notice Requirement 58
    3. Including Essential Elements 59
F. Amending the Information or Indictment 60

G. Use of Grand Jury Subpoenas After Indictment 61
H. Arraignment 62

Chapter 7. Discovery and Notice of Defenses 75
A. The Scope of Criminal Discovery 75
B. Rule 16 Discovery 76
C. Rule 15 Depositions 78
E. Rule 17(c) Trial Subpoenas 79
E. *Brady* Material 80
    1. Favorable or Exculpatory 81
    2. Suppression 81
    3. Material 82
    4. Department of Justice Guidance 82
F. Jencks Act (Rule 26.2) 83
G. Witness Immunity 85
H. Notice of Defenses 87

Chapter 8. The Pretrial Conference 91

PART 3. PRETRIAL MOTIONS

Chapter 9. Pretrial Motions and Rule 12 Procedures 99

Chapter 10. Challenging the Charges and Motions in Limine 103
A. Jurisdiction and Failure to State an Offense 103
B. Venue 104
C. Bill of Particulars 105
D. Joinder of Offenses and Defendants 107
    1. Joinder of Offenses 107
    2. Joinder of Defendants 110
E. Motions in Limine 113
    1. Evidentiary Privileges 113
    2. Character Evidence and Prior Convictions or Bad Acts 114
    3. Unfair Prejudice 116

Chapter 11. Motions to Suppress Evidence for Violations of the Fourth Amendment 117
A. Searches Pursuant to a Warrant 117
    1. Probable Cause 118
    2. Scope of the Warrant 119
    3. Rule 41 Requirements 119
B. Warrantless Searches and Seizures 120
    1. Search or Seizure Requirement 120
        a. Searches 121
        b. Seizures 122
    2. Exceptions to the Warrant Requirement 122
        a. Search Incident to Arrest 123
        b. Protective Sweep 124

		c.	Exigent Circumstances.. 124
		d.	Plain View/Perception 125
		e.	Vehicle Searches 125
		f.	Inventory or Booking Exception 125
		g.	"Stop and Frisk"... 126
		h.	Administrative and Special Needs 127
	3.	Consent to Search... 128
C.	Limits on Claims for Fourth Amendment Violations 129
	1.	Who May File Motions to Suppress.................................... 129
	2.	Fruit of an Illegal Search 129
	3.	The Good-Faith Exception 130

Chapter 12. Motions to Suppress Statements and Eyewitness Identifications 133

A. Fifth Amendment *Miranda* Requirements.. 133
  1. Custody... 134
  2. Interrogation.. 135
  3. Content of the Warnings 135
  4. Invocation and Waiver of Miranda Rights......................... 136
  5. Fruit of the Poisonous Tree... 137
  6. Exceptions to *Miranda*... 137
B. The Sixth Amendment Requirements 138
  1. Deliberately Eliciting Information 138
  2. Offense-Specific Limitation 139
  3. Waiver 139
  4. Fruit of the Poisonous Tree... 139
C. Eyewitness Identifications.. 140
  1. Due Process Requirements 140
  2. The Sixth Amendment Right to Counsel 141

Chapter 13. Pretrial Motions, Memoranda of Law, Evidentiary Hearings, and Oral Arguments.. 143

A. Pretrial Motions 144
  1. Structure of motion 144
     a. Caption and Title.. 144
     b. Grounds for Relief.. 145
     c. Request for Relief... 145
     d. Signature Block, Proposed Order and Certificate of Service 145
B. Drafting Memoranda of Law 146
  1. Structure of a Memorandum of Law 146
     a. Caption and Title.. 146
     b. Introduction 147
     c. Statement of Facts.. 147
     d. Argument 148
     e. Conclusion 149

   f. Signature Block, Certificate of Service and Certificate of Compliance 150
  2. Brief Writing Tips 150
   a. Before Writing a Memorandum of Law 150
   b. During the Drafting Process 150
   c. Editing the Memorandum of Law 152
   d. Proofreading the Memorandum of Law 153
C. Conducting an Evidentiary Hearing 154
 1. Preparing for an Evidentiary Hearing 154
 2. The Direct Examination 155
   a. The Substance of a Direct Examination 156
   b. Structuring a Direct Examination 156
   c. The Form of Direct Examination Questions 159
 3. The Cross-Examination 159
   a. The Substance of a Cross-Examination 160
   b. Structuring a Cross-Examination 160
   c. The Form of Cross-Examination Questions 163
D. Preparing for Oral Argument 164

PART 4. PLEA AGREEMENT AND SENTENCING

Chapter 14. Plea Agreements 181
A. Types of Guilty Pleas 182
B. Contents of Plea Agreements 183
C. Withdrawal of Guilty Pleas 186

Chapter 15. Sentencing 199
A. Section 3553(a) Factors 199
B. The Sentencing Guidelines 201
C. Presentence Investigation Report and Sentencing Hearing 203
D. Probation and Supervised Release Violations 204

INDEX 207

TABLE OF CASES

Aguilar v. Texas 118
Agurs, United States v. 89
Allen, United States v. 106
Apprendi v. New Jersey 60
Arizona v. Evans 130
Arizona v. Gant 125
Arizona v. Hicks 119, 125
Arizona v. Johnson 127, 175
Arizona v. Mauro 135
Arvizu, United States v. 176
Bagley, United States v. 82
Bailey v. United States 119
Bain, Ex parte 60
Barker v. Wingo 27
Beauchamp, United States v. 177
Berghuis v. Thompkins 136
Berkemer v. McCarty 134
Berkermer v. McCarty 134
Biswell, United States v. 128
Board of Educ. of Ind. School District
  No. 92 of Pottawatomie County v.
  Earls 128
Bond v. United States 104
Booker, United States v. 200
Brady v. Maryland 75, 80, 89, 93
Branzburg v. Hayes 50
Braswell v. United States 54
Brewer v. Williams 138
Brunette, United States v. 37
California v. Acevedo 125
California v. Ciraolo 121
California v. Greenwood 122
California v. Hodari D. 126
California v. Prysock 136
Camera v. Municipal Court 128
Campbell, United States v. 176
Carroll v. United States 118, 125
Carter, United States v. 176
Ceccolini, United States v. 130
Chadwick, United States v. 124
Chimel v. California 123
Coleman v. Alabama 43, 47
Coleman, United States v. 109
Colorado v. Bertine 126
Colorado v. Connelly 136
Cortez, United States v. 126, 127
Crawford v. Washington 45
Cupp v. Murphy 124
Daubert v. Merrell Dow
  Pharmaceuticals 116
Davis v. United States 130, 136
Davis, United States v. 177
Dickerson v. United States 134
Dionisio, United States v. 50, 51
Doe v. United States 137
Doe, United States v. 54

Donnell, United States v. 112
Doss, United States v. 61
Dow Chemical Co. v. United
  States 121
Doyle v. Ohio 138
Drayton, United States v. 126
Duckworth v. Eagan 136
Dunaway v. New York 127
Dunn, United States v. 121
Dyke v. Taylor Implement Mfg.
  Co. 126
Edwards v. Arizona 136
El Hage, United States v. 37
Fernandez v. California 129
Fisher v. United States 53
Flemmi, United States v. 62
Florence v. Bd. of Chosen Freeholders
  of the County of Burlington 124
Florida v. Harris 118
Florida v. Jardines 122
Florida v. Powell 135, 136
Franks v. Delaware 3
Frost, United States v. 111
Gall v. United States 200
Garrett, United States v. 109
Gaviria, United States v. 37
Georgia v. Randolf 129
Gerstein v. Pugh 19
Giffen, United States v. 106
Giglio v. United States 81, 93
Giordenello v. United States 4
Gonzalez-Servin v. Ford Motor
  Company 149
Grand Jury Subpoena Duces Tecum,
  In re 62
Greer v. Miller 138
Groh v. Rameriz 119
Hamling v. United States 58
Harris v. New York 154
Heien v. North Carolina 118
Henry, United States v. 139
Herring v. United States 130
Hess, United States v. 58
Holliday, United States v. 103
Horton v. California 125
Hubbell, United States v. 54
Huddleston v. United States 116
Hudson v. Michigan 6, 129, 130
Illinois v. Caballes 122
Illinois v. Gates 4, 5, 118
Illinois v. Krull 130
Illinois v. Lafayette 125
Illinois v. Perkins 137
Illinois v. Rodriguez 128
Illinois v. Wardlaw 176
Indianapolis, City of, v. Edmond 128

Table of Cases

Inmates of Attica Correctional Facility v. Rockefeller 7
J.D.B. v. North Carolina 134
Jaben v. United States 4
Jacobsen, United States v. 121, 122
Jaffee v. Redmond 113
Jawara, United States v. 110
Jencks v. United States 83
Johnson v. Zerbst 128
Jones, United States v. 122
Kansas v. Ventris 138, 139
Kastigar v. United States 85
Katz v. United States 121
Kentucky v. King 125
Kirk v. Louisiana 121, 124
Kuhlman v. Wilson 138
Kyllo v. United States 122
Leon, United States v. 5, 119, 130
Lopez, United States v. 104
Los Angeles, City of v. Patel 122, 128
Mackin v. United States 57
Maine v. Moulton 138, 139
Mandujano, United States v. 51
Manson v. Brathwaite 140
Mara, United States v. 51
Marshall v. Barlow's, Inc. 127
Maryland v. Buie 123, 124
Maryland v. Pringle 4
Maryland v. Shatzer 136
Massiah v. United States 138
Matlock, United States v. 154
Mendenhall, United States v. 126
Mezzanatto, United States v. 86
Michigan v. DeFellippo 4
Michigan v. Mosely 137
Michigan v. Summers 119
Minaya, United States v. 106
Minnesota v. Carter 129
Minnesota v. Olson 129
Miranda v. Arizona 133, 136
Missouri v. Seibert 137
Mohawk Industries v. Carpenter ... 114
Montejo v. Louisiana 139
Montoya de Hernandez, United States v. 128
Muehler v. Mena 119
Myers, United States v. 108
Nadone v. United States 130
Naverette v. California 127
Neil v. Biggers 140
New Jersey v. T.L.O. 120
New York v. Belton 123
New York v. Charles 137
Nguyen, United States v. 110
Nix v. Williams 130, 139
Nixon, United States v. 80
North Carolina v. Butler 136
Oregon v. Mathiason 135

Oregon v. Olstead 137
Orozco v. Texas 135
Pace, United States v. 116
Pasciuti, United States v. 37
Patane, United States v. 137
Patterson v. Illinois 139
Paulette, United States v. 177
Pearce, United States v. 176
Perez, United States v. 176
Perry, United States v. 38
Petite v. United States 108
Peyton v. New York 5, 121
Powell v. Alabama 20
R. Enterprises, United States v. 51, 52, 61
Rakas v. Illinois 129
Ramirez, United States v. 5
Ramsey, United States v. 128
Rhode Island v. Innis 135
Ricketts v. Adamson 186
Riley v. California 123, 124
Robinson, United States v. 123
Rodriguez v. United States 122, 127
Rodriguez-Moreno, United States v. 105
Roviaro v. United States 78
Russell v. United States 59, 60
Saadey, United States v. 108
Safford Unified School Dist. No. 1 v. Redding 128
Salerno, United States v. 35
Schaffer v. United States 112
Schmerber v. California 137
Schneckloth v. Bustamonte 128
Scott v. Illinois 21
Sharpe, United States v. 127
Silverthorne Lumber Co. v. United States 130
Simmons v. United States 154
Smith, United States v. 37
Sokolow, United States v. 43, 127
Sorich, United States v. 106
Terry v. Ohio 122, 126
Texas v. Cobb 139
Tinklenberg, United States v. 29
Trammel v. United States 113
(Under Seal), United States v. 61
Upjohn Co. v. United States 113
Virginia v. Moore 123
Wade, United States v. 141
Washington v. Chrisman 125
Washington, United States v. 51
Weatherford v. Bursey 75
Wong Sun v. United States 5, 129, 130
Wyoming v. Houghton 125
Young, United States v. 176
Zafiro v. United States 107, 112
Zedner v. United States 31
Zolin, United States v. 114

CRIMINAL PRETRIAL ADVOCACY
Second Edition

PART 1
PRELIMINARY PROCEEDINGS
■ ■ ■

CHAPTER 1

COMPLAINT AND ARREST

∎ ∎ ∎

A. CONTENTS OF A CRIMINAL COMPLAINT

Federal criminal proceedings often begin with the filing of a criminal complaint. Federal Rule of Criminal Procedure 3 provides:

> The complaint is a written statement of the essential facts constituting the offense charged. Except as provided in Rule 4.1, it must be made under oath before a magistrate judge or, if none is reasonably available, before a state or local judicial officer.

A complaint is not needed when the government obtains an indictment or files an information prior to an arrest or issuance of a summons. See Chapter 6. Moreover, if an indictment is obtained after the arrest, the indictment supersedes the complaint. When an arrest is made without a warrant, the government is required to present the person arrested to a magistrate judge "without unnecessary delay." Rule 5(a)(1)(A). After a warrantless arrest, a complaint "must be promptly filed in the district where the offense was allegedly committed" to establish probable cause. Rule 5(b).

Under Rule 3, a complaint must: (1) be in writing; (2) contain factual allegations sufficient to make out the offense charged; (3) be made under oath; and (4) be presented to a judicial officer, preferably a federal officer.

The complaint serves as the basis for the government's application for an arrest warrant, and thus, Rule 3 must be read in conjunction with Federal Rule of Criminal Procedure 4, which governs issuance of an arrest warrant. The factual basis for the complaint is usually contained in a detailed affidavit filed by an agent who participated in the investigation of the matter. If the complaint and accompanying affidavit(s) contain sufficient facts to establish that there is probable cause to believe that the person named committed the charged offense, the judicial officer (usually a federal magistrate judge) will issue a warrant for that individual's arrest.

If a complaint contains false or illegally obtained information, the warrant that was issued in reliance on that complaint may be invalidated. A court will not invalidate the warrant if, excluding the tainted information, there is still sufficient allegations to support a probable cause finding. *Franks v. Delaware*, 438 U.S. 154 (1978).

Similarly, even if defects in a complaint render an arrest unlawful, the government may proceed with a criminal prosecution if a valid indictment is returned against the individual.

B. ARREST WARRANTS

Federal Rule of Criminal Procedure 4 sets forth the requirements for the form, the execution, and the return of an arrest warrant. Rule 4(a) provides that warrants may be issued only upon a showing of probable cause. The subsection also provides that a judge, if requested by the government attorney, may issue a summons in lieu of a warrant. Rule 4(b) governs the form of the warrant. Rule 4(c) provides for the return of the warrant to the issuing judge after the warrant is executed.

1. PROBABLE CAUSE

The probable cause standard depends on the "totality of the circumstances." *Illinois v. Gates,* 462 U.S. 213, 231 (1983). In evaluating whether the complaint and any supporting affidavits support a finding of probable cause, the judge decides whether the alleged facts "are sufficient to warrant a prudent person, or one of reasonable caution, in believing, in the circumstances shown, that the suspect has committed, is committing, or is about to commit an offense." *Michigan v. DeFellippo,* 443 U.S. 31, 37 (1979).

Although the Supreme Court has acknowledged that the probable cause standard "is incapable of precise definition or quantification into percentages," *Maryland v. Pringle,* 540 U.S. 366, 371 (2003), the Court does require sufficient information for the magistrate judge to determine if the standard is met. Conclusory allegations or a recitation of the elements of the underlying criminal statute are not sufficient to satisfy the probable cause standard. *Giordenello v. U.S.,* 357 U.S. 480, 486 (1958). However, the complaint and supporting affidavits do not have to contain "each and every fact" contributing to the officer's conclusion that the suspect committed the offense. *Jaben v. United States,* 381 U.S. 214, 224 (1965).

The complaint and supporting affidavit(s) must provide the magistrate judge with some indication of the source of the information contained in the application. If the source is the personal knowledge and beliefs of the officer completing the complaint or affidavit, the officer may simply inform the judge how that knowledge was obtained. In addition, the affidavit may contain hearsay, as long as the judge is provided with sufficient information to evaluate the credibility of the source of the information. Victims and identified witnesses are generally deemed credible. When the government is relying on confidential or anonymous sources, the complaint must explain the basis for the reliance on the source of the information. *Illinois v. Gates,* 462 U.S. 213 (1983).

A defendant may challenge an arrest on the ground that the complaint failed to establish probable cause in a motion to suppress. See Chapter 11. If the arrest is determined to be invalid, any evidence obtained as a consequence of the arrest may be suppressed. Where, however, the police were acting in reliance on an objectively valid warrant, the evidence will not be suppressed, even if the warrant is later invalidated. *United States v. Leon,* 468 U.S. 897 (1984). This good faith exception makes it difficult for defendants to have evidence suppressed when it was obtained in reliance on an invalid warrant. However, the evidence will be suppressed if the official completing the complaint knew the information supporting the complaint was false, the complaint was lacking in credible information, or the warrant was so facially defective that reliance on the warrant issued was not reasonable.

2. CONTENT AND EXECUTION OF A WARRANT

An arrest warrant must contain the suspect's name or adequately identify the suspect if there is no name available. U.S. Const. amend. IV; Rule 4(b)(1). When there is an error in the name, the warrant is only likely to be deemed invalid if there is a substantive problem, such as the wrong person was arrested or the description was so vague as to fail to identify the defendant. *Wong Sun v. United States,* 371 U.S. 471, 481 (1963). By contrast, when there is simply a typographical error or a misspelling of the suspect's name, the warrant will be valid. When the government does not know the suspect's name and wants a "John or Jane Doe" warrant, it must provide sufficient information to identify the person who is the target of the warrant. The warrant must describe the offense charged and command that the defendant who is being arrested be brought before a judge "without unnecessary delay." Rule 5(a)(1)(A).

The warrant is executed by the arrest of the defendant, and the defendant is entitled to examine the warrant. Rule 4(c)(3)(A). If the arresting official does not have the warrant in her possession, she must tell the defendant that the warrant exists and explain the charges it contains. Rule 4(d)(3)(A).

When officers are in possession of an arrest warrant, they may enter a suspect's home if they have reason to believe that the suspect is present in the home. *Peyton v. New York,* 445 U.S. 573, 603 (1980). The officers executing a warrant, however, must use reasonable means to execute it. Thus, in the absence of exigent circumstances, police officers must announce their presence and demand entry to a home before they may break down a door to execute a warrant. *United States v. Ramirez,* 523 U.S. 65, 73 (1998). However, the exclusionary rule does not apply to violations of this "knock-and-announce" rule. *Hudson v. Michigan*, 547 U.S. 586, 591 (2006). Finally, the officer who executes the arrest warrant must return the warrant to the magistrate judge before whom the defendant is brought.

C. THE DECISION TO FILE CHARGES

Prosecutors have enormous discretion on whether to file charges and which violations to pursue in a case. Each prosecutor's office has an important screening function in deciding which cases will be pursued, which will be dropped, and whether the conduct warrants referral to a civil enforcement agency if no criminal charges will be filed. The police and investigative agencies have significant influence over whether a case will be pursued, but the final decision rests ultimately with the prosecutor. Yet, as Professors Green and Zacharias pointed out, "for better or worse, prosecutors are among the least accountable public officials." Bruce A. Green & Fred C. Zacharias, *Prosecutorial Neutrality*, 2004 WIS. L. REV. 837.

In the federal system, the Department of Justice, which operates through the 93 United States Attorney's Offices and various operating groups, such as the Criminal, Tax, and Antitrust Divisions, is responsible for federal criminal prosecutions. The United States Attorneys are nominated by the President and approved by the Senate under its "advice and consent" authority. While they are political appointees, United States Attorneys, along with the Attorney General, are expected to exercise independent judgment and not be beholden to a particular party or faction. In the states, the Attorney Generals, most of whom are elected, are responsible for the administration of the criminal justice system. County and municipal prosecutors receive their authority through the state, and many are also elected to their position and operate with only minimal supervision.

Of course, the vast majority of the prosecuting decisions are made by so-called "career" prosecutors who are neither appointed nor elected and are hired in large part based on merit. The day-to-day work of prosecutors' offices are conducted by lawyers who are largely free from political pressure, and most cases do not have any broad social significance even though they are quite important to the victims and offenders. Offices tend to have a set of guidelines for various categories of cases, and prosecutors have varying degrees of discretion over what to charge and how to resolve a case by a plea bargain.

The standard for filing a criminal charge, whether by complaint, information, or indictment, is probable cause. But the actual decision by the prosecutor usually requires more than having just enough evidence to conclude the defendant probably committed the violation. A criminal charge has an enormous impact on an individual and others, and so prosecutors should be cautious about filing a charge when there is a good chance that a jury will not find the defendant guilty.

Model Rule of Professional Conduct 3.8(a) provides that "[t]he prosecutor in a criminal case shall . . . refrain from prosecuting a charge that the prosecutor knows is not supported by probable cause." The ABA Criminal Justice Standards, Prosecution Function Standard 3–3.9(a), goes a step further in stating that the "prosecutor should not institute, cause to be instituted, or permit the continued pendency of criminal charges in the absence of sufficient admissible evidence to support a conviction." Charging a defendant with the expectation, or hope, that the person will plead guilty and cooperate is a problematic decision, even if there is enough evidence to charge the person. Someone accused of a crime may believe in their innocence and decide to fight the charge. There have been any number of cases in which a defendant peripheral to the main misconduct has been charged and takes the case to trial while others more culpable pleaded guilty, so that the prosecutor is left trying to prove the weakest case.

Prosecutors therefore can—and should—decide not to charge a crime when they conclude that there is insufficient evidence to support a conviction. Courts are reluctant to second-guess the prosecutor's decision to drop an investigation and not pursue charges. For example, in *Inmates of Attica Correctional Facility v. Rockefeller*, 477 F.2d 375 (2d Cir. 1973), a group of prisoners sued to require the Department of Justice to pursue civil rights charges against state correctional officers for their role in retaking control of a prison after a riot that left 29 inmates and 10 hostages dead, later called "the bloodiest encounter between Americans since the Civil War."[1] The Second Circuit rejected the claim that the courts should exercise their supervisory authority over prosecutors to require a case be pursued: "On balance, we believe that substitution of a court's decision to compel prosecution for the U.S. Attorney's decision not to prosecute, even upon an abuse of discretion standard of review and even if limited to directing that a prosecution be undertaken in good faith, would be unwise."

FORMS:

Criminal Complaint:

http://www.uscourts.gov/forms/law-enforcement-grand-jury-and-prosecution-forms/criminal-complaint

Arrest Warrant:

http://www.uscourts.gov/forms/law-enforcement-grand-jury-and-prosecution-forms/arrest-warrant.

---

[1] Preface, New York Special Commission on Attica (1972).

SAMPLE CRIMINAL COMPLAINT
Bank Fraud Conspiracy

UNITED STATES OF AMERICA

v.

DEFENDANT 1 and

DEFENDANT 2

CRIMINAL COMPLAINT

I, Jane R. Jones, being duly sworn, state the following is true and correct to the best of my knowledge and belief. Between on or about September 14, 2013 and on or about November 8, 2014, in the Eastern District of Wayne and elsewhere, DEFENDANT 1 and DEFENDANT 2 did

knowingly and intentionally conspire and agree with each other and others to execute a scheme and artifice to defraud a financial institution, specifically Spencer Savings Bank in Elmwood Park, Wayne, and to obtain moneys, funds, credits, assets, securities, and other property owned by, and under the custody and control of Spencer Savings Bank, by means of materially false and fraudulent pretenses, representations, and promises, contrary to Title 18, United States Code, Section 1344,

in violation of Title 18, United States Code, Section 1349.

I further state that I am a Special Agent with the Federal Bureau of Investigation and that this complaint is based on the following facts:

SEE ATTACHMENT A

_____

Jane R. Jones, Special Agent

Federal Bureau of Investigation

Sworn to before me and subscribed in my presence, February 23, 2015, at Cook City, Wayne.

_____

HONORABLE MICHAEL V. JOHNSON

UNITED STATES MAGISTRATE JUDGE

Attachment A

AFFIDAVIT

I, Jane R. Jones, am a Special Agent with the Federal Bureau of Investigation. I am fully familiar with the facts set forth herein based on my own investigation, my conversations with law enforcement officers, and my review of reports, documents, and items of evidence. Since the complaint is being submitted for the limited purpose of establishing probable cause to believe that the defendants have committed the referenced federal offense, I have not set forth each and every fact that I have learned concerning this investigation:

1. At all times relevant to this complaint, DEFENDANT 1 was the managing member and owner of LVI Realty, LLC, a Wayne limited liability company ("LVI"), and a police officer for the Cook City, Wayne Police Department.

2. LVI, by its principal, DEFENDANT 1, applied for a commercial real estate mortgage loan with Shipley Savings Bank, located in Elmwood Park, Wayne, with principal offices located in Garfield, Wayne ("SHIPLEY SAVINGS") in an application dated September 14, 2014.

3. At all times relevant to this Complaint, SHIPLEY SAVINGS was a financial institution that offered loans and other financing arrangements, and its deposits were insured by the Federal Deposit Insurance Corporation.

4. DEFENDANT 2 was an employee of SHIPLEY SAVINGS from on or about January 1991 through on or about January 2014 and served as the loan officer for LVI's commercial loan application.

5. On or about September 14, 2014, SHIPLEY SAVINGS documented in its Commercial Loan Submission that LVI, by its principal, DEFENDANT 1, requested a commercial loan in the amount of $1,920,000 for the purpose of purchasing apartment buildings located at 416–424 and 430–436 East Washburn Avenue in Elizabeth, Wayne (the "Elizabeth Properties") for $2,400,000. The Elizabeth Properties were owned at that time by Smithson Realty Group ("SMITHSON REALTY"). The Commercial Loan Submission further provided that the loan amount constituted 80% of the purchase price and that DEFENDANT 1, among satisfying other conditions, would need to provide SHIPLEY SAVINGS with sufficient evidence of the source of funds for the remainder of the purchase price in the amount of $480,000. DEFENDANT 2 recommended approval of the loan as evidenced by his signature on the Commercial Loan Submission following the words "Recommended By."

6. By letter dated September 29, 2014, which was executed by both SHIPLEY SAVINGS and DEFENDANT 1, SHIPLEY SAVINGS advised DEFENDANT 1 of its commitment to finance the purchase of the

Elizabeth Properties subject to the terms and conditions outlined in the letter. Paragraph 20(8) provided that there should be no secondary financing of the Elizabeth Properties by LVI and DEFENDANT 1 and that no subordinate liens or encumbrances affecting the Elizabeth Properties should be created or permitted by NI and DEFENDANT 1 during the term of the financing. Paragraph 24(0)(6) of the commitment letter further provided that among other conditions, SHIPLEY SAVINGS must receive and be satisfied with its review of the source of funds for the $480,000 equity contribution. DEFENDANT 1 signed the September 29, 2014 letter as Managing Member of LVI.

7. On or about November 1, 2014, SHIPLEY SAVINGS was informed that DEFENDANT 1 intended to submit a real estate contract, demonstrating his sale of a property located on Jabez Street in Cook City, Wayne (the "Jabez Street Property") as the source of the $480,000 equity contribution for the purchase of the Elizabeth Properties. By letter dated November 1, 2014, SHIPLEY SAVINGS provided DEFENDANT 1's attorney with closing figures for a scheduled closing of November 5, 2014. In the letter, SHIPLEY SAVINGS indicated, that among other documents, it had to receive a copy of the agreement for the sale of real estate for the Jabez Street Property.

8. Between on or about November 1, 2014, and on or about November 5, 2014, SHIPLEY SAVINGS received as part of the loan documents, a Contract for Sale of Real Estate purporting to be executed on or about October 4, 2014 (the "Fraudulent Contract"), as evidence of the source of funds in the amount of $480,000 which was to serve as the down payment on the Elizabeth Properties. The Fraudulent Contract that SHIPLEY SAVINGS received indicated that DEFENDANT 1 had sold the Jabez Street Property to an individual for the purchase price of $540,000. The Fraudulent Contract further stated that the individual paid DEFENDANT 1 $54,000 upon signing the Fraudulent Contract and that the anticipated closing on the sale was scheduled for November 8, 2014. In fact, DEFENDANT 1 did not own the Jabez Street Property in October 2014 at the time that the Fraudulent Contract purported that it was sold to the individual. Review of the deed for the property revealed that DEFENDANT 1 and his brother sold the Jabez Street Property on or about April 23, 2014 to a completely different individual for approximately $480,000.

9. On November 5, 2014, SHIPLEY SAVINGS entered into a Mortgage & Security Agreement with LVI to pay LVI the sum of $1,920,000 which would be returned in accordance with the Mortgage & Security Agreement, Promissory Note that was executed that same day, along with other loan documents. The Mortgage & Security Agreement with LVI that was signed by DEFENDANT 1 prohibited DEFENDANT 1

from encumbering or mortgaging the Elizabeth Properties without the written consent of SHIPLEY SAVINGS.

10. LVI, through defendants DEFENDANT 1 and DEFENDANT 2, subsequently secured a second mortgage from SMITHSON REALTY on the Elizabeth Properties, contrary to the terms of the Mortgage & Security Agreement with SHIPLEY SAVINGS. Although the sale agreement of the Elizabeth Properties between SMITHSON REALTY and NI was dated September 16, 2014, the property was deeded from SMITHSON REALTY to LVI on November 5, 2014, with the understanding that LVI would need to secure a second mortgage from SMITHSON REALTY in order to have enough money to purchase the Elizabeth Properties. By mortgage and mortgage note dated November 8, 2014, defendants DEFENDANT 1 and DEFENDANT 2 agreed on behalf of LVI Realty to a second mortgage with SMITHSON REALTY, a five-year interest only loan in the amount of $300,000. The $300,000 loan was used as part of the $480,000 equity contribution to purchase the Elizabeth Properties. Both defendants DEFENDANT 1 and DEFENDANT 2 signed the mortgage and mortgage note as corporate officers of LVI. DEFENDANT 2 never disclosed his relationship with LVI and/or DEFENDANT 1 to SHIPLEY SAVINGS: (a) when LVI applied for its initial loan with SHIPLEY SAVINGS and (b) when DEFENDANT 2 recommended approval of LVI's loan application and otherwise represented SHIPLEY SAVINGS while serving as the loan officer.

11. On or about November 10, 2014, DEFENDANT 1 made his last payment on the $1,920,000 mortgage with SHIPLEY SAVINGS before causing LVI to default on the loan. On or about February 2, 2013, DEFENDANT 1 turned over the deed to the Elizabeth Properties to SHIPLEY SAVINGS in lieu of foreclosure. After SHIPLEY SAVINGS sold the Elizabeth Properties in mitigation of its loss on the defaulted mortgage loan, the loss amount to SHIPLEY SAVINGS totaled over $400,000.

12. On or about March 17, 2015, DEFENDANT 1 caused LVI to file for bankruptcy in federal court. As part of the bankruptcy filing, DEFENDANT 1 represented that he took out a second mortgage on the Elizabeth Properties in November 2012 in the amount of approximately $300,000. The second mortgage was prohibited by the conditions of the commitment letter and Mortgage & Security Agreement that (a) DEFENDANT 1 and SHIPLEY SAVINGS executed as described in part in paragraphs 6 and 9 of this complaint and (b) for which DEFENDANT 2 served as the loan officer with SHIPLEY SAVINGS.

13. For the reasons set forth above, I believe that probable cause exists to believe that:

DEFENDANT 1 and DEFENDANT 2 did

knowingly and intentionally conspire and agree with each other and others to execute a scheme and artifice to defraud a financial institution, specifically Spencer Savings Bank in Elmwood Park, Wayne, and to obtain moneys, funds, credits, assets, securities, and other property owned by, and under the custody and control of Spencer Savings Bank, by means of materially false and fraudulent pretenses, representations, and promises, contrary to Title 18, United States Code, Section 1344,

in violation of Title 18, United States Code, Section 1349.

/s/ *Jane R. Jones*

Jane R. Jones, Special Agent

Federal Bureau of Investigation

SAMPLE CRIMINAL COMPLAINT
Narcotics Distribution

UNITED STATES OF AMERICA

v.

Jimmy Joe FUQUA

CRIMINAL COMPLAINT

I, James R. Johnson, being duly sworn, state the following is true and correct to the best of my knowledge and belief. On or about December 31, 2014, in the Eastern District of Wayne and elsewhere, DEFENDANT Jimmy Joe Fuqua violated: 21 U.S.C. § 841(a); 18 U.S.C. § 924(c); 18 U.S.C. § 922(g)(1); and 21 U.S.C. § 856(a)(1).

I further state that I am a Special Agent with the Bureau of Alcohol Tobacco and Firearms and that this complaint is based on the following facts:

SEE ATTACHMENT A

_____

James R. Johnson, Special Agent

Federal Bureau of Investigation

Sworn to before me and subscribed in my presence, January 2, 2015, at Cook City, Wayne.

_____

HONORABLE MICHAEL V. JOHNSON

UNITED STATES MAGISTRATE JUDGE

Attachment A
AFFIDAVIT

I, James R. Johnson, being duly sworn, depose and state the following:

1. I make this affidavit with personal knowledge based on my participation in this investigation, including witness interviews by myself and/or other law enforcement agents, communications with others who have personal knowledge of the events and circumstances described herein, and information gained through my training and experience. The information outlined below is provided for the limited purpose of establishing probable cause and does not contain all details or all facts of which I am aware relating to this investigation.

2. I am a Special Agent with the Bureau of Alcohol, Tobacco, Firearms, and Explosives (ATF), the U.S. Justice Department, and have been so employed since May 2008. I am currently assigned to the Cook City, Wayne Field Division, Group 1. I am charged with investigating violations of the federal arson, explosives, firearms and narcotics laws. I have successfully completed the Criminal Investigation Training Program (CITP), which is a 12 week full-time program held at the Federal Law Enforcement Training Center (FLETC) in Glynco, Georgia. I have also completed the Special Agent Basic Training (SABT) program at FLETC. In addition, I have received a Bachelor of Science degree in Criminal Justice from Cook State University, Wayne. I have been involved in numeous investigations of violations of federal firearm and narcotics laws.

3. I, along with other law enforcement personnel, am currently investigating Jimmy Joe FUQUA, DOB **/**/1969, for violations of federal firearm and narcotics laws.

4. A criminal history check of FUQUA revealed that FUQUA was convicted of Felony, Assault with intent to rob while armed, 11/22/1992, and two counts Felony, Criminal Sexual Assault (Weapon Used), 10/05/2008.

5. On December 31, 2014, at 12:25 p.m., Cook City Police, Narcotics Section, executed a state search warrant at 20410 Mullberry, Cook City, Wayne, in the Eastern District of Wayne. A computerized check of the Enniton County Register of Deeds shows that Jimmy FUQUA purchased 20410 Mullberry, Cook City, Wayne, in November 2010. Once entry was made into 20410 Mullberry, Officer Tangrey encountered and ordered FUQUA from the rear of the residence and detained FUQUA in the living room.

6. During the search of the residence, Officer Carvelle located and seized one (I) grocery bag containing a large brick of marijuana from the

refrigerator of the residence. Officer Carvelle also located and seized from the upstairs bedroom, on top of the dresser, a Remington, Pistol, .45 caliber, Model 1911, Serial number *****71, loaded with 7 rounds. Along with the pistol, were three (3) zip lock baggies containing suspected marijuana, a digital scale and cut and folded lotto slips. From my training and experience, I know that the packaging, scales, and lotto slips are consistent with drug trafficking, and not personal use.

7. While searching the upstairs bedroom closet, Officer Rhodey located and seized a New England Firearms Rifle, .22 caliber, Model SB2, Serial Number NW2***24. A subsequent computer records check of the serial number indicated that the rifle was stolen. From my training and experience, I know that narcotics traffickers carry firearms for protection of their drugs and themselves.

8. During a search of the remainder of the residence, Officers located and seized a large amount of United States Currency, additional amounts of suspected marijuana and heroin.

9. A Cook City ATF Special Agent, an expert in interstate nexus of firearms, determined that the firearms that were confiscated from 20410 Mullberry on December 31, 2014, in Cook City, Wayne, were manufactured outside the state of Wayne after 1898 and therefore traveled in and affected interstate commerce.

10. Based on the above information, I have probable cause to believe Jimmy Joe FUQUA, year of birth 1969: (1) knowingly and intentionally possessed controlled substances, including marijuana and heroin. with intent to distribute, in violation of 21 U.S.C. § 841(a); (2) knowingly and intentionally possessed firearms in furtherance of a drug trafficking offense, in violation of 18 U.S.C. § 924(c); (3) as a convicted felon, knowingly possessed firearms, in violation of 18 U.S.C. § 922(g)(1); and (4) knowingly used or maintained any place for the purpose of manufacturing, distributing, or using any controlled substance, in violation of 21 U.S.C. § 856(a)(1).

13. For the reasons set forth above, I believe that probable cause exists to believe that FUQUA violated 21 U.S.C. § 841(a); 18 U.S.C. § 924(c); 18 U.S.C. § 922(g)(1); and 21 U.S.C. § 856(a)(1).

/s/ *James R. Johnson*

James R. Johnson

Bureau of Alcohol, Tobacco, Firearms and Explosives

SAMPLE CRIMINAL COMPLAINT
Sex Trafficking of a Minor

UNITED STATES OF AMERICA

v.

Natasha HARPER

CRIMINAL COMPLAINT

I, Michael J. Jones, being duly sworn, state the following is true and correct to the best of my knowledge and belief. On or about March 8, 2015, in the Eastern District of Wayne, the defendant, Natasha HARPER, knowingly recruited, enticed, transported, provided, or maintained a person (17-year old Minor Victim born in 1998), in or affecting interstate commerce, and knowing and with reasonable opportunity to observe that such person had not attained the age of 18 years and would be caused to engage in a commercial sex act, all in violation of Title 18, United States Code, Section 1591(a).

I further state that I am a Detecive with the Enniton County Sherriff's Department and that this complaint is based on the following facts:

SEE ATTACHMENT A

_____

Micheal J. Jones, Detective (Badge No. 1544)

Enniton County Sherriff's Department

Sworn to before me and subscribed in my presence, March 9, 2015, at Cook City, Wayne.

_____

HONORABLE MICHAEL V. JOHNSON

UNITED STATES MAGISTRATE JUDGE

Attachment A

AFFIDAVIT

I, Michael J. Jones, being duly sworn, depose and state the following:

1. I make this affidavit with personal knowledge based on my participation in this investigation, including witness interviews by myself and/or other law enforcement agents, communications with others who have personal knowledge of the events and circumstances described herein, and information gained through my training and experience. The information outlined below is provided for the limited purpose of establishing probable cause and does not contain all details or all facts of which I am aware relating to this investigation.

2. I am a Detective with the Enniton County Sherriff's Department, Cook City, Wayne assigned to the Exploited and Missing Child Unit. I have been a Detective for four years, and a member of the Sherriff's Department for 11 years. I have investigated numerous cases involving the sexual exploitation of children and child sexual abuse.

3. I, along with other law enforcement personnel, assisted in the investigation (Case No. 199-8415) of child sexual exploitation through advertisements placed on internet bulletin boards.

4. On Thursday March 8, 2015, Officers and Detectives of the Enniton County Sherriff's Department and the Federal Bureau of Investigation were conducting a sting operation in regards to underage human trafficking and child sexual exploitation.

5. Officers made contact with MINOR VICTIM in this case, a 17-year old female born in 1998. Officers arranged for MINOR VICTIM to meet them at the Cook City Inn, located at 6633 W. Grand, Cook City, Enniton County, Wayne.

6. MINOR VICTIM was transported to the above location by Natasha Harper, a 33-year old female born in 1982. Officers observed MINOR VICTIM exit Harper's vehicle. Harper was taken into custody and transported to the Exploiten and Missing Child Unit for an interview.

7. FBI Special Agent David Downs and I interviewed Harper after having advised her of her *Miranda* Rights. Harper waived her rights and agreed to talk. Harper said that she has known MINOR VICTIM for a long time. She said that MINOR VICTIM has been advertising on Backpage.com and that she transports MINOR VICTIM to different locations to make her "calls." She said that she furnished her with a phone and that she and MINOR VICTIM both used the phone to answer calls in regards to their ads. Harper also said that she has answered the phone for MINOR VICTIM in regards to the "calls." Harper said that she and MINOR VICTIM have been doing this together for the last couple of

months. She said that MINOR VICTIM pays her approximately $20-$30 for transporting her to a "call." She said she has made approximately a couple hundred dollars transporting MINOR VICTIM to her "calls."

8. Harper also advised that she too is a prostitute. She said that she has told MINOR VICTIM not to use a pimp because they only cause more trouble. She said tonight MINOR VICTIM called her and asked her to take her to this "call." Harper advised that going on the call usually meant having sex with someone who answered the Backpage.com ad.

9. MINOR VICTIM told Detectives that Harper had transported her to all of her "calls." MINOR VICTIM said that Harper would take the photographs of her for the ads and that Harper was the one who placed the ads on Backpage.com. She said that she had to pay $50 to Harper for each of the "calls" she went on. MINOR VICTIM said that earlier today Harper texted her and asked her if she wanted to make some money. MINOR VICTIM said she knew that meant to post an ad on Backpage.com and go on a date to exchange sex for money. MINOR VICTIM said that on a date she would exchange sex acts including intercourse for $150 for thirty minutes or $200 for an hour. MINOR VICTIM said that when she went on a date the person paying her for the sex would have to place the agreed upon amount of money on the table prior to her performing any sex acts. MINOR VICTIM said that Harper would always pay to rent the motel rooms but MINOR VICTIM would pay part of the rent if she had money on her at the time.

10. Based on the above information, I believe that probable cause exists to believe that Harper violated 18 U.S.C. § 1591(a).

/s/ *Michael J. Jones*

Michael J. Jones

Enniton County Sherriff's Office

Chapter 2

Initial Appearance and Appointment of Counsel

■ ■ ■

Federal Rule of Criminal Procedure 5 requires the arresting official to bring the defendant "without unnecessary delay" before a magistrate judge. Rule 5(a)(1)(B). At this initial appearance, Rule 5(d) requires the judge to inform the defendant of the offenses he is being charged with and the complaint and affidavit that have been filed against him. The judge also must inform the defendant of his right to remain silent and the right to retain counsel. Moreover, if the arrest was made without a warrant, the government must demonstrate the existence of probable cause to charge the defendant at this hearing. Rule 5(b). The Constitution requires that a determination on the probable cause issue be made by a judge within forty-eight hours of the arrest. *Gerstein v. Pugh*, 420 U.S. 103 (1975).

At this initial appearance, the judge will inquire into the defendant's ability to pay for counsel. If the defendant also asserts that he is unable to pay for counsel, then the defendant fills out a financial affidavit, and the judge determines whether the person is entitled to have counsel provided at the government's expense. Finally, the judge will turn to the issue of bail. Bail considerations are described in Chapter 4.

A. INITIAL APPEARANCE

A defendant's first appearance after an arrest is usually before a magistrate judge. Under Federal Rule of Criminal Procedure 5(f), the initial appearance may be conducted by video teleconference if the defendant requests. If the arrest was made without a warrant, the magistrate judge will direct the prosecutor to promptly prepare and file a criminal complaint.

For a felony charge, Rule 5(d)(1) requires the magistrate judge to inform the defendant of the following:

(A) the complaint against the defendant, and any affidavit filed with it;

(B) the defendant's right to retain counsel or to request that counsel be appointed if the defendant cannot obtain counsel;

(C) the circumstances, if any, under which the defendant may secure pretrial release;

(D) any right to a preliminary hearing;

(E) the defendant's right not to make a statement, and that any statement made may be used against the defendant; and

(F) that a defendant who is not a United States citizen may request that an attorney for the government or a federal law enforcement official notify a consular officer from the defendant's country of nationality that the defendant has been arrested — but that even without the defendant's request, a treaty or other international agreement may require consular notification.

Federal Rule of Criminal Procedure 58(b)(2) describes what the magistrate judge must inform a defendant about in misdemeanor prosecutions—a list that basically includes the same items listed in Rule 5(d)(1).

At the initial appearance, the defendant must be allowed a "reasonable opportunity to consult with counsel." Rule 5(d)(2). The magistrate judge may also consider whether to detain or release the defendant, although if there is the possibility of detention, a separate detention proceeding is usually held. The government has the right to have a defendant held for up to three business days pending a detention hearing. See Chapter 4.

If the magistrate judge has any doubts about a defendant's ability to speak and understand English, then the judge will appoint a certified interpreter in accordance with 28 U.S.C. § 1827. If a defendant is a foreign national, regardless of the person's immigration status, the magistrate judge will advise the defendant of the right to consular notification and access.

Federal Rule of Criminal Procedure Rule 60(a) requires the prosecution to "use its best efforts to give the victim reasonable, accurate, and timely notice of any public court proceeding involving the crime." Rule 60(b) states that the "court must not exclude a victim from a public court proceeding involving the crime" unless there are good reasons not to allow a victim to be present. Consequently, the magistrate judge will usually inquire of the prosecutor whether any victims have been properly notified of the hearing.

B. APPOINTMENT OF COUNSEL

The Sixth Amendment provides defendants with the right to the "Assistance of Counsel" for their defense in serious criminal prosecutions. In *Powell v. Alabama*, 287 U.S. 45, 68–69 (1932), the Supreme Court explained the importance of counsel in a criminal prosecution: "The right to be heard would be, in many cases, of little avail if it did not comprehend the right to be heard by counsel. Even the intelligent and educated layman has small and sometimes no skill in the science of law." In *Scott v. Illinois*, 440 U.S. 367, 372 (1979), the Supreme Court limited the availability of the Sixth Amendment right to counsel to those cases which result in the actual imprisonment of a defendant, regardless of the length of time.

Prior to 1964, in federal criminal proceedings there was no statutory authority to compensate counsel appointed for an indigent defendant, so federal judges depended on the local bar to provide *pro bono* representation to defendants unable to retain counsel. Congress adopted the Criminal Justice Act (CJA), 18 U.S.C. § 3006A, in 1964 to create a mechanism for appointing and compensating lawyers to represent defendants unable to retain counsel on their own in federal criminal proceedings. The CJA authorizes reimbursement of appointed counsel for time spent representing a client, along with reasonable expenses and payment of expert and investigative services necessary for an adequate defense. The rates paid to lawyers appointed to represent clients are substantially below those usually charged to retained clients, although appointments are still actively sought by members of the bar.

In 1970, Congress amended the CJA to authorize judicial districts to establish federal defender organizations to serve as the counterpart to federal prosecutors working in the local United States Attorney's Offices. There are two types of federal defender organizations: federal public defender organizations and community defender organizations. Federal public defender organizations are part of the federal government, and staff members are federal employees. The chief federal public defender in a district is appointed to a four-year term by the court of appeals of the circuit in which the district operates. Community defender organizations are non-profits designated in the judicial district's CJA plan, and these organizations operate under the supervision of an independent board of directors. These offices are often a component within a larger defendant organization that may also represent clients in state, county, and municipal courts in the area.

In addition to the defender offices, there are more than 10,000 private lawyers who accept CJA assignments annually. These so-called "panel attorneys" represent many individuals prosecuted in the federal courts. The federal defenders are appointed in approximately 60% of cases made under the CJA, and the remaining 40 percent are assigned to the CJA panel. Especially in multi-defendant cases, panel attorneys frequently work alongside federal defenders.

As of January 1, 2015, a panel attorney is paid $127 per hour in non-capital cases, and, in capital cases, a maximum rate of $181 per hour. The limits on compensation are $9,900 for felonies, $2,800 for misdemeanors, and $7,100 for appeals. The maximum statutory amount can be exceeded when greater amounts are recommended by the district judge presiding over the case as necessary to provide fair compensation. The chief judge of the district must approve any payments above the limits set by the CJA, and that decision is not subject to appeal.

In order to exceed the maximum amounts set in the CJA, the court must first determine that the case is either "complex" or "extended." A "complex" case involves legal or factual issues that are unusual and require the lawyer to expend more time, skill, and effort than usually required in an average case. If more time is required for the representation than the average case, including both pre-trial and post-trial proceedings, then the case is deemed "extended." Once it is determined the case is "complex" or "extended," the court must determine whether the excess payment is necessary to provide fair compensation to the attorney in light of the following factors:

- The responsibilities involved in relation to the magnitude and importance of the case;
- The manner in which those responsibilities were performed;
- The knowledge, skill, efficiency, professionalism, and judgment shown by defense counsel;
- The nature of the lawyer's practice and the impact on it from the appointed representation;
- Any extraordinary time pressure or other circumstances affecting the representation; and
- Any other circumstances relevant to determining a fair and reasonable fee.

Although the Sixth Amendment right to appointed counsel only applies in cases in which the defendant was actually incarcerated, the CJA requires a federal court to appoint counsel to any financially eligible person who is:

- Charged with a felony or with a Class A misdemeanor;
- A juvenile alleged to have committed an act of juvenile delinquency as defined in 18 U.S.C. § 5031;
- Charged with a probation violation;
- Under arrest, when such representation is required by law;

- Charged with a violation of supervised release or faces modification, reduction, or enlargement of a condition, or extension or revocation of a term of supervised release;
- Subject to a mental condition hearing;
- In custody as a material witness;
- Entitled to appointment of counsel under the Sixth Amendment, or faces loss of liberty in a case and a separate federal law requires the appointment of counsel;
- Seeking to set aside or vacate a death sentence in proceedings under 28 U.S.C. § 2254 or § 2255; or
- Entitled to appointment of counsel in connection with prisoner transfer proceedings under 18 U.S.C § 4109.

The CJA provides discretionary authority to the district court to appoint counsel for a financially eligible person in the following circumstances:

- Defendants charged with a petty offense (Class B or C misdemeanor, or an infraction) for which a sentence to confinement is authorized;
- Defendants seeking relief under 28 U.S.C. §§ 2241, 2254, or 2255 (except in capital cases, in which the appointment of counsel is mandatory);
- A person charged with civil or criminal contempt who faces loss of liberty;
- A witness before a grand jury, a court, the Congress, or a federal agency or commission which has the power to compel testimony, counsel may be appointed where there is reason to believe, either prior to or during testimony, that the witness could be subject to a criminal prosecution, a civil or criminal contempt proceeding, or face loss of liberty;
- A person proposed by the prosecutor for processing under a "pretrial diversion" program;
- A person held for international extradition; or
- In an "ancillary" matter, such as a related civil asset forfeiture action or a claim for the return of personal property.

Determining whether a person is "financially unable to retain counsel" does not involve any precise rules, and courts have a measure of discretion in deciding whether to appoint counsel for a defendant. The first step in the process is completion of the Form CJA 23 financial affidavit that provides the information needed for a court to evaluate whether a person's financial resources and income are insufficient to retain counsel. In assessing financial eligibility, a court must consider the costs of providing the person (and any dependents) with necessities, such as food and shelter, and the cost of any bond imposed on a defendant if required for release from custody. The assessment of financial eligibility usually does not include the resources of the defendant's family unless family members indicate a willingness to retain counsel with their own resources. The court can ask a defendant about the financial situation of a spouse (or parent(s), if the person is a juvenile), and if the family member indicates a willingness to pay all or part of the costs of counsel, the judicial officer may direct the retention of private counsel.

Courts are admonished that doubts about a person's eligibility should be resolved in favor of the making the appointment because any errors in the financial assessment can be corrected later, while denying a person appointed counsel can have a devastating impact on the defense. The judge inform the defendant of the penalties for making a false statement on the Form CJA 23, as well as the obligation to inform the court and the appointed attorney of any change in financial status. Prosecutions for perjury for lying on the financial affidavit have been brought.

> **Practice Note:** Prosecutors are generally barred from using the information in the financial affidavit against the defendant. If there is a concern that it contains sensitive information which could affect the defense of a case, such as identifying the location of accounts or assets, defense counsel can move to have the affidavit sealed and submitted to the court ex parte.

The determination of financial eligibility is not a one-time event, so that a defendant who was able to afford private counsel at one point may apply later for an appointed lawyer under the CJA. If the defendant's original lawyer is a panel attorney who is willing to continue the representation, courts will usually appoint that same attorney in order to maintain continuity in the representation and save the expense of having a new attorney spend time mastering the case. If a defendant has sufficient resources to provide for personal and family necessities but not enough to pay all the costs of retained counsel, the court can appoint counsel and direct the person to pay an amount to the clerk of the court on a regular basis to help defray the cost of the lawyer. 18 U.S.C. § 3006(f).

Once counsel is appointed to represent a defendant, the lawyer must adhere to the requirements set by the Administrative Office of the United States Courts for submitting vouchers for payment of fees on Form CJA

20 and, when required, creating a budget on Form CJA 28A if the case may become extraordinary in terms of potential costs that exceed the CJA limits on reimbursement. Defense counsel is required to submit vouchers electronically.

FORMS:

Appointment of and Authority to Pay Court-Appointed Counsel (CJA 20) and Instructions:

http://www.uscourts.gov/forms/vouchers/appointment-and-authority-pay-court-appointed-counsel

Financial Affidavit (CJA 23):

http://www.uscourts.gov/forms/cja-forms/financial-affidavit

CJA eVoucher Program:

https://evsdweb.ev.uscourts.gov/CJA_c09_prod/CJAeVoucher/

CHAPTER 3

SPEEDY TRIAL ACT

■ ■ ■

The Sixth Amendment provides that a defendant has a right to a "speedy and public trial." The Supreme Court has found that both the defendant and society have an interest in a prompt adjudication of charges. *Barker v. Wingo,* 407 U.S. 514, 519–20 (1972). In light of this interest, Congress adopted the Speedy Trial Act (STA), 18 U.S.C. § 3161 et seq., providing specified time limits for criminal prosecutions. Pursuant to the STA, each district court must adopt a Speedy Trial Act plan setting forth how judges will schedule criminal cases, time limits for filing motions and briefs, and periods in which the court should decide an issue. These plans can and often do go beyond the statute's requirements.

A. BASIC REQUIREMENTS OF THE SPEEDY TRIAL ACT

The basic timing requirement of the STA provides that a trial must start no less than 30 days after a defendant's first appearance with counsel on the charges and not more than 70 days after the commencement of the case by filing an indictment or criminal information, or the defendant's appearance before a judicial officer, whichever is later. The 30-day minimum is designed to ensure that there is adequate time to prepare, and the 70-day maximum effectuates the constitutional guarantee of a prompt adjudication of charges.

The 30-day limit starts the STA clock, but the starting date can be changed if certain subsequent events occur. For example, if the government files a superseding indictment, then that restarts the clock. In addition, not all criminal proceedings trigger the STA's guidelines. For example, a state arrest does not trigger the STA, even if federal charges are later filed based on the same underlying conduct, because the STA only applies to the commencement of the federal prosecution. Many states have their own speedy trial laws and rules, which govern criminal prosecutions in those jurisdictions.

Under the STA, prosecutors must file an indictment or information within 30 days of a defendant's arrest on a criminal complaint or service of a summons requiring the person to appear. Failure to do so within the required time limit can result in dismissal of the indictment or information. The 30-day time limit does not apply if a defendant is arrested and then released without charges being filed, and the limit only applies to charges listed in the original complaint and not to new counts added at a later time.

The 70-day limit is frequently an issue in prosecutions. Trials rarely commence within 70 calendar days, and the exclusions provided in the STA mean that federal proceedings often take months, and sometimes even years, to commence. The 70-day period does not begin until the later of the filing of an indictment or criminal information, if the defendant has been arrested, or of the first appearance of the defendant before a judicial officer. If a charge is dismissed and then later refiled, the clock is restarted and the earlier period is not counted, absent abusive conduct by the prosecutor. Similarly, the time after a charge is dismissed by the trial court and later reinstated after a government appeal of that decision is not counted toward the 70-day limit.

The STA provides for excludable time which stops the clock for certain periods while specified proceedings in the case take place. Some Speedy Trial Act Plans limit the use of excludable time by setting a basic time table for criminal cases, regardless of the excludable time provided in the STA, For example, the United States District Court for the Southern District of Iowa's Plan provides that "[e]xcept in complex cases, trial should ordinarily occur within 120 calendar days from arraignment."

The STA's provisions for excluding time can roughly be broken down into two categories: delays related to proceedings involving the defendant and delays in the case that do not necessarily involve actions taken in relation to the defendant. The date a triggering event occurs is when the clock stops, so that day is not included in the 70-day limit, and the clock is not restarted until the day *after* the event that restarts the clock, such as the issuance of a decision by the court.

These exclusions of time are crucial to counting the time toward the 70-day limit because any error in properly calculating the availability or amount of excludable time may result in a trial beginning after the prescribed starting date. The remedy for a violation of the STA's time limits is dismissal of the charges under 18 U.S.C. § 3162(a), which can be with or without prejudice. The statute provides that in deciding what type of dismissal to order for a violation, the court should consider the following: "the seriousness of the offense; the facts and circumstances of the case which led to the dismissal; and the impact of a reprosecution on the administration of this chapter and on the administration of justice." Most dismissals for violating the STA are without prejudice, but some cases have resulted in dismissal with prejudice, which prevents the government from refiling the charges.

B. DELAY RELATED TO THE DEFENDANT

Section 3161(h)(1) provides for the following exclusions from the 70-day limit to commence trial:

(A) Delay resulting from any proceeding, including any examinations, to determine the mental competency or physical capacity of the defendant;

(B) Delay resulting from trial with respect to other charges against the defendant;

(C) Delay resulting from any interlocutory appeal;

(D) Delay resulting from any pretrial motion, from the filing of the motion through the conclusion of the hearing on, or other prompt disposition of, such motion;

(E) Delay resulting from any proceeding relating to the transfer of a case or the removal of any defendant from another district under the Federal Rules of Criminal Procedure;

(F) Delay resulting from transportation of any defendant from another district, or to and from places of examination or hospitalization, except that any time consumed in excess of ten days from the date an order of removal or an order directing such transportation, and the defendant's arrival at the destination shall be presumed to be unreasonable;

(G) Delay resulting from consideration by the court of a proposed plea agreement to be entered into by the defendant and the attorney for the Government; and

(H) Delay reasonably attributable to any period, not to exceed 30 days, during which any proceeding concerning the defendant is actually under advisement by the court.

The exclusion in § 3161(h)(1)(D) for pretrial motions is the most common ground for permissible delay in a federal criminal case because of the number of filings with the district court in a typical case, including motions required to be filed under Rule 12(b)(3). See Chapter 9. In *United States v. Tinklenberg*, 563 U.S. 647 (2011), the Supreme Court held that "the filing of a pretrial motion falls within this provision irrespective of whether it actually causes, or is expected to cause, delay in starting a trial." Thus, the clock will be stopped by the filing of any motion until its disposition, including the 30-day period under § 3161(h)(1)(H) that the judge has to issue a decision once a matter is taken under advisement.

C. OTHER DELAYS

Section 3161(h)(2)–(8) provides for the following additional exclusions from the 70-day limit to commence trial:

- A deferred prosecution agreement with the defendant during which the defendant can establish good behavior;

- The absence or unavailability of the defendant or an essential witness, which occurs "whenever his whereabouts are known but his presence for trial cannot be obtained by due diligence or he resists appearing at or being returned for trial";

- Any period during which the defendant is mentally incompetent or physically unable to stand trial;

- The period after dismissal of a charge and refiling of the same charge by the prosecutor;

- A reasonable period when the defendant is joined for trial with a codefendant, and the STA time for commencing trial as to the other defendant has not run and no motion for severance has been granted; and

- A period not to exceed one year to obtain evidence from a foreign country.

In addition, time made be excluded under the so-called "ends of justice" delay, which allows a trial court to stop the clock for an extended period because of considerations related to the case that are not governed by the other provisions of the STA. Section 3161(h)(7)(A) authorizes a continuance granted by any judge on his own motion or at the request of the defendant or his counsel or at the request of the attorney for the Government, if the judge granted the continuance on the basis of a finding that the ends of justice served by granting a continuance outweigh the interest of the public and the defendant in a speedy trial.

Section 3161(h)(7)(B) list the factors a court should consider in determining whether to grant a continuance in a case under the "ends of justice" exception to the 70-day requirement:

- Whether the failure to grant such a continuance in the proceeding would be likely to make a continuation of such proceeding impossible or result in a miscarriage of justice;

- Whether the case is so unusual or so complex, due to the number of defendants, the nature of the prosecution, or the existence of novel questions of fact or law, that it is unreasonable to expect adequate preparation for pretrial proceedings or for the trial itself within the time limits established by this section;

- Whether, in a case in which arrest precedes indictment, delay in the filing of the indictment is caused because the arrest occurs at a time such that it is unreasonable to expect return and filing of the indictment within the period specified in § 3161(b), or because the facts upon which the grand jury must base its determination are unusual or complex; and

- Whether the failure to grant a continuance in a case which, taken as a whole, is not so unusual or so complex as to fall within clause (ii), would deny the defendant reasonable time to obtain counsel, would unreasonably deny the defendant or the Government continuity of counsel, or would deny counsel for the defendant or the attorney for the Government the reasonable time necessary for effective preparation, taking into account the exercise of due diligence.

There is no limit imposed on the length of the permissible delay under § 3161(h)(7)(B), so postponement of trial on this ground can last for a significant period of time. In order to authorize an "ends of justice" delay, the trial court must set forth on the record, orally or in writing, "the reasons for finding that the ends of justice served by the granting of such continuance out-weigh the best interests of the public and the defendant in a speedy trial." § 3161(h)(7)(A). In *Zedner v. United States*, 547 U.S. 489 (2006), the Supreme Court made clear that the trial court must put its findings on the record about the basis for an ends-of-justice delay, at the very latest when ruling on a motion to dismiss for impermissible delay but more properly at the time the decision is made on the delay. The Court explained that under the STA a court's failure to make these required findings will result in the delay being counted in for STA purposes and that "if as a result the trial does not begin on time, the indictment or information must be dismissed." *Id.* at 508. Examples of a motion to exclude time and an order excluding time are included at the end of this chapter.

It is the obligation of attorneys for both sides, along with the court, to monitor the timing of the case to ensure compliance with the STA. Counsel should create a separate calendar for each case so that the crucial dates can be entered, and any continuances can be counted as excludable time in calculating the date when a trial must take place. If a question arises regarding whether time should be excluded from the 70-day limit to commence trial, or if there is a new basis on which time should be excluded, then it is imperative that the grounds for the delay and its basis in the STA be placed on the record so that an appellate court is not forced to guess at the reasons.

SAMPLE SPEEDY TRIAL ACT MOTION

United States District Court
For the Eastern District Of Wayne

UNITED STATES OF AMERICA,
Plantiff

v.   Case No. _____

D-1 _____   Honorable_____

Defendant

STIPULATION CONTINUING TRIAL DATE AND EXCLUDING TIME UNDER THE SPEEDY TRIAL ACT

A. The United States of America and the Defendant, _____, through their respective attorneys, hereby agree and stipulate to continue the trial in this case and to exclude the time period from [date of hearing or stipulation] and the new trial date from computation under the Speedy Trial Act. The reason(s) for the continuance is (are): [*insert explanation here*]

B. The parties further agree that the ends of justice served by the continuance outweigh the best interests of the Defendant and the public in a speedy trial, and [check all that apply, but per the statute 2 and 3 cannot both be checked]:

1. The failure to grant such a continuance would be

    ☐ likely to make a continuation of such proceeding impossible

    ☐ to result in a miscarriage of justice.

2. The case is so

    ☐ unusual

    ☐ complex

due to

   ☐ the number of defendants

   ☐ the nature of the prosecution

   ☐ the existence of novel questions of fact or law

that it is unreasonable to expect adequate preparation for pretrial proceedings or for the trial itself within the time limits established by the Speedy Trial Act.

3. The failure to grant the continuance would

    ☐ deny the defendant reasonable time to obtain counsel

    ☐ unreasonably deny the defendant continuity of counsel

    ☐ unreasonably deny the government continuity of counsel.

☐ deny counsel for the defendant the reasonable time necessary for effective preparation, taking into account the exercise of due diligence

☐ deny counsel for the government the reasonable time necessary for effective preparation, taking into account the exercise of due diligence.

4. (Other factors considered).

C. The parties further agree that the period of time from [date of hearing or stipulation] to and including [new trial date], constitutes a period of delay which shall be excluded in computing the time within which the trial in this case must commence pursuant to the Speedy Trial Act, 18 U.S.C. §§ 3161(h)(8)(A) and (h)(8)(B).

DATED _____.

By: _____

Assistant U.S. Attorney

By: _____

Attorney for Defendant

SAMPLE PROPOSED ORDER

United States District Court
For the Eastern District Of Wayne

UNITED STATES OF AMERICA,
Plantiff

v.   Case No. _____

D-1 _____   Honorable_____

Defendant

ORDER CONTINUING TRIAL AND EXCLUDING
SPEEDY TRIAL ACT TIME

The above Stipulation Continuing Trial Date And Excluding Time Under the Speedy Trial Act is hereby approved, and the agreements set forth in paragraphs A, B, and C of the Stipulation is adopted as findings by the court.

For the reasons stated, IT IS HEREBY ORDERED:

(1) the jury selection and trial are set for [date];

(2) the final pretrial conference is set for [date] at 10:00 a.m.;

(3) [if applicable] defense motions are due on [date], and the government's responses are due on [date].

IT IS FURTHER ORDERED that the period of time from [date of hearing or stipulation] to and including [new trial date], constitutes a period of delay which shall be excluded in computing the time within which the trial in this case must commence pursuant to the Speedy Trial Act, 18 U.S.C. §§ 3161(h)(8)(A) and (h)(8)(B).

DATED _____.

/s/ _____

United States District Judge

CHAPTER 4

PRETRIAL DETENTION AND BAIL

■ ■ ■

The Bail Reform Act, 18 U.S.C. § 1341 et seq., governs bail and pretrial detention for federal defendants. This statute requires that a defendant generally be afforded pretrial release, but permits pretrial detention for enumerated reasons, including when the defendant presents a particular flight risk or danger to a person or the community. Although the Eighth Amendment mandates that "[e]xcessive bail shall not be required," the Supreme Court has concluded that neither the Eighth Amendment nor the Due Process Clause prohibit pretrial detention. *United States v. Salerno*, 481 U.S. 739 (1987). As the Court explained, "the pretrial detention contemplated by the Bail Reform Act is regulatory in nature, and does not constitute punishment before trial in violation of the Due Process Clause." *Id.* at 748.

A. PRETRIAL DETENTION

18 U.S.C. § 3142 sets forth the procedures governing the bond and detention determinations at the trial-court level. Bond is a pledge of cash or property by the defendant or others to secure release on the condition that if the defendant fails to appear at future proceedings, the bond will be forfeited to the government.

The question whether the defendant will be detained or released on bond is first taken up at a defendant's initial appearance. At that hearing, the government has the absolute right, without any showing of cause, to require that the defendant be "temporarily detained" for up to three business days. As a practical matter, however, when the government requests temporary detention, the resulting detention hearing typically takes place the following business day. The defendant may also request that the detention hearing be extended for five business days to prepare for the hearing.

If the government seeks to have the defendant detained until trial, it has the burden of establishing that the defendant presents a risk of flight or a danger to a particular person, such as a victim or witness, or to the community. The government's position on detention will be considered at a hearing, usually conducted before a magistrate judge in the first instance. 18 U.S.C. § 3142(f)(2). The level of proof required at this hearing depends on the government's claim. The government must prove a risk of nonappearance by a preponderance of the evidence, while it must show a danger to any person or the community by clear and convincing evidence.

There are a limited number of statutorily-defined "presumption" cases in which "[s]ubject to rebuttal by the [defendant], it shall be presumed that no condition or combination of conditions will reasonably assure the appearance of the [defendant] as required and the safety of the community." 18 U.S.C. § 3142(e)(3). The presumptions only apply to determining whether to detain a defendant, and do not affect the presumption of innocence applicable at trial. 18 U.S.C. § 3142(j). The most common presumption cases include:

- Drug trafficking offenses subject to imprisonment for ten years or more (in practice, almost every controlled substance offense other than those involving less than 50 kilograms of marijuana);
- Terrorism-related offenses;
- Offenses involving the use and carrying of a firearm during, or possession of a firearm in furtherance of, a crime of violence or drug trafficking offense; and
- Human trafficking and child exploitation offenses, other than simple possession of child pornography.

For the statutory presumption to apply, there must be a finding that there is probable cause to conclude that the defendant committed the charged offense. If an indictment has not yet been returned, and the defendant is charged by criminal complaint, the government must show the magistrate judge at the detention hearing that there is probable cause for the statutory presumption to apply. By contrast, if the defendant has been charged by an indictment, that satisfies the probable cause requirement.

If the government establishes that the statutory presumption applies, the defendant bears the burden of producing some evidence to refute this showing. If the defendant does not produce any evidence, the presumption can be sufficient to authorize pretrial detention. If, on the other hand, the defendant produces evidence in support of the claim that the presumption should not apply, the government retains the burden to persuade the court that there is a risk of flight or danger to the community. In deciding whether that burden is met, § 3142(g) sets forth a list of four non-exhaustive factors to be considered by the magistrate judge at the detention hearing "in determining whether there are conditions of release that will reasonably assure the appearance of the person as required and the safety of any other person and the community." These are:

- The nature and circumstances of the offense, including in particular whether the alleged crime involves violence, child exploitation, terrorism, controlled substances or firearms;
- The weight of the evidence against the defendant;
- The history and characteristics of the defendant, including family and community ties, history of employment, financial resources, and prior interaction with the criminal justice system (*i.e.*, criminal history, any record of prior nonappearances, and whether on probation, parole, or other form of release at the time of the current offense); and
- The nature and seriousness of the danger to any person or the community that would be posed by the defendant's release.

At the detention hearing, "the rules concerning admissibility of evidence in criminal trials do not apply to the presentation and consideration of information." 18 U.S.C. § 3142(f)(2). Accordingly, the government often proceeds by proffer, with the prosecutor recounting the relevant facts in lieu of calling a live witness. In fact, the weight of authority holds that the government can proceed by proffer at a detention hearing, irrespective of a defendant's demand that the government proceed through live testimony. *See United States v. El Hage*, 213 F.3d 74, 82 (2d Cir. 2000) ("While the defendant may present his own witnesses and cross examine any witnesses that the government calls, either party may proceed by proffer and the rules of evidence do not apply"); *United States v. Smith*, 79 F.3d 1208, 1210 (D.C. Cir. 1996) ("We join our sister circuits in holding that it 'literally goes without saying' the government has the right to proceed by proffer. A right to require the Government to produce its witnesses against him would complicate the hearing to a degree out of proportion to the liberty interest at stake"); *United States v. Brunette*, 839 F. Supp. 2d 449, 453 (D. Mass. 2012) ("Although the statute, 18 U.S.C. § 3142(f), allows the defendant to 'present information by proffer or otherwise,' there is no provision permitting the Government to do the same but neither is there a prohibition against the Government going this route.").

The defendant generally has the right to present relevant information by proffer, as well as to testify (although that is uncommon), to call his own witnesses, and to cross-examine any witnesses that are called by the government. Some courts have recognized a defendant's "conditional right to call adverse witnesses," either in the trial court's discretion or if "he can proffer to the court in reasonable detail how he expects their testimony to negate substantial probability." *United States v. Gaviria*, 828 F.2d 667, 670 (11th Cir. 1987); *see United States v. Pasciuti*, 958 F.2d 361 (1st Cir. 1992) (finding no abuse of discretion in district court's refusal to subpoena officer). A defendant's testimony at a detention hearing generally may not be used by the government at a later trial if it was given to overcome a presumption of dangerousness that will result in being detained prior to trial. *See United States v. Perry*, 788 F.2d 100, 116 (3d Cir. 1986). Even if a defendant's testimony cannot be used in the prosecution's case-in-chief, however, it can be used to impeach the defendant should he or she testify at trial.

Prior to the detention hearing, the district court's Pretrial Services Office prepares a report, based on an interview of the defendant and any available family members, employers, or other acquaintances, setting forth facts relevant to each of the § 3142(g) factors. The Pretrial Services Report also presents the magistrate judge with the Office's recommendation as to whether detention is appropriate in the particular case. Because the Pretrial Services Office has the responsibility for monitoring the defendant if he is released, its recommendation carries significant weight in the court's ultimate determination.

B. RELEASE ON BAIL

In most cases, especially non-violent ones, the prosecution does not seek pretrial detention, but rather asks the court for release of the defendant with certain conditions, including bond and restrictions on the defendant's activities. When the prosecution does not seek pretrial detention, or if it fails to establish that detention is necessary and appropriate, the defendant is released, subject to a personal recognizance/unsecured appearance bond and such "least restrictive further condition, or combination of conditions, that ... will reasonably assure the appearance of the person as required and the safety of any other person and the community." 18 U.S.C. § 3142(c)(1)(B). Because the Bail Reform Act prohibits "a financial condition that results in the pretrial detention of the person," 18 U.S.C. § 3142(c)(2), cash bonds, as opposed to a pledge of cash, jewelry, or other property, are disfavored in the federal system.

Standard bond conditions imposed in every case include: (1) maintaining or seeking employment; (2) not committing any additional crimes; (3) resolving any outstanding warrants; (4) refraining from possession of firearms; and (5) avoiding the use of drugs or excessive use of alcohol. In child exploitation cases, electronic monitoring (*i.e.,* a tether) is also required as a mandatory bond condition. 18 U.S.C. § 3142(c).

The magistrate judge may also impose additional bond conditions, including:

- Requiring the defendant to provide a DNA sample;
- Prohibiting contact with co-defendants, witnesses, and victims;

- Requiring mental, psychological or psychiatric treatment, including for drug and alcohol dependency;
- Appointing a third-party custodian;
- Requiring the defendant to be subject to electronic monitoring (*i.e.*, a tether);
- Requiring home confinement, which precludes leaving the home other than for employment, religious activities, visits with counsel, and court appearances; and
- Imposing house arrest, which precludes leaving the home other than for court appearances.

Both the government and the defendant have the right to appeal a magistrate's detention determination to the district court. 18 U.S.C. § 3145. If the defendant has been indicted, the district court judge assigned to the case will hear the appeal. If the defendant has not yet been indicted, the appeal will be heard by the "duty" district court judge. Review is *de novo* and the district judge may take evidence. As a practical matter, however, the district judge usually will hear arguments based on the record developed before the magistrate judge. Both the defendant and the government may appeal immediately a district court decision to the circuit court.

> **Practice Note:** The plain language of § 3145 makes clear that a defendant may only appeal a magistrate judge's detention order to one district court judge, with any further recourse being to the circuit court of appeals. That is, a pre-indictment defendant may not appeal his detention to the miscellaneous district court judge and, if he loses, appeal again to the district court judge later assigned to the case post-indictment. But at least one district court has held that such internecine review may be possible where there is a "clear error of law or changed circumstances." *United States v. Logan*, 613 F. Supp. 1227, 1228 (D. Mont. 1985).

After conviction and pending sentencing, courts revisit the issue of detention for defendants. For presumption offenses, detention becomes mandatory post-conviction, unless the trial court finds a substantial likelihood that a motion for acquittal or new trial will be granted or unless the government states its intention not to seek a sentence of imprisonment and the court finds by clear and convincing evidence that the defendant is neither likely to flee nor pose a danger to any other person or the community. 18 U.S.C. § 3143(a)(2). For non-presumption offenses, detention is also required post-conviction, unless the court finds by clear and convincing evidence that the person is not likely to flee or pose a danger if released. 18 U.S.C. § 3143(a)(1). As a practical matter, however, and notwithstanding the prescriptive language of the Bail Reform Act, defendants who are on bond at the time of conviction generally are permitted to remain on bond through sentencing, particularly those who plead guilty.

Finally, release pending appeal is disfavored. For presumption offenses, detention is mandatory barring exceptional circumstances. 18 U.S.C. § 3143(b)(2), 3145(c). For non-presumption offenses, to warrant release, the court must find that the appeal raises a substantial question of law or fact likely to result in reversal, a new trial, or a non-custodial sentence, and that the defendant is neither a risk of flight nor a danger to the community. 18 U.S.C. § 3143(b)(1).

FORMS:

Order Scheduling a Detention Hearing (AO 470):
http://www.uscourts.gov/forms/pretrial-detention-forms/order-scheduling-detention-hearing

Order to Detain a Defendant Temporarily Under 18 U.S.C. § 3142(d) (AO 471):
http://www.uscourts.gov/forms/pretrial-detention-forms/order-detain-defendant-temporarily-under-18-usc-ss-3142d

Order of Detention Pending Trial (AO 472):
http://www.uscourts.gov/forms/pretrial-detention-forms/order-detention-pending-trial

Appearance Bond (AO 98):
http://www.uscourts.gov/forms/pretrial-release-and-appearance-bond-forms/appearance-bond

Bail Information Sheet (AO 100A):
http://www.uscourts.gov/forms/criminal-forms/bail-information-sheet

Surety Information Sheet (AO 100B):
http://www.uscourts.gov/forms/criminal-forms/surety-information-sheet

Order Setting Conditions of Release (AO 199A):
http://www.uscourts.gov/forms/pretrial-release-and-appearance-bond-forms/order-setting-conditions-release

Additional Conditions of Release (AO 199B):
http://www.uscourts.gov/forms/pretrial-release-and-appearance-bond-forms/additional-conditions-release

Advice of Penalties/Acknowledgment (AO 199C):
http://www.uscourts.gov/forms/pretrial-release-and-appearance-bond-forms/advice-penaltiesacknowledgment

PART 2

PREPARING THE CASE FOR PROSECUTION

■ ■ ■

CHAPTER 5

PRELIMINARY HEARING

■ ■ ■

A. PROCEDURES

Federal Rule of Criminal Procedure 5.1 requires a magistrate judge to hold a preliminary hearing unless a grand jury returns an indictment or the defendant waives the right to the hearing. A preliminary hearing is not a mini-trial on the guilt of the defendant. Rather, the magistrate judge examines the government's evidence and determines whether that evidence is sufficient to show probable cause the defendant committed the offense(s) alleged in the complaint. Because the preliminary hearing is an adversarial proceeding and considered a "critical stage" of the prosecution, an indigent defendant has the right to appointed counsel at this hearing. *Coleman v. Alabama,* 399 U.S. 1 (1970).

Rule 5.1(c) governs the general timing for a preliminary hearing: within 10 days of the initial appearance for a defendant in custody and within 20 days for a defendant who is not in custody. But, a preliminary hearing may be postponed if the defendant consents and there is good cause for the delay under Rule 5.1(d). If a defendant does not consent to the delay, a preliminary hearing can be postponed only if the prosecution shows "extraordinary circumstances exist and justice requires the delay."

At the hearing, the prosecution bears the burden of showing that there is probable cause to conclude that a crime was committed and that the defendant committed the charged offense(s). In order to satisfy this burden, the prosecution calls witnesses and submits documentary or forensic evidence. The magistrate judge then renders a judgment as to whether the government has shown that there is probable cause to believe the defendant committed the offense. As with the standard for issuance of a warrant, the probable cause standard is lower than the typical preponderance of the evidence requirement in civil litigation. *United States v. Sokolow,* 490 U.S. 1 (1989). Thus, while the magistrate judge assesses the credibility of any witnesses who testify, the standard is whether a reasonable juror *could* credit the testimony and not whether magistrate judged actually believed the witness.

Federal Rule of Evidence 1101(d) specifically exempts preliminary hearings from the requirements for admission of evidence. Constitutional and evidentiary testimonial privileges, however, are available. For example, a witness can assert the Fifth Amendment privilege and refuse to testify, and evidentiary privileges, such as those for attorney-client or spousal communications, may be asserted unless an exception to the privilege applies. Because the rules of evidence do not apply at these hearings, the government can rely on hearsay statements to show there is sufficient evidence to proceed to trial. In fact, at these hearings, an investigative agent frequently recounts what an eyewitness or confidential informant reported about the crime—testimony that would not be admitted at trial unless the demands of both the Confrontation Clause and the evidence rules were satisfied. Permitting such testimony reflects the reality that prosecutors do not want to expose witnesses who might be in danger, especially if the investigation is on-going.

Although the government is permitted to use hearsay statements at preliminary hearings, the Advisory Committee note to Rule 5.1 points out that a magistrate judge may require "a showing that admissible evidence will be available at the time of trial." Thus, a prosecutor should explain to the magistrate judge the reason for using hearsay evidence and discuss whether the person is likely to be available to testify at trial.

In addition to using hearsay evidence, the government may use evidence that could be suppressed at trial because it was unlawfully obtained. Under Rule 5.1(e), a defendant is not permitted to object to evidence "on the ground that it was unlawfully acquired." Rule 5.1(e) also permits defendants to cross-examine the government's witnesses and introduce evidence. However, because the purpose of the preliminary hearing is limited to a probable cause determination, the magistrate judge may curtail the defendant's presentation of evidence if the government established probable cause.

A preliminary hearing is not required in every case. A defendant can waive the proceeding and proceed directly to trial. Even when a defendant does not consent to waive a hearing, a prosecutor may avoid a preliminary hearing by proceeding with a grand jury indictment. Because a grand jury determines whether there is probable cause for a charge, an indictment eliminates the need for a preliminary hearing. Thus, because the Fifth Amendment requires a grand jury indictment for any felony, the prosecution can avoid preliminary hearings as long as the indictment is returned by the grand jury within the time period permitted by Rule 5.1(c).

Rule 5.1(a)(3) also provides that when a defendant consents pursuant to Federal Rule of Criminal Procedure 7(b) to the filing of a criminal information charging a felony, this consent effectively waives the right to have a preliminary hearing. This procedure is commonly used when a defendant agrees to plead guilty to the charge. And, Rule 5.1(a) provides that a preliminary hearing is not required when a defendant is charged with a misdemeanor in a criminal information or when the defendant consents to a trial before a magistrate judge on a misdemeanor charge.

B. BENEFITS OF A PRELIMINARY HEARING

Preliminary hearings permit weak cases to be dismissed before requiring defendants to expend significant time and resources defending themselves. In addition, preliminary hearings may benefit both the government and defendants. These hearings give both sides the opportunity to evaluate the credibility of prosecution witnesses and their ability to hold up on cross-examination. In addition, the hearings allow the parties to evaluate the risks of trial and the benefits of a plea offer.

For the government, a preliminary hearing allows for the possibility of preserving evidence, which can be important for meeting the requirements of the Confrontation Clause under *Crawford v. Washington*, 541 U.S. 36 (2004). As a general matter, a magistrate judge may limit cross-examination at a preliminary hearing because the proceeding's purpose is only to determine whether there is sufficient evidence to go to trial, not a determination of guilt. The Confrontation Clause, however, requires that the defendant must be afforded a full and fair opportunity to cross-examine the witness or the testimony is not admissible at trial. Thus, if a prosecutor wishes to preserve the ability to use the testimony provided at a preliminary hearing, that prosecutor should notify the magistrate judge and defense counsel of any concerns about the possible unavailability of the witness so that the defendant can be afforded the right to fully cross-examine the witness.

The defendant can also realize significant benefits from a preliminary hearing. The proceeding gives the defense a preview of the government's case, including discovery of the prosecution's theory of the case and at least some of the evidence it intends to use at trial to prove the violation. Because pre-trial depositions of witnesses are largely unavailable in federal prosecutions, the opportunity to hear direct testimony and then cross-examine a witness may provide invaluable information not otherwise available.

Witness testimony at a preliminary hearing also provides the defense with several additional benefits. First, the defense may obtain witness statements that it might not otherwise receive until trial. Rule 5.1(h) establishes that Rule 26.2 applies to preliminary hearings. As a result, the government must turn over prior recorded statements of any witnesses it calls to testify at the preliminary hearing. In the absence of the witness testifying, the defense may not have access to these statements until trial. See Chapter 7. Second, the testimony may also give the defense impeachment material at trial. For example, a witness who is tentative at the preliminary examination in identifying a defendant or recalling the details of a crime, but who is much firmer in that recollection at trial, may be cross-examined regarding how the person's memory suddenly improved. Defense counsel may be able to impeach the witness by suggesting that the witness had assistance in developing an improved memory.

The defense counsel can also try to use the preliminary hearing as an opportunity to question a witness beyond the scope of the direct examination, such as asking the person about any prior crimes or agreements with the government. Asking such questions serves two goals. First, the answers to those questions may provide useful information in developing a defense. Second, if the prosecution successfully objects to these questions, defense counsel may use the successful objection to bar the introduction of the witness's preliminary hearing testimony at trial if the witness is later unavailable on the ground that there was not an opportunity for full cross-examination as required by *Crawford*.

Although the defendant has the right to a preliminary hearing, there may be good reasons for the defense to waive the proceeding and allow the case to move forward to trial. Most commonly, defendants waive the right to a preliminary hearing to avoid adverse publicity. Because almost all preliminary hearings are open to the public, and because in large part only the government's evidence will be introduced at the hearing, the publicity generated by these hearings can have an adverse effect on the jury pool. The defense may conclude that this adverse impact outweighs any benefit if might receive from the preliminary hearing.

> **Practice Note:** As a general proposition, prosecutors do not want to put on the entire case during the preliminary examination, so some evidence may be held back from the hearing. The prosecutor can also pursue a case after dismissal of the charge by the magistrate judge by seeking a grand jury indictment. Because the probable cause standard for an indictment is the same as for a preliminary hearing, a grand jury indictment would be valid and obviate the need for another preliminary hearing. The prior dismissal is irrelevant to the validity of a subsequent grand jury indictment.

C. THE BINDOVER DECISION

If the magistrate judge finds that there is probable cause that the defendant committed the charged offense(s), the case proceeds forward, i.e., it is "bound over." On the other hand, if the magistrate judge determines the government did not produce sufficient evidence to establish probable cause, the court "must dismiss the complaint and discharge the defendant." Rule 5.1(f).

Even if the complaint is dismissed, however, the case against the defendant does not necessarily end. Rule 5.1(f) provides that dismissal "does not preclude the government from later prosecuting the defendant for the same offense." Double jeopardy does not apply to a pre-trial dismissal of charges, so there is no constitutional prohibition on pursuing the same charges in a subsequent proceeding. In fact, the government is not required to obtain additional evidence before charging the defendant again after charges were dismissed, although as a strategic matter the government may choose to do some additional investigation.

A defendant does not have a right to appeal the decision that there is probable cause for the charge. Moreover, once a fact finder validly finds the defendant guilty beyond a reasonable doubt in a subsequent trial, any failure to dismiss the charge after the preliminary hearing is considered harmless error. In addition, the harmless error standard applies to any allegations of constitutional errors at the preliminary hearing. For example, while the denial of counsel at a preliminary hearing is a constitutional violation, courts still inquire as to whether this error tainted the subsequent conviction. *Coleman v. Alabama*, 399 U.S. 1 (1970). Thus, a defendant may not appeal any alleged errors during a preliminary hearing after receiving a guilty verdict.

Chapter 6

The Grand Jury Indictment

■ ■ ■

A. HISTORICAL BACKGROUND

At the time of the adoption of the Constitution, the grand jury was renowned as "the people's panel," serving as both a "shield" and a "sword." The colonists before the American Revolution viewed the grand jury as protecting against unfounded and oppressive initiation of prosecutions when the Crown's evidence was insufficient or the prosecution simply appeared unjust. Exercising that screening authority, colonial grand jurors showed their independence by refusing to issue indictments against those who had spoken against royal power, such as the refusal to indict Peter Zenger for seditious libel (although the British authorities then proceeded against him by a prosecutor's information). The grand jury served as a sword when it investigated on its own initiative and brought criminal charges, even over the opposition of the colonial government, by issuing a presentment against British officials and soldiers. Thus, it was not surprising that the grand jury's powers were given constitutional recognition in the Fifth Amendment, which provides that no person shall "be held to answer for a capital or otherwise infamous crime, unless on a presentment or indictment of a Grand Jury."

By the end of the nineteenth century, however, the grand jury had lost much of its luster. Its value as a shield was questioned by critics who contended that the grand jury was unrepresentative and inefficient, and inferior to magistrates in screening out cases in which the prosecution's evidence was insufficient. A number of states abolished the requirement that all felony prosecutions be initiated by indictment, thereby allowing prosecutions to proceed by criminal information, which is a set of charges drafted by the prosecutor's office. In the federal system, where the constitutional requirement still applies, Federal Rule of Criminal Procedure 7(b) authorizes federal prosecutors to proceed by filing a criminal information if the defendant waives the right to indictment for an offense punishable by more than one year imprisonment.

B. INVESTIGATORY POWER

In its earliest form, the grand jury relied on the observations and information provided by individual grand jurors, who were often leading members of the community, to determine whether a crime occurred. A grand jury today obtains evidence, which includes compelling witnesses to appear, through the use of subpoenas. The grand jury is entitled to "every man's evidence" as part of its investigation. "Because its task is to inquire into the existence of possible criminal conduct and to return only well-founded indictments, its investigative powers are necessarily broad." *Branzburg v. Hayes*, 408 U.S. 665, 688 (1972). The grand jury "may act on tips, rumors, evidence offered by the prosecutor, or their own personal knowledge." *United States v. Dionisio*, 410 U.S. 1, 16 (1973).

A grand jury can require a person to appear before it by issuing a subpoena *ad testificandum* and to provide documents and other physical evidence by means of a subpoena *duces tecum*. The grand jury's authority is buttressed by the contempt power of the court. Federal Rule of Criminal Procedure 17(g) provides, "The court . . . may hold in contempt a witness who, without adequate excuse, disobeys a subpoena issued by a federal court in that district." A witness may be jailed for civil contempt in which the person "holds the keys" to the jail cell and can be released upon compliance with the subpoena or if the court determines there is no possibility the person will comply. In addition, a person who refuses to comply with a grand jury subpoena may also be charged with criminal contempt under 18 U.S.C. § 403.

In the modern grand jury, the prosecutor's role in the process is to serve as the grand jury's legal advisor. The prosecutor and not—except in very rare cases—individual grand jurors make the decisions regarding which witnesses to subpoena and what evidence to seek. A subpoena need not be approved in advance by the grand jurors, and frequently prosecutors issue subpoenas on behalf of the grand jury before its members even begin to review evidence or hear testimony. In addition, investigative agencies, like the FBI, often conduct a preliminary review of a case before any decision is made about whether to present evidence to the grand jury for possible charges.

Using a grand jury as the vehicle to investigate a case in conjunction with law enforcement officers, such as FBI special agents, can provide significant advantages to prosecutors. Unlike a search warrant, which requires the approval of a judicial officer based on probable cause, a grand jury subpoena can be issued without prior judicial approval and without the need to establish probable cause. In addition, witnesses testifying before a grand jury are usually placed under oath, and, if they lie, may be subject to a perjury prosecution.

At the same time, a grand jury investigation can be more cumbersome because of the time it takes to receive a response to a subpoena. Investigators lose the element of surprise that they have when they interview a suspect or execute a search warrant because most grand jury subpoenas give the recipient a period of time to comply. And, during this time period, the evidence remains in the control of the recipient who may delay responding, destroy the evidence, or otherwise place it beyond the reach of the authorities.

The Fourth Amendment is largely inapplicable to grand jury investigations, and the government is not precluded from submitting evidence to the grand jury that may have been obtained in violation of the Fourth Amendment. Moreover, in *United States v. Dionisio*, 410 U.S. 1, 15 (1973), the Supreme Court rejected the argument that a grand jury subpoena for voice exemplars violated the Fourth Amendment requirements for a search because "neither the summons to appear before the grand jury nor its directive to make a voice recording infringed upon any interest protected by the Fourth Amendment. . . ." Thus, a subpoena can be used to require a person to provide certain items, such as material to conduct a DNA test or a handwriting or voice exemplar, because the witness does not have a reasonable expectation of privacy regarding certain external characteristics, and, therefore, there is no search for purposes of the Fourth Amendment. *See United States v. Mara*, 410 U.S. 19 (1973). If, however, a subpoena is the functional equivalent of a search because of its breadth, some lower courts have ordered that the subpoena be quashed and only allow for a narrower one.

Along the same line, the Fifth and Sixth Amendments are generally not implicated by grand jury proceedings. *Miranda* warnings need not be given to the witness because testifying in a grand jury is not considered a custodial interrogation, despite the fact that a failure to appear and answer questions may be subject to judicial contempt. *United States v. Mandujano*, 425 U.S. 564 (1976). And, unlike a police custodial interrogation where a person has the right to counsel, a witness has no right to be accompanied by counsel in connection with an appearance before a grand jury. The witness may be permitted to consult with counsel outside the grand jury room, but because neither *Miranda* nor the Sixth Amendment right to counsel attach to an appearance before the grand jury, there is no constitutional requirement to furnish counsel to a witness. Nor does a witness appearing before a grand jury have a constitutional right to a warning that the person is a target of the investigation. *United States v. Washington*, 431 U.S. 181 (1977). Finally, a person who is target of a grand jury investigation does not have a right to require the prosecutor to call him or her to testify before the grand jury.

The grand jury's investigative authority is not unlimited. Witness privileges, such as the protection for attorney-client or marital communications and the Fifth Amendment right against compelled self-incrimination, apply in the grand jury and may be a valid basis to resist providing evidence and testimony. In addition, in *United States v. R.*

Enterprises, 498 U.S. 292, 300 (1991), the Supreme Court noted that a grand jury is not "licensed to engage in arbitrary fishing expeditions, nor may they select targets of investigation out of malice or an intent to harass."

Federal Rule of Criminal Procedure 17(c)(1) sets forth the requirements for subpoenas issued in federal investigations:

> A subpoena may order the witness to produce any books, papers, documents, data, or other objects the subpoena designates. The court may direct the witness to produce the designated items in court before trial or before they are to be offered in evidence. When the items arrive, the court may permit the parties and their attorneys to inspect all or part of them.

A subpoena may be directed to a natural person or a legal entity. Where records of a corporation or other type of organization, such as a labor union or law partnership, are sought, the subpoena may be directed to a "custodian of records" for the entity. The description of the subpoenaed records often includes phrases like "any and all documents reflecting, referring, or relating to" and "any and all documents in the possession, custody, or control of" an identified person or organization. This broad language makes it more difficult for the recipient to avoid producing potentially incriminating records by claiming the records were not included in the subpoena from the grand jury.

Federal prosecutors often are willing to make arrangements for service of the subpoena and delivery of documents and other materials so that the recipient does not have to appear before the grand jury. In addition, counsel for the subpoena recipient frequently request an extension of time for delivery of the materials and seek clarification about the scope of the subpoena. Consequently, counsel and prosecutors may negotiate over limiting the time frame for the records sought or to allow for production in stages as documents are retrieved and reviewed if the subpoena seeks a large number of business records.

C. CHALLENGING GRAND JURY SUBPOENAS

When the challenge goes to the underlying validity of the subpoena, it is presented through a motion to quash under Rule 17(c)(2) on the ground that compliance with the subpoena would be "unreasonable or oppressive." The Supreme Court gave a broad reading to the validity of grand jury subpoenas in *United States v. R. Enterprises*, 498 U.S. 292 (1991), which considered a challenge to subpoenas on the ground that the items sought were irrelevant to the investigation because they were outside the grand jury's jurisdiction. The Court stated, "[A] grand jury subpoena issued through normal channels is presumed to be reasonable, and the burden of showing unreasonableness must be on the recipient who seeks to avoid compliance." *Id.* at 301. When assessing the validity of a grand jury subpoena, *R. Enterprises* held that "the motion to quash must be denied unless the district court determines that there is no reasonable possibility that the category of materials the government seeks will produce information relevant to the general subject of the grand jury's investigation." *Id.* Given the broad reach of the federal criminal law and the grand jury's expansive authority to investigate possible violations, *R. Enterprises* makes it very difficult to challenge a subpoena on the ground that the information sought is irrelevant to the investigation or not within the power of the grand jury to review.

Because it is so difficult to quash a subpoena, the most common challenges are those based on a common law, statutory, or constitutional privileges. The full range of privileges applicable in federal courts, such as the Fifth Amendment right against self-incrimination and the attorney-client privilege, applies to grand jury proceedings. These types of challenges do not contest the validity of the subpoena itself, but seek to interpose the privilege claim to prevent having to respond to certain questions or produce particular records.

Any witness may assert the Fifth Amendment right against self-incrimination as the basis for refusing to testify before the grand jury. The Supreme Court, however, significantly limited the ability to raise a Fifth Amendment challenge to the production of documents in *Fisher v. United States*, 425 U.S. 391, 411 (1976). In *Fisher,* the Court held that the contents of voluntarily created records were not protected by the Fifth Amendment because there was no compulsion in their creation, and, therefore, they did not qualify for the protection afforded by the privilege against self-incrimination. The Court did not dispense completely with the Fifth Amendment protection of documents. Instead, it recognized that the act of production in response to a subpoena communicated information about the existence, possession, and authenticity of the records sought could implicate the privilege against self-incrimination. Thus, the Court recognized that the act-of-production privilege can be asserted if turning over the documents—considered a communicative act—would be incriminating by providing the government with information that could be used against the witness.

There is no privilege for providing documents if the information conveyed by producing the documents is not incriminating because it was "a foregone conclusion and the [witness] adds little or nothing to the sum total of the Government's information by conceding that he in fact has the papers." *Id.* at 411. In other words, if the government can show that it already knows about the existence, possession, and authenticity of the records sought, there is no incriminating communication by producing them and the witness can be compelled to comply with the subpoena. The foregone conclusion analysis requires the government to show that it possessed information about the existence, possession, and authenticity of the records at the time it issued the subpoena.

If prosecutors are unable to establish the foregone conclusion regarding the records, they still can compel production of the records if the witness is given use/fruits immunity. See Chapter 7. This type of immunity prohibits the government from making any direct or derivative use of the communicative aspect of the act of production. Use immunity prevents the government from both referring to the defendant's act of production and, in most cases, using the content of the records at trial. *United States v. Hubbell*, 530 U.S. 27 (2000). In *Hubbell,* the Court held that any use of the documents would violate the immunity provided to the defendant because "[i]t is abundantly clear that the testimonial aspect of respondent's act of producing subpoenaed documents was the first step in a chain of evidence that led to this prosecution." *Id.* at 42.

Fisher's act-of-production privilege applies to a sole proprietorship. *United States v. Doe*, 465 U.S. 605 (1984). But, for corporations and larger business organizations, there is no Fifth Amendment right to resist producing the organization's documents. In *Braswell v. United States*, 487 U.S. 99 (1988), the Court reaffirmed its long-standing position denying the privilege against self-incrimination to corporations under the "collective entity doctrine." *Braswell* held a custodian of records "may not resist a subpoena for corporate records on Fifth Amendment grounds," regardless of the size or complexity of the organization. *Id.* at 109. The entity at issue was a small corporation, with only a single shareholder, but because a corporate form was chosen, there was no right to resist a subpoena *duces tecum* directed to it.

Although the collective entity doctrine bars an organization from asserting the Fifth Amendment in response to a subpoena for its records, there are limits on the use of the testimony of the witness producing the documents. First, the act of producing those records cannot be used against the custodian in a subsequent prosecution of that person. *Braswell* explained in a footnote that limiting the evidentiary use of the corporation's document production was a "necessary concomitant of the notion that a corporate custodian acts as an agent and not an individual when he produces corporate records in response to a subpoena addressed to him in his representative capacity." *Id.* at 119 n.11. Second, if the person holding the records is no longer an employee of the organization, the records may be considered personal documents for which the act-of-production privilege could be asserted to resist supplying them to the grand jury in response to a subpoena.

D. THE CHARGING AUTHORITY

Under Federal Rule of Criminal Procedure 6(a)(1), a grand jury ranges in size from 16 to 23 members, who are selected largely in the same way as members of petit juries who decide a defendant's guilt. Unlike a petit jury, a grand jury sits for a designated period of time rather than deciding a particular case, and usually hears evidence from a number of investigations that may result in returning indictments in hundreds of prosecutions. Pursuant to Rule 6(g), a grand jury is impaneled for eighteen months, although its term can be extended six months, and in certain special situations a statute authorizes a grand jury to sit for up to three years. The frequency with which the grand jurors must attend sessions depends on a prosecutor's caseload and the number of grand juries in a district. In a larger urban area, there are likely to be multiple grand juries with at least one meeting every day.

There are no peremptory challenges to remove a grand juror, and there is no involvement of prosecutors or defense counsel in their selection. Rule 6(b)(1) authorizes challenges to the composition of a grand jury by either the prosecution or defense "on the ground that it was not lawfully drawn, summoned, or selected, and may challenge an individual juror on the ground that the juror is not legally qualified." These challenges would be brought after an indictment, not during a grand jury investigation.

The chief judge of the district usually administers the oath and gives the grand jurors general instructions about their duties. This marks the end of the judge's formal involvement in the process. From that point forward, the federal prosecutors control the course of the proceedings. The press and public are barred from the proceedings, as are suspects (unless testifying before the grand jury) and their counsel. Even judges are not allowed in the room while a grand jury is sitting. Rule 6(e)(2)(B) provides that only the following individuals are permitted to attend a grand jury proceeding and must not disclose any matter occurring before it: "(i) a grand juror; (ii) an interpreter; (iii) a court reporter; (iv) an operator of a recording device; (v) a person who transcribes recorded testimony; (vi) an attorney for the government; or (vii) a person to whom disclosure is made under Rule 6(e)(3)(A)(ii) or (iii)."

An important feature of grand jury investigations is their secrecy under Rule 6(e). Those participating in the proceeding, except for a witness, are sworn to secrecy, and any violation of the rule by disclosing information about matters occurring before the grand jury is subject to civil or criminal contempt. Moreover, unless the defendant is entitled to the testimony under *Brady v. Maryland* or the Jencks Act, see Chapter 7, the defendant may not obtain transcripts of the grand jury proceedings.

The grand jury's primary task is to review the evidence presented to it by the prosecutor and to determine whether there is probable cause to charge an individual with an offense. The prosecutor calls witnesses, questions them, and presents documentary and forensic evidence related to the conduct in question. Unlike jurors at a trial, grand jurors may freely ask questions of the witnesses and discuss the case with the prosecutor as evidence is submitted, rather than waiting until the end of the presentation. After the witnesses have testified and the evidence is provided, the prosecutor usually summarizes the law and asks the jurors to vote to return an indictment accusing one or more persons of any crimes that the prosecutor believes are supported by the evidence.

Under Rule 6(d)(2), "No person other than the jurors, and any interpreter needed to assist a hearing-impaired or speech-impaired juror, may be present while the grand jury is deliberating or voting." Pursuant to Rule 6(f), "A grand jury may indict only if at least 12 jurors concur." If there is an affirmative vote, the grand jury foreperson or deputy foreperson returns the indictment "to a magistrate judge in open court." On the other hand, if a defendant has been charged by an information and 12 grand jurors do not vote in favor of the indictment, the foreperson "must promptly and in writing report the lack of concurrence to the magistrate judge." In addition, if the grand jury concludes that the evidence is insufficient, it returns a "no bill" (or "no true bill"). A "no bill" does not preclude the government from seeking an indictment from a second grand jury, however, because the protection against double jeopardy does not attach to the grand jury's decision.

E. REQUIREMENTS FOR A VALID INDICTMENT

Prosecutors have enormous discretion in deciding whether to file charges and what charges to pursue. A decision not to file charges is virtually unreviewable by the courts. For example, a police officer who observes a minor transgression of the law could decide not to pursue the matter with a formal arrest or citation, perhaps by giving the person a warning. Similarly, a prosecutor can review the evidence in a case and decide that it is insufficient to establish criminal liability for an offense, or that there are insufficient resources to pursue the matter further. In addition, a prosecutor may determine that the matter should be pursued in a civil or administrative proceeding or referred to state or local authorities.

While less broad than the prosecutor's discretion not to charge a crime, the prosecutor has substantial control over what particular violation(s) to charge, when to initiate the prosecution (subject to the applicable statute of limitations), and in certain instances where the prosecution will be pursued. The breadth of federal criminal law often means that a variety of charges can be filed arising from a single course of conduct, and the law does not limit the government's authority to file multiple charges so long as the elements of each offense can be established.

The Fifth Amendment requires that federal criminal prosecutions for all capital or "otherwise infamous" crimes be brought by grand jury indictment. The Supreme Court has defined an "infamous crime" as one punishable by imprisonment in a penitentiary or for a term of years at hard labor. *Mackin v. United States*, 117 U.S. 348 (1886). The Indictment Clause applies to charges, not the actual punishment, and any crime with a potential penalty of at least one year is considered "infamous" because the defendant can be confined in a penitentiary.

If a grand jury indictment is not required, or the defendant waives the right to an indictment, the prosecutor can initiate a case by filing a criminal information. Indictments or criminal informations must give the defendant sufficient notice of the charge(s) to allow for a determination whether the defendant's double jeopardy rights have been implicated. Once a case goes to trial, the government is generally bound by the terms of the charging instrument, and a variance between the charges and the proof may result in a conviction being overturned.

At one time, courts applied hyper-technical pleading rules that were often a trap for the unwary or a means by which courts could vacate convictions in cases in which it found the government's evidence of questionable quality. The Federal Rules of Criminal Procedure put an end to the technical and formalized pleading rules. Rule 7(c)(1) requires that an indictment or information "must be a plain, concise, and definite written statement of the essential facts constituting the offense charged and must be signed by an attorney for the government. It need not contain a formal introduction or conclusion."

Each count of an indictment or information is considered as if it were a separate charging document, so a count must be sufficient in itself. However, prosecutors can satisfy this requirement by expressly incorporating allegations from one count into other counts. The government can also allege that the means by which the defendant committed the offense are unknown, or that he or she committed the crime by one or more specified means. This eliminates the use of multiple counts in which each alleges the commission of the offense by a different means or in a different way.

1. DUPLICITY AND MULTIPLICITY

Defendants may attack an indictment as being "duplicitous" or "multiplicitous." An indictment or information that charges two (or more) different offenses in a single count is called "duplicitous," although a charge that alleges different means to commit a single offense is not duplicitous. For example, a charge of distribution of a controlled substance that alleges the defendant sold different types of drugs is not duplicitous. Duplicity in an indictment or information is not necessarily fatal to the case if it comes to the court's attention before the jury begins its deliberations. Courts usually allow the prosecution to correct the error by selecting a single crime on which it will proceed for each count.

An indictment or information that charges the same offense in different counts is termed "multiplicitous." Multiplicity is improper because the defendant may receive more than one sentence for a single offense and this result would violate the Double Jeopardy Clause. Separate charges related to a single course of conduct are not necessarily considered multiplicitous, however, if each charge requires proof of facts that the other count does not. For example, under the federal mail fraud statute, each separate mailing can be charged as a separate offense even though there is only one scheme to defraud. Similarly, a defendant who makes a series of attempts to steal another person's identity could be charged with the same crime in multiple counts.

2. NOTICE REQUIREMENT

An indictment or criminal information must provide a defendant with sufficient notice of the charge in order to prepare a defense and, if necessary, invoke the Double Jeopardy Clause to bar a second prosecution. In *Hamling v. United States*, 418 U.S. 87, 118 (1974), the Supreme Court explained that "an indictment is sufficient if it, first, contains the elements of the offense charged and fairly informs a defendant of the charge against which he must defend, and, second, enables him to plead an acquittal or conviction in bar of future prosecutions for the same offense." Reciting the words of the statute allegedly violated can be sufficient to provide the defendant with adequate notice of the charge so long as it is "accompanied with such a statement of the facts and circumstances as will inform the accused of the specific offence, coming under the general description, with which he is charged." *United States v. Hess*, 124 U.S. 483, 487 (1888). Rule 7(c)(1) requires the indictment to cite the statute or rule claimed to have been violated, although Rule 7(c)(2) provides that "[u]nless the defendant was misled and thereby prejudiced, neither an error in a citation nor a citation's omission is a ground to dismiss the indictment or information or to reverse a conviction."

An indictment or criminal information must provide the defendant with certain factual information about the charged offense(s). Simply alleging that defendant "committed a burglary" without including the location of the crime, the approximate date (and time) of its occurrence, and the intended offense upon entry would not provide a basis to discern what the government intends to prove. The prosecution, however, is not required to plead its theory of guilt, nor must it provide detailed information or a description of the evidence or witnesses it intends to call to prove the case. For certain types of offenses, such as those involving a single act or result, providing a general statement of the date—and perhaps the time—of the crime, which need not be exact, and the location and identity of the defendant and victim(s) is often sufficient. For example, it is common for a criminal charge to state that the offense took place "on or about July 1" so that any error in the exact date cannot be the basis for dismissing a charge or overturning a conviction.

3. INCLUDING ESSENTIAL ELEMENTS

The indictment must contain all of the relevant elements of the alleged charge. Sometimes this can be done by quoting the statute. The danger of simply reciting the statuory language alone is that it may not expressly include a crucial element. Some statutes do not contain an express *mens rea* element, but an intent element has been required by courts in construing the provision. For example, proof of securities fraud for insider trading requires that the defendant breach a "duty of trust and confidence" owed to the source of the confidential information, even though this requirement is not found in the language of the statute. This requirement is only found in Supreme Court decisions that analyzed the meaning of "deceptive" in the relevant statute. Just quoting the statute in the charging document without including the intent required for the offense could result in a determination that the indictment or information was inadequate and could lead to dismissal of a charge or reversal of a conviction.

For the purpose of establishing venue, the charge need only state that the offense took place in the district in which the prosecution occurs. The government bears the burden of proving venue, but the indictment need not establish that by pleading all the facts necessary to establish the location of the prosecution is proper. When the government charges more complex crimes, such as conspiracy or a fraudulent scheme, it is required to provide greater detail in the charging document, such as the manner and means of the criminal agreement or illegal object of the scheme.

In federal prosecutions, a defendant must raise a challenge to the institution of a prosecution before trial. But Federal Rule of Criminal Procedure 12(b)(2) provides that "[a] motion that the court lacks jurisdiction may be made at any time while the case is pending." A failure to allege an essential element of the crime means that the indictment does not "state an offense" and the charge could be dismissed at any point when the case is pending.

In short, prosecutors must draft the charging instrument with some care or risk reversal of a conviction. In *Russell v. United States*, 369 U.S.

749 (1962), the Supreme Court overturned convictions because the indictment simply tracked the statute but did not adequately identify a key aspect of the crime. The defendants were charged with contempt of Congress for refusing to testify before a House Subcommittee, but there was no identification of the subject matter of the hearing in the indictment. The statute at issue made it a crime to refuse to answer questions "pertinent to the question under inquiry" by the congressional subcommittee, so the failure to allege the subject matter of the proceeding was a fatal error in the indictment. According to the Court, "A cryptic form of indictment in cases of this kind requires the defendant to go to trial with the chief issue undefined. It enables his conviction to rest on one point and the affirmance of the conviction to rest on another. It gives the prosecution free hand on appeal to fill in the gaps of proof by surmise or conjecture." *Id.* at 766.

F. AMENDING THE INFORMATION OR INDICTMENT

Although Rule 7(e) permits amendment of an information before a verdict, an indictment is treated differently. Because an indictment reflects the decision of the grand jury regarding what should be charged based on the evidence presented, federal courts do not allow substantive changes to the indictment, apart from dropping a count or a means of committing the offense. *Ex parte Bain*, 121 U.S. 1 (1887). In *Russell v. United States*, 369 U.S. 749, 770 (1962), the Supreme Court recognized that minor changes to an indictment could be made, stating that "an indictment may not be amended except by resubmission to the grand jury, unless the change is merely a matter of form." Permissible changes to an indictment include a correction in the spelling of a defendant's name or the location of an offense, but anything more extensive requires reindictment by the grand jury.

Rule 7(d) permits a court to remove language from an indictment if the defendant so requests. The Rule does not authorize the prosecutor to move to delete language from the charging document. Nevertheless, a court may accede to a prosecutor's request, or even act on its own initiative, to remove surplusage absent an objection by the defendant.

The traditional rule was that an indictment need not set forth allegations relevant only to sentencing and not guilt. In *Apprendi v. New Jersey*, 530 U.S. 466 (2000), and its progeny, the Supreme Court has held that any fact—other than a prior conviction—that increases the penalty for an offense beyond the statutory maximum must be submitted to a jury and proved beyond a reasonable doubt. These decisions mean that prosecutors must add certain facts in the charging document to establish the defendant's liability for a sentencing enhancement. For example, if an assault is punishable by five years' imprisonment, but is punishable by a ten-year sentence where the motivating factor for the attack is racial animus, then that factor must be alleged in the indictment and proven to the jury beyond a reasonable doubt.

Defendants frequently seek greater detail from the prosecutor about the charges through discovery requests seeking the government's evidence. Many states and the federal government explicitly authorize a court to order the prosecutor to provide additional information through a bill of particulars. See Chapter 10. Even those jurisdictions that do not specifically provide for such a procedure generally allow a court to order the government to provide additional information to overcome shortcomings in an indictment or information.

G. USE OF GRAND JURY SUBPOENAS AFTER INDICTMENT

The investigation of wrongdoing is not necessarily complete when a defendant is charged with a crime. Investigators may continue to look into the charged offenses as well as additional crimes beyond those in the indictment or information. However, while the grand jury's broad power to gather evidence and compel witnesses to appear before it continues, there are limitations on its authority to gather evidence to aid the pending criminal prosecution as opposed to investigating new or different violations.

The grand jury cannot be used as an aid to discovery for the criminal charges, which is governed by Federal Rule of Criminal Procedure 16. See Chapter 7. The fact that the information sought by the grand jury may be useful in a pending prosecution is not in itself reason to quash a subpoena. Rather, the validity of a grand jury subpoena related to a defendant who was previously charged depends on whether it is issued for the sole or dominant purpose of preparing for trial on an already pending indictment. *United States v. Doss*, 563 F.2d 265, 276 (6th Cir. 1977) (en banc). On the other hand, when a grand jury seeks information that may be useful in prosecuting pending criminal charges, the key issue is whether there is any "reasonable possibility that the category of materials the Government seeks will produce information relevant to the general subject of the grand jury's investigation." *United States v. R. Enterprises*, 498 U.S. 292, 301 (1992). The inquiry centers on the information's potential usefulness to the investigation by the grand jury that issued the subpoena, so that "[o]nce it is shown that a subpoena might aid the grand jury in its investigation, it is generally recognized that the subpoena should issue even though there is also a possibility that the prosecutor will use it for some other purpose than obtaining evidence for the grand jury." *United States v. (Under Seal)*, 714 F.2d 347, 350 (4th Cir. 1983).

If the subpoena is issued for an improper purpose, then the available remedies are to quash the subpoena. Alternatively, a court may "enforce the rule against using a grand jury subpoena predominantly for trial preparation simply by barring use at trial of evidence obtained pursuant to the subpoena, thereby leaving the grand jury's access to the evidence unimpaired." *In re Grand Jury Subpoena Duces Tecum Dated Jan. 2, 1985 (Simels)*, 767 F.2d 26, 30 (2d Cir. 1985).

Courts have generally permitted defendants to challenge grand jury subpoenas issued after an indictment, even when the subpoena is directed to a third party, such as a financial institution, telecommunications or internet service provider, or travel agency. In addition, when the government adds counts or expands the scope of charges through a superseding indictment based on information gathered by the grand jury after the return of the first indictment, the new charges can be challenged based on misuse of the grand jury if there is no substantial difference between the original charge and those in the superseding indictment. In *United States v. Flemmi*, 245 F.3d 24, 30 (1st Cir. 2001), the First Circuit explained:

> A prosecutor's renewed resort to the grand jury for evidence-gathering purposes cannot be validated simply by having the grand jury return any old superseding indictment. If, say, a superseding indictment merely corrects peripheral details or adds something trivial to the pending charges, an inquiring court has every right to be skeptical. But when the new indictment charges new crimes, adds new defendants, or otherwise works a major change in the prior indictment that is sufficiently analogous, for these purposes, to charging new crimes or adding new defendants, it adequately evinces the propriety of the prosecutor's purpose and thus becomes a safe harbor for the government.

H. ARRAIGNMENT

The arraignment is usually held after an indictment or information has been filed. Under Federal Rule of Criminal Procedure 10(a), these proceedings, which must be in open court, consist of reading the indictment or information to the defendant, unless that is waived, and asking the defendant to plead to the charges. Pursuant to Federal Rule of Criminal Procedure 11(a)(1), the defendant may plead guilty, not guilty, or nolo contendere. A nolo contendere plea, in which the defendant states he is not contesting the government's charges, requires the court's permission.

Guilty pleas are discussed in detail in Chapter 14. Briefly, if the defendant pleads guilty or nolo contendere, the court must question the defendant and determine that the defendant understands his constitutional right and the consequences of the guilty plea. Rule 11(b)(1). The court must also determine that the plea is voluntary and that there is a factual basis for the plea. Rule 11(b)(2)–(3). If the guilty plea is reached pursuant to a plea bargain, that bargain is required to be disclosed in open court, unless the court excuses this requirement. Rule 11(c)(2). If the court rejects a plea agreement, the court must give the defendant an opportunity to withdraw his guilty plea. Rule 11(c)(5).

If a defendant pleads not guilty, the magistrate judge will issue a scheduling order and inform the defendant what federal district judge will preside of the remainder of the case. This scheduling order may include evidentiary hearings necessitated by motions to suppress evidence, as well as a date for a pretrial conference and the trial itself.

SAMPLE INDICTMENT—Bank Fraud

United States District Court
For the Eastern District of Wayne

UNITED STATES OF AMERICA

v.

D-1 DEFENDANT 1 and

D-2 DEFENDANT 2

INDICTMENT

The grand jury charges:

COUNT ONE

(18 U.S.C. § 1349—*Conspiracy to Commit Bank Fraud*)

DEFENDANT 1 and DEFENDANT 2

The Defendants and Other Related Parties

1. At all times relevant to this Indictment, DEFENDANT 1 was a resident of Cook City, Wayne, and was a real estate agent licensed by the State of Wayne. As a real estate agent, DEFENDANT 1 acted on behalf of buyers and sellers of residential and commercial real estate in Wayne.

2. At all times relevant to this Indictment, DEFENDANT 2 was a resident of Cook City, Wayne, and was a real estate agent licensed by the State of Wayne. DEFENDANT 2 worked with DEFENDANT 1, and also acted on behalf of buyers and sellers of residential and commercial real estate in Wayne.

3. At all times relevant to this Indictment, BOS Asset Management, LLC ("BOS"), was a limited liability company organized under the laws of the State of Wayne for which DEFENDANT 1 was the sole member. DEFENDANT 1 used BOS to facilitate the purchase of real property in Wayne.

4. At all times relevant to this Indictment, a trust formed under the laws of the State of Wayne, which trust's identity is known to the Grand Jury and which hereinafter is referred to as the "Trust," was an entity which provided funding for the purchase of real property by BOS and DEFENDANT 1, and on its own account, during the period from 2012 to 2013, as described herein.

5. At all times relevant to this Indictment, the Trust held assets, including accounts, which were managed by an investment adviser firm located in New York, New York, the identity of which is known to the Grand Jury ("Investment Adviser"). DEFENDANT 2 was able to communicate requests for funds to the Investment Advisor directly, and the grantor of the Trust would then authorize the Investment Advisor to transfer funds from the Trust to an entity designated by DEFENDANT 2.

6. At all times relevant to this Indictment, Wells Fairview Bank, N.A., was a financial institution headquartered in San Francisco, California, the deposits of which are insured by the Federal Deposit Insurance Corporation, and Wells Fairview Home Mortgage was a division of Wells Fairview Bank, N.A. (jointly, "Wells Fairview").

7. At all times relevant to this Indictment, Regional Bank was a financial institution headquartered in Alabama, the deposits of which are insured by the Federal Deposit Insurance Corporation.

The Conspiracy

8. From in or about November 2012, and continuing through in or about December 2013, in the Eastern District of Wayne and elsewhere, DEFENDANT 1 and DEFENDANT 2, and others known and unknown to the Grand Jury, willfully and knowingly did combine, conspire, confederate and agree together and with each other to commit the offense of bank fraud against the United States. The object of the conspiracy was that the defendants would and did knowingly and willfully, and with intent to defraud, devise a scheme or artifice to defraud Wells Fairview, Regional Bank and other financial institutions known and unknown to the Grand Jury, and to obtain moneys, property, credits, assets, securities or other property owned by or under the custody or control of financial institutions, by means of materially false and fraudulent pretenses, representations, and promises, which scheme and artifice in substance as set forth herein, is contrary to 18 U.S.C. § 1344.

The Manner and Means of the Conspiracy

9. It was part of the conspiracy that DEFENDANT 1 and DEFENDANT 2, or either of them or others acting at the direction of either of them, made material misrepresentations to financial institutions about the price buyers had offered to pay for real property on which the financial institutions held or controlled mortgages and other property rights. Because the mortgage balances were more than the amount of the proposed offers to sell the properties, the banks had to approve a proposed "short sale" price and agree to release their liens at a loss before a sale transferring clear title to a buyer could take place.

10. It was further part of the conspiracy that DEFENDANT 1 used his company, BOS, to make straw purchases of real estate which were funded primarily by the Trust. DEFENDANT 1 then caused the properties to be resold within a day or two of the initial transaction.

11. During the course of the conspiracy, DEFENDANT 2 identified certain real estate transactions for which she was the listing real estate agent, and negotiated "short sales" with various lenders. DEFENDANT 2 also arranged for the Trust's funds to be available to BOS in order to make straw purchases of real estate. At DEFENDANT 2's direction, the Trust itself acted as a straw buyer of various properties on at least two occasions.

12. It was further part of the conspiracy that DEFENDANT 1 and DEFENDANT 2 executed, or caused to be executed, purchase and sale agreements between homeowners of real property and BOS at a price that was substantially lower than a price already offered by a third party purchaser (the "Preexisting Price(s)"). During the course of the conspiracy, either DEFENDANT 2 or DEFENDANT 1 would be the listing agent for the subject properties and they worked together from the same office where they would have access to written offers to purchase the subject properties at the Preexisting Prices. DEFENDANT 2 and DEFENDANT 1 created the straw buyer contracts at a lower price than Preexisting Prices. The purpose of the straw buyer contracts was to create a circumstance where, for a subject property, neither the mortgage holder or property owner received the benefit of the difference between the short sale price and the Preexisting Price.

13. During the course of the conspiracy, DEFENDANT 2, DEFENDANT 2 or others acting at the direction of DEFENDANT 2 or DEFENDANT 2: (a) contacted the relevant financial institution holding a mortgage or other property right relating to real estate or the mortgage servicing agent; (b) disclosed the purchase and sale agreement between the homeowner and BOS, or between the homeowner and the Trust; (c) did not disclose the higher priced purchase and sale agreement between the homeowner and the third party purchaser of which DEFENDANT 1 or DEFENDANT 2 or both were aware; and (d) requested that the financial institution or its agent agree to release its mortgage in exchange for a payment that was less than the outstanding balance on the mortgage.

14. It was further part of the conspiracy that once a financial institution agreed to release its mortgage for a sum based on the price in a BOS purchase and sale agreement or a Trust purchase and sale agreement, DEFENDANT 1 or DEFENDANT 2 would arrange for two transfers of title for the property. At the first transfer of the property, or the first closing, either the Trust or BOS would purchase the real property at the lower price using funds provided directly by the Trust, through BOS or from others known and unknown to the Grand Jury. At the second closing, the property was then sold to the third party purchaser who had originally offered the higher price, although the financial institution did not know of the second sale and received none of the proceeds from the second sale.

15. It was further part of the conspiracy that DEFENDANT 1 and DEFENDANT 2 concealed the identity of the true owner of the real property from the third party purchasers, and concealed the circumstances surrounding the sale of the property including the final sale price and the identity of the buyers from the homeowners. In addition, DEFENDANT 1 and DEFENDANT 2 concealed the true identity of the third party purchaser, and the terms of the third party purchaser's agreement, from the financial institutions and their agents.

Overt Acts

16. In furtherance of the conspiracy and to effect the objects thereof, within the Eastern District of Wayne and elsewhere, defendants DEFENDANT 1 and DEFENDANT 2, did commit and cause to be committed the following overt acts, among others:

a. On or about January 15, 2013, DEFENDANT 2 in her capacity as a listing real estate agent obtained a purchase and sale agreement for residential real property in Enniton, Wayne, the identity of which is known to the Grand Jury ("Property #1") at a price of $160,000 from an individual whose identity is known to the Grand Jury ("Purchaser #1"). b. On or about January 2013, DEFENDANT 2 advised the owner of Property # 1 whose identity is known to the Grand Jury ("Property Owner #1") to stop paying her mortgage so that the mortgage would go into default and the bank holding the mortgage on the property, Wells Fairview, would be more likely to agree to a short sale transaction.

b. On or about May 12, 2013, DEFENDANT 1, acting as the sole member of BOS, executed a purchase and sale agreement for Property #1 as the purchaser at a price of $128,000.

c. In or about May 2013, DEFENDANT 2 acting as a listing real estate agent and with a power of attorney from Property Owner # 1 agreed with Purchaser #1 to change the price of the January 15, 2013 purchase and sale agreement to be $150,000.

d. On or about May 12, 2013, DEFENDANT 2 acting as a listing real estate for and as a power of attorney or agent of Property Owner #1, sent correspondence to America's Servicing Company, the servicing agent for Wells Fairview, via facsimile transmission, stating that she represented Property Owner #1.

e. On or about June 9, 2013, DEFENDANT 1 and DEFENDANT 2 caused or directed that a deed be executed transferring title to Property #1 from Property Owner #1 to BOS for a sale price of $128,000, free and clear of the mortgage held by Wells Fairview or its successors or agents.

f. On or about June 12, 2013, DEFENDANT 1 caused or directed title to Property #1 to be transferred from BOS to Purchaser #1 for a sale price of $150,000.

g. On or about June 30, 2013, DEFENDANT 2 acting as a listing real estate agent received a written offer to purchase residential real property in Monroe, Wayne, the identity of which is known to the Grand Jury ("Property #2") at a price of $410,000 from individuals whose identity is known to the Grand Jury (jointly, "Purchaser #2").

h. On or about July 28, 2013, DEFENDANT 2 acting as a listing real estate agent and as an agent of a property owner whose identity is known to the Grand Jury ("Property Owner #2") sent correspondence to Select Portfolio Servicing, Inc., the servicing agent for SMI—Credit Swiss Financial Corp.

("Credit Swiss"), via facsimile transmission, including a copy of a HUD-1 form reflecting a proposed sale of Property #2 to the Trust at a price of $370,000.

i. On or about August 7, 2013, DEFENDANT 2 acting as a listing real estate agent received a second written offer to purchase Property #2" for $462,500 from Purchaser #2.

j. On or about August 30, 2013, DEFENDANT 2 caused or directed that a deed be executed transferring title to Property #2 from Property Owner #2 to the Trust based on a sale price of $363,000 free and clear of all mortgages.

k. On or about October 8, 2013, DEFENDANT 2 caused or directed that title to Property #2 to be transferred from the Trust to Purchaser #2 for a sale price of $462,500.

l. On or about August 14, 2013, DEFENDANT 2 acting as a listing real estate agent received a written offer to purchase residential real property located in Cook City, Wayne, the identity of which is known to the Grand Jury ("Property #3"), from individuals whose identities are known to the Grand Jury (jointly, "Purchaser #3"), for a price of $90,000.

m. On or about October 17, 2013, DEFENDANT 1 executed an "Affidavit of Arm's Length Transaction" with regard to the sale of Property #3.

n. On or about October 17, 2013, DEFENDANT 1 and DEFENDANT 2 caused or directed that a deed be executed transferring title to Property #3 to the Trust based on a sale price of $55,000 free and clear of all mortgages.

o. On or about October 30, 2013, DEFENDANT 1 and DEFENDANT 2 caused or directed title to Property #3 to be transferred from the Trust to Purchaser #3 for a sale price of $90,000.

p. On or about December 5, 2012, DEFENDANT 2 acting as a listing real estate agent received a written offer to purchase residential real property located in Enniton, Wayne, the identity of which is known to the Grand Jury ("Property #4"), from an individual, whose identity is known to the Grand Jury ("Purchaser #4") for a price of $132,500.

q. On or about April 14, 2013, DEFENDANT 1, acting as the sole member of BOS, executed a purchase and sale agreement from the property owner or owners of Property #4, whose identity is known to the Grand Jury ("Property Owner #4") for a price of $102,375.

r. On or about June 9, 2013, DEFENDANT 1 and DEFENDANT 2 caused or directed that a deed be executed transferring title to Property #4 from Property Owner #4 to BOS for a sale price of $102,375, free and clear of all mortgages.

s. On or about June 9, 2013, DEFENDANT 1 and DEFENDANT 2 caused or directed that title to Property #4 to be transferred from BOS to Purchaser #4 for a sale price of $132,500.

All in violation of Title 18, United States Code, § 1349.

COUNT TWO

(18 U.S.C. § 1344—Bank Fraud) (18 U.S.C. § 2—Aiding and Abetting)

DEFENDANT 1 and DEFENDANT 2

17. The allegations set forth in paragraphs 1 through 5 and paragraphs 7 through 16 of Count One of this Indictment are hereby realleged and incorporated as though set forth in full herein.

18. On or about June 9, 2013, in the Eastern District of Wayne and elsewhere, DEFENDANT 1 and DEFENDANT 2, knowingly and for the purpose of executing or attempting to execute a fraudulent scheme and artifice to defraud Regional Bank, and to obtain any of the moneys, funds, credits, assets, securities, or other property owned by, or under the custody or control of Regional Bank, by means of false or fraudulent pretenses, representations, or promises, did cause Regional Bank to release its mortgage recorded in the land records of the City of Harperteen, Wayne, against real property known to the Grand Jury as Property #4, for approximately $30,125 less than full consideration.

All in violation of 18 U.S.C. § 1344 and 18 U.S.C. § 2.

JANE DOAH

UNITED STATES ATTORNEY

AL NOONE

ASSISTANT UNITED STATES ATTORNEY

A true bill:

_____

Grand Jury Foreperson

SAMPLE INDICTMENT—Narcotics Distribution

United States District Court
For the Eastern District of Wayne

UNITED STATES OF AMERICA

v.

D-1 DEFENDANT 1

D-2 DEFENDANT 2 and

D-3 DEFENDANT 3

INDICTMENT
COUNT 1 (Conspiracy)

The Grand Jury Charges That:

Between in or about July 2011, the exact date being unknown, and on or about May 31, 2014, in the Eastern District of Wayne, and elsewhere, the defendants, **DEFENDANT 1, DEFENDANT 2,** and **DEFENDANT 3,** did knowingly, willfully and unlawfully combine, conspire and agree together and with others, known and unknown, to commit the following offenses, that is, to manufacture 1,000 or more marijuana plants, a Schedule I controlled substance, in violation of Title 21, United States Code, Sections 841(a)(1)and 841(b)(1)(A); to possess with intent to distribute, and to distribute, marijuana, a Schedule I controlled substance, in violation of Title 21, United States Code, Section 841(a)(1); and to use and maintain a place for the purpose of manufacturing and distributing marijuana, a Schedule I controlled substance, in violation of Title 21, United States Code, Section 856(a)(1).

All in violation of Title 21, United States Code, Section 846.

COUNT 2 (Manufacturing Marijuana)

The Grand Jury Further Charges That:

Between in or about July 2011, the exact date being unknown, and on or about May 31, 2014, at 2157 South Park Avenue, Cook City, Wayne, in the Eastern District of Wayne, the defendants, **DEFENDANT 1, DEFENDANT 2** and **DEFENDANT 3,** did knowingly, intentionally and unlawfully manufacture 100 or more marijuana plants, a Schedule I controlled substance.

All in violation of Title 21, United States Code, Sections 841(a)(1) and 841(b)(1)(B), and Title 18, United States Code, Section 2.

COUNT 3 (Maintaining a Drug-Involved Premises)

The Grand Jury Further Charges That:

Between in or about July 2011, the exact date being unknown, and on or about May 31, 2014, in the Eastern District of Wayne, the defendants,

DEFENDANT 1, DEFENDANT 2 and **DEFENDANT 3,** did knowingly, intentionally and unlawfully use and maintain a place, that is, the premises at 2157 South Park Avenue, Cook City, Wayne, for the purpose of manufacturing and distributing marijuana, a Schedule I controlled substance.

All in violation of Title 21, United States Code, Section 856(a)(1), and Title 18, United States Code, Section 2.

COUNT 4 (Possession of Firearms in Furtherance of Drug Trafficking Crimes)

The Grand Jury Further Charges That:

On or about May 31, 2014, in the Eastern District of Wayne, the defendant, **DEFENDANT 2,** in furtherance of drug trafficking crimes for which they may be prosecuted in a court of the United States, that is, violations of Title 21, United States Code, Section 846, 841(a)(1) and 856(a)(1), as set forth in Counts 1, 2, and 3 of this Indictment, the allegations of which are incorporated herein by reference, did knowingly and unlawfully possess firearms, namely, a Mossberg, 12 gauge shotgun, bearing serial number L4033076; and a BTS SEM CA, SKS Model, 7.62 caliber rifle, bearing serial number 1813209111.

All in violation of Title 18, United States Code, Section 924(c)(1).

JANE DOAH

UNITED STATES ATTORNEY

AL NOONE

ASSISTANT UNITED STATES ATTORNEY

A true bill:

_____

Grand Jury Foreperson

SAMPLE INDICTMENT—Sex Trafficking and Child Pornography

United States District Court
For the Eastern District of Wayne

UNITED STATES OF AMERICA

v.

D-1 DEFENDANT 1 and

D-2 DEFENDANT 2

INDICTMENT

COUNT 1 (Sex Trafficking of Children and Aiding and Abetting)

The Grand Jury Charges That:

Between on or about July 1, 2014 and on or about June 29, 2015, in the Eastern District of Wayne and elsewhere, the defendants, DEFENDANT 1 and DEFENDANT 2, in and affecting interstate commerce, knowingly recruited, enticed, harbored, transported, provided, obtained, and maintained, or caused to be recruited, enticed, harbored, transported, provided, obtained, and maintained, by any means, M.G., a minor female under the age of 18 years, knowing and in reckless disregard of the fact, and having had a reasonable opportunity to observe M.G., that M.G. had not attained the age of 18 years and would be caused to engage in a commercial sex act.

All in Violation of Title18, United States Code, Sections 1591(a)(1) and (2)).

COUNT 2 (Transportation of Minor for Prostitution and Aiding and Abetting)

The Grand Jury Further Charges That:

Between on or about July 1, 2014 and on or about June 29, 2015, in the Eastern District of Wayne and elsewhere, the defendants, DEFENDANT 1 and DEFENDANT 2, did knowingly transport, or cause to be transported, an individual, that is, M.G., a minor female under the age of 18 years, in interstate commerce, that is between Wayne and Indiana, with the intent that M.G. engage in prostitution, a criminal offense under Title 22, Wayne Criminal Code Section 2701 (2008 ed.).

All in violation of Title 18, United States Code, Sections 2423(a) and 2.

COUNT 3 (Production of Child Pornography)

The Grand Jury Further Charges That:

On or about October 12, 2014, in the Eastern District of Wayne and elsewhere, the defendant, DEFENDANT 1, did knowingly and intentionally employ, use, persuade, induce, entice, and coerce M.G., a minor female under the age of 18 years, to engage in sexually explicit conduct for the purpose of producing any visual depiction of such conduct, using materials that have been mailed, shipped, and transported in and affecting interstate and foreign commerce by any means, including by computer.

All in violation of Title 18, United States Code, Section 2251(a).

COUNT 4 (Possession of Child Pornography)

The Grand Jury Further Charges That:

Between on or about October 12, 2014 and on or about June 29, 2015, in the Eastern District of Wayne and elsewhere, the defendant, DEFENDANT 1, did knowingly and intentionally possess matter containing one or more visual depictions, to wit: images contained on a Samsung Galaxy phone, which were produced using materials which had been mailed and shipped and transported in or affecting interstate and foreign commerce, by any means, including by computer, the production of such visual depictions having involved the use of a minor engaging in sexually explicit conduct, and such visual depictions were of such conduct.

All in violation of Title 18, United States Code, Section 2252(a)(4)(B).

JANE DOAH

UNITED STATES ATTORNEY

AL NOONE

ASSISTANT UNITED STATES ATTORNEY

A true bill:

_____

Grand Jury Foreperson

CHAPTER 7

DISCOVERY AND NOTICE OF DEFENSES

■ ■ ■

A. THE SCOPE OF CRIMINAL DISCOVERY

The scope of discovery in a federal criminal prosecution is very different from that available in a civil case. In a civil case, each party has the right to depose other individuals, including any opponent, and to require the production of a range of documents from individuals and organizations. By contrast, in criminal cases, the government and defendant have only limited discovery rights.

The government has a constitutional obligation to turn over material exculpatory evidence to a defendant. *Brady v. Maryland,* 373 U.S. 83 (1963). However, the Supreme Court has made clear that "[t]here is no general constitutional right to discovery in a criminal case." *Weatherford v. Bursey*, 429 U.S. 545, 559 (1977). A defendant's ability to obtain evidence and interview witnesses, therefore, is governed for the most part by statutes and rules.

Federal Rule of Criminal Procedure 16 prescribes reciprocal discovery rights for the government and the defense in federal criminal prosecutions. In addition, although witness depositions are uncommon in federal cases, courts can authorize them under Federal Rule of Criminal Procedure 15 when necessary "because of exceptional circumstances and in the interest of justice." Federal Rule of Criminal Procedure 17 allows each side to issue subpoenas for records and evidence that will be used at trial. Subpoenas under Rule 17, however, cannot be used to sidestep the limits on discovery under other rules.

The government has significant investigative resources, such as the police and other civil and criminal law enforcement agencies, as well as the power of the grand jury to compel the production of evidence as part of its investigation of a crime. Individuals may assert their Fifth Amendment privilege against self-incrimination and refuse to provide the government with statements and—in some circumstances—evidence from the person. But, this right is not absolute. The government can compel an individual to testify under a grant of immunity. This ability to compel testimony by providing immunity gives the government a powerful weapon to obtain evidence from uncooperative witnesses.

By contrast, a defendant may struggle to obtain discovery of the government's evidence. The defense may not compel an interview with an uncooperative witness. Unless a hostile witness is called to testify at a preliminary hearing, the defense may not have the opportunity to question that person until the trial. And, while a defendant has the right, upon request, to receive copies of the evidence that the prosecution plans to introduce at trial, a defendant does not have a right to the list of the witnesses the government intends to call well in advance of trial. Most federal judges, however, require the two sides to exchange witness lists at least before the start of trial. The defense also does not have a right to review any prior statements before a witness testifies. Instead, Federal Rule of Criminal Procedure 26.2 provides that the defense has the right to receive witness statements only after the person has testified. Again, in practice, this information is frequently provided before the trial to allow the proceeding to move forward without delays. Finally, although the defendant's right to receive "*Brady* material" is effectively a form of discovery, prosecutors must disclose only information that is both exculpatory and material.

B. RULE 16 DISCOVERY

The original discovery rule adopted in 1946 was quite limited. The rule required that the government produce only two types of evidence: (1) items that the defendant showed might be material to the preparation of a defense, and (2) any documents obtained from or belonging to the defendant and documents obtained from others by seizure or by process. Federal Rule of Criminal Procedure 16 was greatly expanded in 1966 and provided the prosecution as well as the defense with discovery rights. A sample discovery motion is provided at the end of this Chapter.

Under Rule 16(a)(1), the government must provide, *upon request,* the following information to the defendant:

- The substance of any oral statement by the defendant;
- The defendant's written or recorded statement;
- Any statements made by a representative of an organization charged as a defendant;
- The defendant's prior criminal record;
- Any documents or objects that are: (1) material to preparing the defense; (2) will be used in the government's case-in-chief; or (3) obtained from or belonging to the defendant;
- Any reports of examinations and tests; and
- Any written summaries of expert testimony to be used in the government's case in chief.

While this listing may appear extensive, Rule 16(a) contains two significant limitations on the government's obligation to disclose information to the defendant. First, Rule 16(a)(2) provides that the government is not required to make available to a defendant any reports, memoranda, or internal documents made by an attorney or agent as part of the investigation or prosecution of a case. This protection functions much like the protection afforded by the attorney-client privilege and work product doctrine. Second, Rule 16 excludes witness statements from the discovery. Witness statements are covered by Rule 26.2. And, that Rule provides that statements previously made by a witness must be produced only after the witness testifies at a judicial proceeding, although in practice most federal judges require disclosure earlier in the proceeding.

Practice Note: In developing a defense, defense attorneys may wish to review items and information held by agencies and local police departments, such as 9-1-1 tapes, officer communications, prison recordings, drugs and other paraphernalia, and weapons. Defense counsel should be aware that this type of evidence may be destroyed pursuant to standard retention policies. For example, many jurisdictions maintain recordings and video tapes from police cruisers for 30 to 60 days and then erase them. A defense attorney concerned about such evidence should file a motion requesting an order directing that the government retain these items in an unaltered state.

Rule 16(b) provides the prosecution with reciprocal discovery from the defendant. The prosecution may request discovery once it has complied with the defendant's discovery requests. After the government has fulfilled any discovery requests from the defendant, the defendant must, on request, provide the prosecution with documents or objects that the defense intends to use in its case in chief. If requested, the defense must also provide any reports of examinations and tests done by a witness whom the defense intends to call and any reports of expert witnesses who will testify on behalf of the defense. The reciprocal disclosure obligation does not include reports prepared by the defendant or counsel, or statements made by the defendant. Nor does it include statements to the defendant or defense counsel by any actual or prospective defense or government witness. Rule 16(b)(2). Although this information is protected from discovery, the defendant is required to give notice for certain defenses that may be offered at trial, as discussed below.

Neither the government nor the defendant has a right to demand disclosure of proposed witnesses. As a practical matter, however, judges usually require each side to identify its witnesses in advance of trial. The government is generally not required to disclose the identity of a confidential informant or what that person communicated, at least when the person will not be a witness at trial. In limited circumstances, however, the government could be required to disclose the identity of an informant if that information "is relevant and helpful to the defense of an accused, or is essential to a fair determination of" a case. *Roviaro v. United States*, 353 U.S. 53, 60 (1957).

Rule 16(c) imposes on both sides a continuing duty to disclose evidence throughout the proceeding. In addition, the Rule gives courts the authority to impose a protective order, for good cause, on the information disclosed in discovery, or otherwise "deny, restrict, or defer discovery or inspection." Rule 16(d). Trial judges also have broad authority to remedy a party's failure to comply with the discovery obligations imposed by Rule 16, including continuing a case, prohibiting the introduction of evidence, or "any other order that is just under the circumstances."

Rule 16 does not contain specific timing requirements for turning over discovery. The federal courts usually address the timing issues in their local rules for criminal cases or in standing orders issued by the district judges. For example, the Local Rules for the United States District Court for the District of Massachusetts require the government to produce all evidence governed by Rule 16 and *Brady*, along with the names of any unindicted coconspirators, within 28 days of arraignment unless the defendant waives the right to receive the evidence.

C. RULE 15 DEPOSITIONS

Federal Rule of Criminal Procedure 15 permits a court to authorize a deposition when it is justified by "exceptional circumstances and is in the interest of justice." The original version of Rule 15 only allowed the defendant to request witness depositions. In 1975, the rule was amended, and now both the government and the defendant can seek judicial approval to depose a witness in advance of trial. If the court permits a deposition, the deposition is conducted in the same manner as one taken in a civil proceeding under the Federal Rules of Civil Procedure.

The party wishing to depose a witness must request permission of the court to conduct a deposition, and the opposing side must have the opportunity to object to the request. The party asking for the deposition must show that there are "exceptional circumstances" that justify the deposition. Because neither party can immediately appeal a decision to permit (or deny) a motion to depose a witness, the trial court has broad discretion in deciding deposition requests.

Trial courts generally require the party to establish both the materiality of the witness' testimony and the necessity of a deposition based on the particular circumstances of the case. Moreover, although Rule 15 does not specifically mention the need to establish the witness's likely unavailability at trial, courts frequently treat unavailability as a key consideration. The fact that obtaining the testimony by deposition is more convenient does not meet the "exceptional circumstances" standard. Rather, this standard requires the party to show a situation such as a witness residing abroad who cannot be compelled to appear at trial or an aged or seriously infirm witness who may not be able to attend the proceeding.

Any deposition by the prosecution implicates the Confrontation Clause. The Confrontation Clause requires that defendants have a meaningful opportunity for both a face-to-face meeting with the witness and for full cross-examination. As a result, Rule 15(c) has strict requirements to ensure the presence of a defendant and counsel at a deposition. When the government conducts a deposition, a defendant being held in custody must be produced for the examination and kept in the presence of the witness through the questioning, unless the defendant tries to obstruct the deposition. Similarly, a defendant not in custody must be given the opportunity to attend the deposition, and if necessary, the government must pay the expenses to permit the defendant and counsel to attend. Rule 15(d).

Finally, under Rule 15(f), a deposition may be introduced as evidence "as provided by the Federal Rules of Evidence." Consequently, court approval for a deposition does not necessarily mean that the transcript will be admitted at trial. For example, if the witness were present and able to testify at trial, a court could preclude a party from introducing the person's deposition into evidence. In addition, the court could limit the use of the deposition to impeachment or refreshing recollection.

E. RULE 17(c) TRIAL SUBPOENAS

A defendant has a Sixth Amendment right to use the court's compulsory process to require a witness to be present at trial. This is usually done by means of a subpoena. The government is required to serve defense subpoenas and to pay the requisite witness fees and expenses for indigent defendants.

Rule 17(c)(1) permits subpoenas requiring a witness "to produce any books, papers, documents data, or other objects." A party generally does not need to seek a court's permission to issue a subpoena. But, Rule 17(c)(3) requires court authorization for subpoenas seeking information from third parties about a victim. In addition, some judges require prior authorization if the subpoena seeks the production of records before trial.

The recipient of a subpoena can file a motion to quash a trial subpoena. If the subpoena is opposed, or requires a judge's approval, the burden is on the party issuing the subpoena to establish that the records sought are properly within the court's authority to compel production.

Courts have been quite explicit in pointing out that a subpoena is not a means of obtaining discovery and should focus solely on obtaining evidence for use at trial. In *United States v. Nixon*, 418 U.S. 683, 700 (1974), the Supreme Court held that, to be enforceable, a trial subpoena for evidence "must clear three hurdles: (1) relevancy; (2) admissibility; (3) specificity." Courts frequently reject subpoenas, particularly those issued by defendants, because they do not meet the *Nixon* requirements and instead appear to be a "fishing expedition" for potentially useful evidence.

> **Practice Note:** In seeking a trial subpoena for documents, a defendant may effectively reveal a potential defense to the prosecutor. First, the type of records sought and the party subpoenaed may provide sufficient information to a prosecutor for the prosecutor to infer defense strategy. Second, if the recipient of the subpoena challenges the subpoena with a motion to quash, the defense counsel will have to explain how the information sought is material to a defense at trial, further revealing potential trial strategy. Thus, a defendant must be willing to disclose the purpose of the subpoena to the government if there is opposition to its issuance or forego the subpoenaed information.

To be enforceable, a subpoena for documents must be reasonably particular regarding what the recipient must provide. Phrases like "any and all" or "including but not limited to" may be a sign that the subpoena does not meet the specificity element. When a subpoena is challenged, the party issuing the subpoena does not need to establish conclusively that the evidence is admissible. But a court will scrutinize the terms of the subpoena to ensure that it seeks at least arguably admissible evidence that is relevant to an issue at trial.

E. *BRADY* MATERIAL

The Supreme Court's decision in *Brady v. Maryland*, 373 U.S. 83 (1963), requires the government to turn over to a defendant all exculpatory, material evidence in its possession. This requirement stems from the Due Process Clause of the Fifth and Fourteenth Amendments and applies in all federal and state criminal prosecutions. The rule does not depend on establishing the prosecutor acted in bad faith. Moreover, the government cannot defend a failure to produce exculpatory information on grounds that the government was merely mistaken or acted in good faith.

Although *Brady* is not formally a rule granting a defendant discovery rights, it effectively provides defendants with discovery of some information in the possession of the government. *Brady* requires the prosecution to provide exculpatory evidence to the defendant so that defense counsel can effectively use the information at trial. Most courts require the government to turn over all *Brady* material near the outset of the case. But, the prosecution has a continuing obligation to disclose exculpatory information throughout the proceeding.

Most of the information that comes within *Brady* will also fall within the required production of evidence under Rule 16. Even if the evidence need not be disclosed under the discovery rules, *Brady* trumps any limitations that the discovery rules may impose. Thus, the government may still be required to produce information that is protected under the discovery rules. Defense counsel frequently add a demand for *Brady* material to a discovery request under Rule 16 to ensure that all possible avenues for obtaining information have been covered.

There are three components to *Brady*:

- The evidence must be favorable to the accused;
- The government must have suppressed information in its possession, either actual or constructive; and
- The evidence must be material, so that withholding it caused prejudice to the defendant.

1. FAVORABLE OR EXCULPATORY

Brady requires the disclosure of material, exculpatory evidence. Exculpatory evidence means evidence that calls into question either the defendant's guilt or the severity of a punishment. In *Brady*, the government did not turn over a co-defendant's statements in which he admitted to killing the victim. The Court considered this evidence to be exculpatory because it showed that the defendant played a lesser role in the homicide and thus the defense could have used the evidence to argue for a reduced sentence. Evidence that could be used to impeach an adverse witness also comes within *Brady*. *Giglio v. United States*, 405 U.S. 150 (1972). Common types of impeachment evidence include: cooperation agreements with witnesses; promises regarding resolution of civil or tax liability; payments made to confidential informants; rewards to those who furnish information; participation by a witness in other criminal activity, and prior conflicting statements made by a witness.

2. SUPPRESSION

Brady imposes an obligation on the prosecutor to provide exculpatory information to the defense and describes the government's failure to turn over this evidence as "suppression." But the "suppression" requirement does not mean a prosecutor must take any steps to keep it away from a defendant or even be personally aware of the evidence. Instead, "suppression" means that the information was in the possession of the government and was not turned over to the defense.

In essence, the prosecutor is charged with knowledge of what is in the files of other government agencies that are affiliated with the prosecution, such as the police and other investigative agencies. Thus, *Brady* applies to all information that is within the possession of any government agent. If a civil regulatory agency was involved in an investigation, then exculpatory information in its files may be subject to disclosure in the criminal case. This is true even if the agency was not involved in the decision to prosecute. Prosecutors, however, are not required to seek out information from other governments if there was no connection to their work in investigating or prosecuting the defendant.

3. MATERIAL

Even when the prosecution fails to provide the defense with exculpatory information, a defendant will obtain relief only if the suppressed evidence was material to the defendant's guilt or punishment. In *United States v. Bagley*, 473 U.S. 667, 682 (1985), the Court ruled that materiality depended on whether "there is a reasonable probability that, had the evidence been disclosed to the defense, the result of the proceedings would have been different." According to the Court, a "reasonable probability" is "a probability sufficient to undermine confidence in the outcome." *Id.*

The Court in *Bagley* effectively established a prejudice requirement. Any *Brady* claim requires a defendant to establish that the favorable evidence would have had such an impact on the trial that confidence in the guilty verdict or sentence is undermined. A defendant need not, however, establish that the jury likely would have found him "not guilty" of the charge. In addition, in determining whether the evidence was material, the evidence is assessed cumulatively. Thus, the issue is whether the sum total of the withheld evidence calls into question the result, rather than whether an item-by-item analysis would result in such a conclusion.

4. DEPARTMENT OF JUSTICE GUIDANCE

In January 2010, the Department of Justice issued a memorandum that provides guidance to prosecutors on their obligations under both *Brady* and the discovery rules. The Department distributed this memorandum in the wake of the several federal prosecutions in which judges questioned whether federal prosecutors had complied with their disclosure obligation. One of the most notable, or notorious, of these cases was prosecution of former United States Senator Ted Stevens. In that case, Senator Stevens was convicted of receiving improper benefits from a contractor. But, after the trial, the government moved to dismiss the charges because the prosecutors had failed to disclose evidence that called into question the veracity of a key government witness.

The Department of Justice memorandum directs prosecutors to review the following to determine whether there is information, including potential *Giglio* material, that should be provided to the defendant:

- Investigative agency files;
- Confidential informant/witness/source files;
- Documents gathered by civil attorneys and regulatory agencies in parallel investigations;
- Case-related communications;
- Information gained in witness interviews, including trial preparation sessions; and
- Agent notes.

F. JENCKS ACT (RULE 26.2)

The Supreme Court held in *Jencks v. United States*, 353 U.S. 657 (1957), that the prosecution was required to turn over written reports of statements made by two important government witnesses to investigators so that the defense counsel could use the statements in cross-examining the witnesses. The Court required disclosure of the statement regardless of whether there was any indication the reports contradicted the witnesses' testimony. The *Jencks* decision was viewed—incorrectly—as being too favorable to defendants by allowing them the opportunity to rummage through the government's investigative files searching for evidence.

The Court based its decision in *Jencks* on its supervisory power over federal district courts rather than on any constitutional protection for criminal defendants. In response to the criticism of this decision, Congress adopted 18 U.S.C. § 3500, known as the Jencks Act, to govern when a witness's prior statement must be disclosed. The operative provisions of § 3500 have been incorporated into Federal Rule of Criminal Procedure 26.2, although many courts still refer to the Jencks Act.

As noted above, Rule 16(a) requires the government to provide during discovery any prior statements by the defendant to the defense upon request. The government is not, however, required to provide all witness statements to the defense. Rather, Rule 26.2 provides that once a witness other than the defendant testifies on direct examination, the court may order, upon request, that counsel turn over to the other side "any statement of the witness that is in their possession and that relates to the subject matter of the witness's testimony." The timing of the required disclosure of the witness statement—*after* the direct examination is complete—is critical. This timing can significantly handicap the opposing counsel because there is only limited time to prepare the cross-examination. And, defense attorneys cannot avoid these timing rules by subpoenaing witness statements in advance of trial. Rule 17(h).

Rule 26.2(d), however, does authorize the court to grant a recess to allow time to review the statement. Many judges do not like the potential for interruptions of the trial to allow counsel to review prior witness statements, especially if those statements are voluminous. Consequently, to avoid delays in the proceedings, judges frequently require disclosure of witness statements in advance of either trial or the person's appearance for direct examination to give opposing counsel a reasonable opportunity to review the statements. In addition, of course, where the witness's statement contains *Brady* material, the government must provide that statement to the defense notwithstanding the timing requirements of Rule 26.

Rule 26.2(c) requires the witness's entire statement be produced unless only part of it relates to the subject matter about which the person testified or there is a claim of privilege regarding part of it. If a party contends that either of these exceptions applies to part of the statement, the trial judge inspects the statement *in camera* and can redact any portion that is irrelevant or privileged. Rule 26.2(e) provides that disobeying an order to produce a witness statement results in the testimony being stricken from the record. In addition, if it is the government that refuses to produce the statement, the court "must declare a mistrial if justice so requires."

Rule 26.2(f) provides the following definition of what constitutes a "statement" by a witness:

- A written statement that the witness makes and signs, or otherwise adopts or approves;
- A substantially verbatim, contemporaneously recorded recital of the witness's oral statement that is contained in any recording or any transcription of a recording; or
- A witness's statement to a grand jury, however taken or recorded, or a transcription of such a statement.

A "substantially verbatim" recording of a witness's statement need not be a complete transcription. Instead, in evaluating whether the document is adequate, courts look at whether the recording recites the language used by the witness, whether the written statement was prepared within a short period of the oral statement, and the length of the written statement compared to how long the person spoke.

Notes of an interview are generally not considered to be a "statement" under the Rule, although in some instances a court may order their production if there is a question raised about whether the notes provide a more accurate recitation of what was said. The protection afforded by Rule 16(a)(2) for work product created during an investigation does not shield a witness statement from production under Rule 26.2. Nor can a statement be withheld because there are questions regarding its admissibility as evidence at trial—that is a separate issue from the requirement to produce the statement to the opposing party.

Rule 26.2(g) provides that the disclosure requirement applies when a witness testifies at the following judicial proceedings in addition to trial:

- Suppression hearing;
- Preliminary hearing;
- Sentencing hearing;
- Probation or supervised release revocation or modification hearing;
- Detention hearing; and
- Collateral proceeding after a conviction or sentence under 18 U.S.C. § 2255.

G. WITNESS IMMUNITY

A witness may invoke the Fifth Amendment privilege against self-incrimination and refuse to answer questions before a grand jury or at trial. But, an assertion of this privilege does not prevent the government from obtaining the person's testimony. The government may require the witness to testify by providing the unwilling witness with immunity under the federal immunity statute. In addition, the government and a defendant may agree to either full immunity or a more limited form of immunity as part of a plea bargain agreement.

The federal immunity statute, 18 U.S.C. § 6002, provides that the government may grant a witness immunity from prosecution after the person refuses to answer questions before the grand jury or a federal court. The power to grant immunity belongs largely to the government. A defendant cannot demand that the government provide witnesses favorable to his side with immunity. And, a court can only grant immunity on its own authority in only a very limited situation: when the government is trying to keep relevant evidence from being introduced.

The government can theoretically prosecute a witness who received this immunity, called use or fruits immunity, for crimes other than making a false statement or perjury. But, it is very difficult for the government to do so. In *Kastigar v. United States,* the Court held that when the government pursues criminal charges after a grant of use immunity, the prosecution has "the affirmative duty to prove that the evidence it proposes to use is derived from a legitimate source *wholly independent of the compelled testimony.*" 406 U.S. 411, 461 (1972) (emphasis added). When an immunized witness is subsequently prosecuted, the district court holds a *Kastigar* hearing, usually before trial, to determine whether the prosecution can go forward. At this hearing, the government has the burden of demonstrating that none of its evidence is in any way related to either the immunized testimony or information derived from that testimony.

Prosecutors hesitate to grant immunity to potential witnesses without knowing the kind of testimony they can provide and the extent of their participation in illegal conduct. Because of these concerns, prosecutors commonly require that the defense attorney make a "proffer." A proffer sets forth their client's participation in possible misconduct and the information that person can provide. The proffer allows prosecutors to avoid granting immunity to a person who was too involved in the criminal activity to warrant a grant of immunity. In addition, government attorneys may also be reluctant to grant immunity without evaluating the witness's credibility or the performance of a person in a courtroom setting. Thus, prosecutors may demand an interview with the witness before making a decision about immunity.

The rules exclude the use of any statements from these interviews, except for prosecutions under 18 U.S.C. § 1001 for making a false statement to government officials. Federal Rule of Criminal Procedure 11(f) provides that "[t]he admissibility or inadmissibility of a plea, a plea discussion, and any related statement is governed by Federal Rule of Evidence 410." Rule 410 states that "any statement made in the course of plea discussions with an attorney for the prosecuting authority which do not result in a plea of guilty or which result in a plea of guilty later withdrawn" cannot be admitted in evidence against the person making the statement.

As a practical matter, however, the government may demand that the defendant waive the protections of Rules 11(f) and 410 for statements made during an interview. As the Court explained in *United States v. Mezzanatto*, 513 U.S. 196, 209 (1995), "A defendant can 'maximize' what he has to 'sell' only if he is permitted to offer what the prosecutor is most interested in buying. And while it is certainly true that prosecutors often need help from the small fish in a conspiracy in order to catch the big ones, that is no reason to preclude waiver altogether."

In practice, prosecutors and defense attorneys frequently negotiate the extent to which the government will be able to use any statements made by the defendant during an interview. For example, defense attorneys commonly seek an agreement that no statements made during an interview be used against their client before allowing the interview, while prosecutors may insist on the ability to use the statements to impeach the individual should the person offer contrary testimony at trial. In addition, the defense frequently asks that any commitments made apply to civil proceedings as well as criminal actions.

Finally, prosecutors and defense attorneys frequently negotiate the type of immunity that is granted to the witness. Prosecutors may ask the witness to agree to a more limited form of immunity—sometimes referred to as letter immunity—rather than providing the witness with immunity under the federal statute. Letter immunity typically involves the government agreeing not to use the witness's statement at trial in exchange for the witness's information. But, the government retains the ability to use information derived from the witness in its investigation. This type of agreement allows the government to preview what the witness has to offer without committing to full immunity or a plea bargain. Witnesses are often willing to enter into these agreements when there are several persons trying to make a deal with the government because the letter immunity offers the best chance at negotiating a plea bargain.

> **Practice Note:** Entering into a limited immunity agreement places the witness at significant risk if the negotiations for full immunity or a plea agreement break down. Under the terms of a standard letter agreement, the witness provides information in exchange for a promise from the government that any statements made during the proffer will not be used directly against him or her. If negotiations break down, the letter agreements typically used by the Department of Justice allow prosecutors to use the person's proffer statement in a number of ways. These include using the statement to pursue new investigative leads and to cross-examine the defendant if he or she testifies inconsistently with the proffer statement.

H. NOTICE OF DEFENSES

Although defendants do not have to disclose their strategy, the Federal Rules of Criminal Procedure impose affirmative disclosure obligations on a defendant with respect to two types of defenses: alibi and insanity. The Rules treat the defendant's obligations for these two defenses differently. Disclosure of an alibi defense is only required if requested by the government. Notice of an insanity defense must occur even if not requested.

Rule 12.1 requires that a defendant, within 14 days of the government's written request, provide notice of any intended alibi defense. This rule requires the defendant to disclose: (1) each specific place where the defendant claims to have been at the time of the alleged offense; and (2) the name, address, and telephone number of each alibi witness on whom the defendant intends to rely. Because the duty of disclosure is continuing, the defendant must notify the government of any additional witnesses that come to light prior to trial. Failure to comply with the Rule may lead to the exclusion of any undisclosed witness.

Within 14 days of the defendant's disclosure of this alibi information, Rule 12.1(b) requires the government to disclose the name, address, and telephone number of each witness that the government intends to rely upon to establish that the defendant was present at the scene of the crime or to otherwise rebut the defendant's alibi defense. This obligation includes, on a showing of good cause, the address and telephone number of any victim who may be used by the government to establish that a defendant was present at the scene of the alleged offense. Because of this reciprocal duty to provide information, it is not uncommon for the government to forego making a Rule 12.1 alibi request to avoid premature disclosure of rebuttal witnesses and of a victim's personal information. If a defendant withdraws an alibi defense after giving the notice, it is not admissible in any civil or criminal proceeding. Rule 12.1(f).

Rule 12.2 requires a defendant who intends to assert a defense of insanity to notify the government in writing by the pretrial motion deadline set by the court. A defendant may raise an insanity defense to contest either the issue of guilt or the determination of punishment in a capital case. To rely on an insanity defense, a defendant must disclose any report prepared by his retained expert. The defendant must also submit to a government-sponsored psychiatric or psychological examination. Any statement made by a defendant during these examinations is inadmissible except on the issue of the person's mental condition. The court may exclude a defendant's expert evidence if the defense fails to provide notice as required by the rule or refuses to submit to a government examination. A defendant found not guilty by reason of insanity is remanded to government custody until the person can establish, either by a preponderance or by clear and convincing evidence (depending on the nature of the underlying offense), that "his release would not create a substantial risk of bodily injury to another person or serious damage of property of another due to a present mental disease or defect." 18 U.S.C. § 4243(d).

A defendant must give notice under Rule 12.3 of a defense based on an "actual or believed exercise of public authority on behalf of a law enforcement agency or federal intelligence agency." The notice must be filed within the time frame for filing a motion under Rule 12. Rule 12.3(a)(2) requires that the notice include the agency involved, any member of the agency "on whose behalf the defendant claims to have acted," and the time frame in which the defendant claims to have acted pursuant to public authority. In response to the notice, the government "must admit or deny that the defendant exercised the public authority identified" by the defendant. Rule 12.3(a)(3). Like an alibi defense, each side must disclose the witnesses it will use to support or oppose the public authority defense. If a defendant withdraws an alibi defense after giving the notice, it not admissible in any civil or criminal proceeding. Rule 12e(3).

SAMPLE DEFENSE DISCOVERY NOTICE

United States District Court
Eastern District Of Wayne

UNITED STATES OF AMERICA,
Plantiff

v.   Case No. _____

D-1 _____   Honorable_____

Defendant

_____

REQUESTS AND NOTICES IN COMPLIANCE WITH STANDING ORDER FOR DISCOVERY AND INSPECTION

In compliance with the Standing Pretrial Order ("Standing Order") in effect for this case, Defendant, _____ _____, through his/her attorney, _____ _____, hereby provides the Government with the following requests and notices:

1. It is hereby requested that the Government provide copies or an opportunity to make copies of:

   (a) Any information within the meaning of the "Standing Order", paragraph 2(a) and/or Rule 16(a)(1) of the Federal Rules of Criminal Procedure.

   (b) A written summary of the expert testimony the government intends to use under Rules 702, 703, or 705 of the Federal Rules of Criminal Evidence during its case in chief at trial. This summary must describe the witness's opinions, the bases and the reasons therefore, and the witnesses' qualifications. Rule 16(a)(1)(E).

   (c) Any exculpatory evidence within the meaning of the "Standing Order" paragraph 2(b) and/or *Brady v. Maryland*, 373 U.S. 83 (1963) and *United States v. Agurs*, 427 U.S. 97 (1976).

   (d) Any document which will be used to refresh the memory of a witness within the meaning of the "Standing Order" paragraph 8 and/or Rule 612 of the Federal Rules of Evidence.

   (e) Any statement by persons who have possible knowledge or information relative to this case which are not protected from disclosure by 18 U.S.C. § 3500.

   (f) Any statement of witnesses within the meaning of 18 U.S.C. § 3500 (e).

2. Notice is hereby given pursuant to the "Standing Order" that the foundation for any and all exhibits will be contested.

3. Notice is hereby given pursuant to the "Standing Order" that the chain of custody of any and all exhibits will be contested.

4. Notice is hereby given pursuant to the "Standing Order" that any scientific analysis or summary testimony by experts will be contested unless there has been a proper basis for the witness' testimony under Rule 1006 of the Federal Rules of Evidence.

5. All requests for information, materials, or evidence contained herein are continuing and the prosecution is expected to immediately provide any additional information, materials, or evidence as required by the "Standing Order" and/or Rule 16(c) of the Federal Rules of Criminal Procedure.

6. Notices contained herein will remain in effect unless expressly withdrawn.

7. That written requests have been made by defense counsel to the Assistant U.S. Attorney for discovery materials and there has been no response as of this date.

Respectfully submitted,

s/ _____

Attorney for Defendant

Dated: _____ __, 20__

Chapter 8

The Pretrial Conference

■ ■ ■

Federal Rule of Criminal Procedure 17.1 authorizes judges to hold one or more pretrial conferences "to promote a fair and expeditious trial." After the hearing, the court must issue a memorandum regarding "any matters agreed to during the conference." An important protection afforded to defendants at the pretrial conference is that "[t]he government may not use any statement made during the conference by the defendant or the defendant's attorney unless it is in writing and is signed by the defendant and the defendant's attorney." Under this rule, defendants may assert a potential claim or defense without any concern that any admission of an element of the offense could be used as evidence at trial.

Many courts have local rules and individual judges have standing policies providing more detailed guidelines about the process of exchanging discovery materials, filing of pretrial motions, and the topics that may be covered in a pretrial conference. These local rules often set the timing of pretrial conferences within a certain period after an indictment is returned or a preliminary hearing held. A sample standing order is provided at the end of this Chapter.

Among the issues that may be addressed at the pretrial conference are:

- Production of statements or reports of witnesses;
- Production of grand jury testimony of witnesses intended to be called at the trial;
- Stipulation of facts which may be deemed proved at the trial without further proof by either party;
- Dismissal of certain counts and elimination from the case of certain issues;
- Severance of trial as to any co-defendant or joinder of any related case;
- Pretrial exchange of lists of witnesses, including experts, intended to be called in person or by deposition to testify at trial, except those who may be called only for impeachment or rebuttal;

- Pretrial exchange, with opportunity for mutual inspection of lists of documents, exhibits, summaries, schedules, models, or diagrams intended to be offered or used at trial;

- Marking of intended trial exhibits, except for impeachment and rebuttal materials. As a rule, no exhibits are assigned a number without first contacting the clerk, and the exhibits remain in the same sequence as they appear on the exhibit list;

- Pretrial resolution of objections to exhibits or testimony to be offered at trial; and

- Preparation of trial briefs on disputed points of law likely to arise at trial.[2]

When counsel are preparing for a pretrial conference, they should think though their entire case. As is noted in Chapter 9, Rule 12 requires defense counsel to file pretrial motions if they wish to challenge issues related to a "defect in the prosecution" or if they seek to suppress evidence obtained by the government. Defense counsel should come to the pretrial conference with these motions prepared, if they have not already been filed. Note that many local rules require pretrial motions to be filed within a set time from the date of arraignment, often 20 days. Prosecutors should anticipate defense claims and be prepared to respond to those claims. For example, both government and defense counsel should be able to voice an opinion as to whether evidentiary hearings are required for any pretrial motions at the conference.

---

[2] Source: Local Rules of Procedure, United States District Court, District of Montana.

SAMPLE STANDING PRETRIAL ORDER

United States District Court
For the Eastern District Of Wayne

STANDING PRETRIAL ORDER IN CRIMINAL CASES

It is the court's policy to rely on the standard discovery procedures as set forth in this Order as the sole means of the exchange of discovery in criminal cases except in extraordinary circumstances. This Order is intended to promote the efficient exchange of discovery and to facilitate the pretrial motions process without altering the rights and obligations of the parties, but at the same time eliminating the practice of routinely filing perfunctory and duplicative discovery motions.

MEETING OF COUNSEL

1. Within ten (10) days from the date of arraignment, or such other date as may be set by the Judge to whom the case is assigned, government and defense counsel shall meet and confer about the case.

INITIAL DISCLOSURES

2. **Disclosure by the Government.** At the initial meeting of counsel within ten (10) days of arraignment, or on a date otherwise set as agreed by counsel or by the court for good cause shown, the government shall tender to defendant the following:

   a. *Fed. R. Crim. P. 16(a) Information.* All discoverable information within the scope of Rule 16(a) of the Federal Rules of Criminal Procedure.

   b. Brady *Material.* All information and material known to the government which may be favorable to the defendant on the issues of guilt or punishment, without regard to materiality, within the scope of *Brady v. Maryland,* 373 U.S. 83 (1963).

   c. Giglio *Material.* The existence and substance of any payments, promises of immunity, leniency, preferential treatment, or other inducements made to prospective witnesses, within the scope of *United States v. Giglio,* 405 U.S. 150 (1972).

   d. *Testifying informant's convictions.* A record of prior convictions of any alleged informant who will testify for the government at trial.

3. **Defendant's identification.** If a line-up, show-up, photo spread or similar procedure was used in attempting to identify the defendant, the exact procedure and participants shall be described and the results, together with any pictures, and photographs, shall be disclosed.

4. **Inspection of vehicles, vessels, or aircraft.** If any vehicle, vessel, or aircraft was allegedly utilized in the commission of any offenses charged, the government shall permit the defendant's counsel and any expert

selected by the defense to inspect it, if it is in the custody of any governmental authority.

5. **Defendant's latent prints**. If latent fingerprints, or prints of any type, have been identified by a government expert as those of the defendant, copies thereof shall be provided.

6. **Fed. R. Evid.404(b)**. The government shall advise the defendant of its intention to introduce evidence in its case in chief at trial, pursuant to Rule 404(b) of the Federal Rules of Evidence.

7. **Electronic Surveillance Information**. If the defendant was an aggrieved person as defined in 18 U.S.C. § 2510(11), the government shall so advise the defendant and set forth the detailed circumstances thereof.

OBLIGATIONS OF THE GOVERNMENT

8. The government shall anticipate the need for, and arrange for the transcription of, the grand jury testimony of all witnesses who will testify in the government's case in chief, if subject to Fed. R. Crim. P. 26.2 and 18 U.S.C. § 3500. Jencks Act materials and witnesses' statements shall be provided as required by Fed. R. Crim. P. 26.2 and 18 U.S.C. § 3500. However, the government, and where applicable, the defendant, are requested to make such materials and statements available to the other party sufficiently in advance as to avoid any delays or interruptions at trial. The court suggests an early disclosure of Jencks Act materials.

9. The government shall advise all government agents and officers involved in the case to preserve all rough notes.

10. The identification and production of all discoverable evidence or information is the personal responsibility of the Assistant United States Attorney assigned to the case and may not be delegated without the express permission of the court.

DISCLOSURES TO U.S. PROBATION

11. At arraignment, or on a date otherwise designated by the court upon good cause shown, the government shall tender to the U.S. Probation Office all essential information needed by U.S. Probation to accurately calculate the sentencing guideline range for the defendant, including, but not limited to, information regarding the nature of the offense (offense level), the nature of the victim and the injury sustained by the victim, defendant's role in the offense, whether defendant obstructed justice in the commission of the crime, defendant's criminal history, and any information regarding defendant's status as a career offender/armed career criminal. In addition, in order to comply with the requirements of the Anti-Terrorism Act, the government shall produce to the U.S. Probation Office information regarding the victims of defendant's alleged criminal activity, including, but not limited to, the identity of the victim by name, address, and phone number, and the nature and extent of the victim's loss or injury.

DISCLOSURES BY THE DEFENDANT

12. If the defendant accepts or requests disclosure of discoverable information pursuant to Fed. R. Crim. P. 16(a)(1)(C), (D), or (E), the defendant, on or before a date set by the court, shall provide to the government all discoverable information within the scope of Fed. R. Crim. P. 16(b).

SUPPLEMENTATION

13. The provisions of Fed. R. Crim. P. 16(c) are applicable. It shall be the duty of counsel for all parties to immediately reveal to opposing counsel all newly discovered information, evidence, or other material within the scope of this Rule, and there is a continuing duty upon each attorney to disclose expeditiously.

MOTIONS FOR DISCOVERY

14. No attorney shall file a discovery motion without first conferring with opposing counsel, and no motion will be considered by the court unless it is accompanied by a certification of such conference and a statement of the moving party's good faith efforts to resolve the subject matter of the motion by agreement with opposing counsel. No discovery motions shall be filed for information or material within the scope of this Rule unless it is a motion to compel, a motion for protective order or a motion for an order modifying discovery. See Fed. R. Crim. P. 16(d). Discovery requests made pursuant to Fed. R. Crim. P. 16 and this Order require no action on the part of this court and shall not be filed with the court, unless the party making the request desires to preserve the discovery matter for appeal.

PRETRIAL MOTIONS

15. Any pretrial motion, either permissive or required by Fed. R. Crim. P. 12, including all motions in limine, shall be filed within twenty (20) days of the date of arraignment of the defendant involved.

PRETRIAL CONFERENCE

16. Within thirty (30) days of arraignment, the Judge assigned to the matter will schedule a pretrial conference for the purpose of determining the likely issues for pretrial decision and that may arise during trial. Counsel should, if possible, determine by the time of the pretrial conference whether the defendant is likely to enter a guilty plea, or any other disposition of the charge(s). A firm trial date will be set at the pretrial conference.

PART 3
PRETRIAL MOTIONS
■ ■ ■

CHAPTER 9

PRETRIAL MOTIONS AND RULE 12 PROCEDURES

■ ■ ■

Federal Rule of Criminal Procedure 12 governs the filing of pretrial motions. Defendants may file pre-trial motions challenging the charges and seeking to suppress evidence on constitutional and statutory grounds, as well as motions for discovery, discussed in Chapter 7. In addition, the defense (and less frequently the prosecution) may file motions in limine to obtain a ruling on the admissibility of evidence at trial. The substance of each type of motion is discussed in greater detail in Chapters 10–12, while general considerations for drafting drafting motions and memoranda of law supporting those motions, and preparing for and conducting both evidentiary hearings and oral arguments are discussed in Chapter 13. This Chapter provides an overview of Rule 12.

Practice Note: Rules 12 and 47 provide the basic guidelines for filing of motions. It is important to consult with both the local rules of the district in which the case is pending and the rules or guidelines of the judge or magistrate judge before whom the case is pending prior to submitting any motion to the court. Failure to follow the rules may result in the court refusing to hear the claim.

Rule 12(a) cleared away a clutter of terminology for different types of pleadings by limiting those in a criminal case to "the indictment, the information, and the pleas of not guilty, guilty, and nolo contendere." In addition to establishing the governing rules for pre-trial motions, Rule 12(b)(1) makes clear that Rule 47 governs the form of motions. Rule 47(b) provides that a "motion—except when made during a trial or hearing—must be in writing, unless the court permits the party to make the motion by other means." The Rule further requires that the party's motion "must state the grounds on which it is based and the relief or order sought." Rule 47(d) states that the motion may be accompanied by an affidavit furnishing the court with additional factual information in support of the motion.

Rule 12 divides pretrial motions into two categories: those that can be made at any time, and those that must be made before trial. Rule 12(b)(2) provides that a "motion that the court lacks jurisdiction may be made at any time while the case is pending." Although a defendant could seek the dismissal of charges on the ground that the evidence is insufficient to establish guilt beyond a reasonable doubt, courts are quite hesitant to even consider such a motion and rarely has one been granted. The types of motions that must be raised under Rule 12 "if the basis for the motion is then reasonably available and the motion can be determined without a trial on the merits" are claims challenging a defect in instituting the prosecution, a defect in the indictment or information, for suppression of evidence, severance of charges or defendants, and for discovery of evidence.

Rule 12(b)(3) provides that the following motions *must* be filed before trial, if the basis is reasonably known, or the defendant waives any claim regarding them:

- Improper venue;
- Preindictment delay;
- Violation of the constitutional right to a speedy trial;
- Selective or vindictive prosecution;
- Error in the grand-jury proceeding or preliminary hearing;
- Joining two or more offenses in the same count (duplicity);
- Charging the same offense in more than one count (multiplicity);
- Lack of specificity;
- Failure to state an offense;
- Suppression of evidence;
- Severance of charges or defendants under Rule 14; and
- Discovery under Rule 16.

Rule 12(b)(4) provides for the government to give the defense notice of any evidence it intends to use at the arraignment or as soon as practicable afterwards so that the defendant has the opportunity to object to its use. In addition, the defendant may request notice of the government's intent to use evidence in its case-in-chief that the defendant may be entitled to receive under Rule 16, which sets forth the discovery requirements in a prosecution. See Chapter 7.

Rule 12(c) provides that the court sets the deadline for filing motions "at the arraignment or as soon afterward as practicable." If a defendant fails to file a motion within that time frame, then Rule 12(c)(3) provides that the motion is "untimely" but "a court may consider the defense, objection, or request if the party shows good cause." Consideration of an untimely motion is discretionary with the court. Judges are often reluctant to grant a waiver absent a compelling reason and may limit the nature of the relief even when granting a waiver.

The failure to timely raise the issue before the court's deadline is frequently due to inadvertence or negligence by counsel, not an affirmative decision to forego an otherwise valid claim. The real impact of failing to raise an issue is on appeal, because a defendant claiming that a conviction was improper based on a claim that was required to be raised before trial under Rule 12(b)(3) but was not must establish that the violation constituted "plain error." This is a very high standard to meet and requires a reviewing court to find that allowing the conviction to stand would constitute a miscarriage of justice. Moreover, not all appellate courts allow for a plain error review for a claim waived pursuant to Rule 12(b)(3), and those courts will not consider the issue further due to the failure to file a timely motion in the trial court.

Chapter 10

Challenging the Charges and Motions in Limine

■ ■ ■

Federal Rule of Criminal Procedure 12(b)(3) requires a defendant to file a pretrial motion to raise issues related to "a defect in instituting the prosecution" and "a defect in the indictment or information." The types of claims involved range from challenges to grand jury proceedings and the indictments to venue challenges and requests to sever charges and defendants. They also include motions in limine, such as efforts to preclude the government from using certain types of evidence, including privileged communications or character evidence. Grand jury requirements and the form of the indictment are discussed in Chapter 6 and speedy trial issues are discussed in Chapter 3. This Chapter discussed other common challenges to the charges and non-constitutional challenges to certain evidence.

A. JURISDICTION AND FAILURE TO STATE AN OFFENSE

Rule 12(b)(3) requires that most defense motions must be filed prior to trial if the basis for the motion is reasonably available. Rule 12(b)(2) specifically exempts from this timing requirement a motion that the court lacks jurisdiction over the case. Because the court would not have jurisdiction over a prosecution under an invalid statute, this type of claim can be brought at any time in the proceeding. Nonetheless, defense counsel should pursue these claims before trial, so that a proper record is created.

The federal government has jurisdiction only over those crimes that are identified by statute. There are no federal common law crimes. *United States v. Holliday*, 70 U.S. 407 (1865). While most crimes may in general be prosecuted in either state or federal court, the federal government has exclusive jurisdiction in specified geographical areas, including those on the high seas, on federal land or serious crimes committed by adults in the District of Columbia. The federal government also has exclusive jurisdiction in crimes involving specified subject matters, such as currency counterfeiting and copyrights.

As a general rule, claims that an indictment or information failed to properly invoke the court's jurisdiction because the conduct falls outside the scope of the statute are unlikely to succeed. Defendants can also challenge the validity of the statute under which the prosecution has been brought. One of the most frequent claims of this type is that the statute violates a defendant's due process rights. Other claims to invalidate statutes have been brought under the First Amendment and the Equal Protection Clause of the Fourteenth Amendment. This type of claim, called a facial challenge, asserts that the law was not a proper exercise of legislative authority and therefore is unenforceable against any person, even if the defendant's conduct actually violated the terms of the provision.

While these claims do not often succeed, the Supreme Court pointed out in *Bond v. United States*, 131 S. Ct. 2355, 2365 (2011), "Just as it is appropriate for an individual, in a proper case, to invoke separation-of-powers or checks-and balances constraints, so too may a litigant, in a proper case, challenge a law as enacted in contravention of constitutional principles of federalism." Thus, in *United States v. Lopez*, 514 U.S. 549 (1995), for example, the Supreme Court held that the Gun-Free School Zones Act exceeded Congress's power under the Commerce Clause.

B. VENUE

Jurisdiction over an offense must be distinguished from venue. Venue denotes the location of the prosecution. While the two terms are sometimes used interchangeably, they apply to different aspects of a criminal prosecution. The federal venue rules allocate the authority to pursue prosecutions among the different federal districts. Unlike subject-matter jurisdiction, venue does not involve the power of the court to adjudicate a case, but is a right granted to the defendant to have the case heard in a particular location. Thus, while a court cannot hear a case in which it does not have jurisdiction, a defendant can waive an objection to venue. The location of the prosecution is a protection available to the individual and does not involve judicial authority to decide the case.

The Constitution contains an explicit requirement that part of the right to trial is that the proceeding take place where the crime occurred. Article III, Section 2 provides that the trial of all federal crimes "shall be held in the State where the said Crimes shall have been committed." Because of this constitutional requirement, the indictment needs to establish that venue is proper. The indictment need not provide a complete recitation of the government's evidence supporting venue. Rather, most charges simply state that the crime occurred "in the [_____] District of _____ and elsewhere" with no further detail.

If a federal statute prescribes the appropriate venue for its prosecution, then that provision controls where the case can be filed. Most federal crimes, however, do not have a specific venue provision. In the absence of a specific venue provision, the general federal venue statute, 18 U.S.C. § 3237(a), controls the location of the prosecution. The statute is particularly important for "continuing" offenses that occur in multiple locations by permitting prosecution in different districts. The statute provides:

> Except as otherwise expressly provided by enactment of Congress, any offense against the United States begun in one district and completed in another, or committed in more than one district, may be inquired of and prosecuted in any district in which such offense was begun, continued, or completed.
>
> Any offense involving the use of the mails, transportation in interstate or foreign commerce, or the importation of an object or person into the United States is a continuing offense and, except as otherwise expressly provided by enactment of Congress, may be inquired of and prosecuted in any district from, through, or into which such commerce, mail matter, or imported object or person moves.

A court must ascertain whether the venue chosen by the government was proper by analyzing the conduct that allegedly constitutes the offense. In *United States v. Rodriguez-Moreno*, 526 U.S. 275, 279 (1999), the Supreme Court adopted an expansive—albeit rather imprecise—description of the analysis required under § 3237(a): "[A] court must initially identify the conduct constituting the offense (the nature of the crime) and then discern the location of the commission of the criminal acts." The initial question in a prosecution involving a statute which does not contain a specific venue provision is whether the crime was committed in only a single location. If the crime was committed in a single location, the district court in that location is the sole proper venue for the case. If the alleged criminal activity is a continuing offense that involves multiple locations, § 3237(a) allows charges to be filed in any district where the crime "was begun, continued, or completed."

If it is clear on the face of the indictment that the charge should not have been brought in that district, the defendant must raise a challenge to that court's venue in a pretrial motion. If a defect in venue is not apparent until trial, the failure to file a motion challenging venue will not constitute a waiver under Rule 12(b)(3). Thus, the defendant can raise the issue at the point in time in which the venue defect becomes clear.

C. BILL OF PARTICULARS

A bill of particulars is a formal written statement by the prosecutor providing additional information about the charge(s), sometimes based on areas identified by the defendant as needing further clarification or detail. Rule 7(f) provides, "The court may direct the government to file a bill of particulars. The defendant may move for a bill of particulars before or within 14 days after arraignment or at a later time if the court permits." At the same time, it is a commonly repeated mantra that if the indictment or information is insufficient, the charges must be dismissed and cannot be cured by a bill of particulars. Therefore, while the bill of particulars can assist the defendant in receiving a fair trial, it does not protect the government from a fatally flawed indictment or information.

A bill of particulars serves two functions: first, to give the defendant notice of the essential facts supporting the crimes alleged in the indictment or criminal information; and second, to avoid prejudicial surprise at trial. A defendant is not entitled to a bill of particulars as a matter of right, so the decision whether to order the prosecution to produce one, and the information required in it, is usually left to the discretion of the trial court. In *United States v. Sorich*, 427 F. Supp. 2d 820, 838 (N.D. Ill. 2006), the district court discussed the factors in deciding on a request for a bill of particulars: "(1) complexity of the charges; (2) clarity of the indictment; and (3) degree of discovery available to the defense absent a bill of particulars."

The focus of the bill of particulars is to provide additional facts and not to disclose evidence or the government's theory of the case. Courts usually refuse to order a bill of particulars if the information is available to the defendant through some other means. For example, if sufficient information is already contained in the indictment or information but the defendant simply wants more details, the motion will usually be denied. Similarly, a bill of particulars is not required if the government has provided the desired information through pretrial discovery or in some other acceptable manner, such as a letter from the prosecutor explaining a charge. Courts are more likely to order a bill of particulars to provide a defendant with the time and place of the crime, and the names of those present, including the victim. See *United States v. Minaya*, 395 F. Supp. 2d 28 (S.D.N.Y. 2005); *United States v. Allen*, 289 F. Supp. 2d 230 (N.D.N.Y. 2003).

Courts routinely state that a bill of particulars is not primarily a means of discovery, which is provided through Rule 16. See Chapter 7. The focus of the bill of particulars is to provide additional facts required to defend the case, not a means to obtain evidence or learn the government's theory of the case. But the fact that a bill of particulars will effectively disclose evidence or the government's theory is not a ground to deny one if it is otherwise needed. In *United States v. Giffen*, 379 F. Supp. 2d 337, 346 (S.D.N.Y. 2004), the district court noted that "if necessary to give the defendant enough information about the charge to prepare his defense, a bill of particulars will be required even if the effect is disclosure of the Government's evidence or theories."

D. JOINDER OF OFFENSES AND DEFENDANTS

The prosecution of multiple offenses against a defendant in a single indictment and the joining of two or more defendants for the same trial ensures the efficient use of judicial resources. The Supreme Court noted a preference for joint trials as "play[ing] a vital role in the criminal justice system." *Zafiro v. United States*, 506 U.S. 534, 537 (1993). This preference is reflected in practice. In the federal prosecutions, more than half of all defendants are charged with multiple counts, approximately one-third are joined with one or more other defendants, and one-quarter face are charged with multiple counts along with one or more co-defendants in a single case. Leipold and Abbasi, *The Impact of Joinder and Severance on Federal Criminal Cases: An Empirical Study*, 59 VAND. L. REV. 349 (2006).

Prosecutors make the initial decision whether to bring multiple charges against a defendant. The government also decides whether to join two or more defendants in one criminal information or indictment. Trying defendants together reduces the possibility of inconsistent verdicts, and bringing an array of charges for different crimes against a defendant in one proceeding reduces the delay inherent in the criminal justice system.

There are risks, however, in bringing multiple charges or defendants into a single proceeding. A jury may be confused by multiple counts or defendants. In addition, joinder of offenses or defendants may create prejudicial "spillover" of the evidence from one charge (or defendant) to another. As explained in detail below, Rule 8 governs the joinder of offenses and defendants, while Rule 14 governs the relief defendants may receive in the event the joinder is prejudicial.

1. JOINDER OF OFFENSES

Federal Rule of Criminal Procedure 8(a) describes when it is permissible to join more than one count in a single indictment or information. Prosecutors must be careful in drafting an indictment to avoid issues related to duplicity or multiplicity. See Chapter 6. Beyond those concerns, Rule 8(a) provides that an indictment or information can contain in separate counts two or more offenses, whether felonies or misdemeanors, when they "are of the same or similar character, or are based on the same act or transaction, or are connected with or constitute parts of a common scheme or plan." Because the rule is permissive and not mandatory, a defendant could be subjected to multiple trials, perhaps even in different jurisdictions, for crimes that are similar or arise out of the same basic chain of events. Double jeopardy does not prevent the federal government from pursuing a prosecution after a state has charged a defendant for a crime arising from the same course of conduct. But, principles of federalism and fairness strongly discourage a subsequent federal prosecution absent extenuating circumstances.

The Department of Justice has long had the policy that "several offenses arising out of a single transaction should be alleged and tried together and should not be made the basis of multiple prosecutions, a policy dictated by considerations both of fairness to defendants and of efficient and orderly law enforcement." *Petite v. United States*, 361 U.S. 529, 531 (1960). The United States Attorney's Manual § 9–2.031 explains the requirements for a federal prosecution after a prior proceeding:

> This policy precludes the initiation or continuation of a federal prosecution, following a prior state or federal prosecution based on substantially the same act(s) or transaction(s) unless three substantive prerequisites are satisfied: first, the matter must involve a substantial federal interest; second, the prior prosecution must have left that interest demonstrably unvindicated; and third, applying the same test that is applicable to all federal prosecutions, the government must believe that the defendant's conduct constitutes a federal offense, and that the admissible evidence probably will be sufficient to obtain and sustain a conviction by an unbiased trier of fact. In addition, there is a procedural prerequisite to be satisfied, that is, the prosecution must be approved by the appropriate Assistant Attorney General.

Because this so-called *Petite* Policy is only a guideline for federal prosecutors, a defendant cannot claim any violation of rights if the federal government files charges that violate the Policy.

Rule 8(a) permits joinder of offenses against a single defendant when the various charged offenses arise from the "same act or transaction," are part of "a common scheme or plan," or are "of the same or similar character." Courts have read "transaction" as requiring that there be some logical connection between the charges. Courts consider whether the evidence supporting the different offenses overlaps sufficiently such that the same evidence would be admissible if there were separate trials. The fact that two crimes are contemporaneous may not be sufficient to permit joinder, while a significant gap in time between the offenses does not preclude charging of them as arising from the same transaction. For example, courts have upheld fraud and tax evasion charges when the same financial information would be used to establish both offenses, even though the victims and elements of the offenses are quite different. *E.g., United States v. Saadey*, 393 F.3d 678 (6th Cir. 2005). On the other hand, joinder of theft and assault on a police officer charges has been found improper when the assault occurred when the defendant was arrested for the theft, the arrest occurred well after the theft, and there was no other connection between them. *United States v. Myers*, 700 F. Supp. 1358 (D.N.J. 1988).

Rule 8(a) also allows joinder of offenses against a single defendant if the different charges are "connected with or constitute parts of a common scheme or plan." Courts look for a logical connection between the offenses to find that they are part of a continuous course of conduct. This test is quite similar to the "same act or transaction" basis for joinder. Indeed, courts analyzing whether charges are proper under Rule 8(a) often fail to distinguish between these first two grounds for joinder. For example, courts frequently assert that the evidence is "inextricably intertwined" or "factually interrelated" as the basis to find the joinder was acceptable under the rule without going into further detail.

Although the first two grounds under Rule 8(a) for joinder of offenses against a single defendant are fairly uncontroversial, the third basis for joinder under the Rule—the crimes are "of the same or similar character"—presents more difficult issues. The benefits of joinder are less obvious in this circumstance, and the risk of an unfair trial more pronounced. The connection between the offenses is not based on any particular relationship among the offenses other than their "character"—a broad term. Allowing charges under this prong of Rule 8(a) may make it more difficult for a defendant to testify about one charge but not another or may permit a jury to hear evidence about other crimes that would have been inadmissible if there had been separate trials on the charges.

> **Practice Note:** There are some common types of criminal charges that courts routinely allow to be joined together absent strong evidence from the defendant that the charges are clearly unrelated. For example, many narcotics prosecutions include charges of illegal possession or use of a firearm, money laundering, and conspiracy. Similarly, federal mail and wire fraud offenses often include tax evasion, money laundering, false statements, and conspiracy charges. For certain crimes involving administrative agencies, prosecutors often include false filing, perjury, and obstruction of justice charges in the indictment or information.

Courts take different, and sometimes inconsistent, approaches to determining whether offenses are of a similar character for purposes of Rule 8(a). Some decisions apply a categorical approach, looking at the elements of the crimes charged, not whether there is any temporal or evidentiary overlap between the actual offenses alleged by the government. *E.g., United States v. Coleman,* 22 F.3d 126 (7th Cir. 1994). Other decisions look at both the objective aspects of the crimes along with the particular allegations in the charging document, such as the timing and location of the crimes and whether there is overlapping evidence that justifies the use of a single proceeding to converse judicial resources. *E.g., United States v. Garrett,* 648 F.3d 618 (8th Cir. 2011).

Allowing a trial on similar but otherwise unconnected charges does entail a gain in efficiency because only one jury is needed and the consolidation of the charges will allow for a better use of all participants' time. It is arguable whether this modest benefit overcomes the potential harm to a defendant facing a single trial on multiple charges that are only connected by their similar character. *United States v. Jawara*, 474 F.3d 565 (9th Cir. 2007). Permitting joinder based on the fact that the crimes are of similar character creates a situation in which jurors are presented with evidence on a crime that would not be admissible if there were separate trials on the charges. In such situations, courts may allow joinder and rely on jury instructions requiring segregation of the evidence so that the jurors do not view the evidence to find the defendant guilty on all charges. *E.g., United States v. Nguyen*, 88 F.3d 812 (9th Cir. 1996). Whether an instruction is sufficient to overcome the possibility that the jurors will view the defendant as a bad character deserving of punishment regardless of the sufficiency of the evidence on a particular charge is an open question.

Rule 14(a) allows a court to sever counts of an indictment for separate trial if joinder prejudices the defendant or the prosecution. The Rule provides: "If the joinder of offenses or defendants in an indictment, information, or a consolidation for trial appears to prejudice a defendant or the government, the court may order separate trials of counts, sever the defendants' trials, or provide any other relief that justice requires." Although Rule 14 authorizes the severance of charges, courts are generally reluctant to do so if the joinder was proper under Rule 8. One reason for this is the difficulty defendants face in demonstrating prejudice. Defendants do not satisfy this burden merely by asserting that they would have a better chance of acquittal if the counts were tried separately. Because the severance motion is filed before trial, there is always an element of speculation as to the asserted harm, and courts tend to reject vague claims that a defendant will suffer unfairness or prejudice from a single proceeding.

2. JOINDER OF DEFENDANTS

Rule 8(b) provides for the joinder of two or more defendants in a single prosecution "if they are alleged to have participated in the same act or transaction, or in the same series of acts or transactions, constituting an offense or offenses." Courts approach the joinder of defendants in much the same way as they examine joinder of offenses. Even though only Rule 8(a) mentions joinder of felony and misdemeanor charges, courts permit felony and misdemeanor charges to be joined against multiple defendants.

One important difference between the two subsections is that Rule 8(a) allows offenses to be joined if they are of "the same or similar character" and Rule 8(b) does not. Courts do not permit joinder of charges of a similar character for one defendant under Rule 8(a) and then in the same proceeding join additional defendants who have no connection with the added charges. In other words, what is permissible under Rule 8(a) may not be under Rule 8(b). For example, A committed armed robberies of three banks in the same area. In the first two robberies, B assisted by acting as a lookout. A committed the third robbery with a different person's help. Under Rule 8(a), A could be charged for all three robberies in the same indictment because they are of similar character. If B is added to the indictment on the first two robberies, however, A could not be charged in that indictment for the third robbery. Rule 8(b) bars joinder of the third robbery, or requires severance of B, because the potential prejudice to B is too great, even though it is arguably more efficient to include all of A's crimes in a single proceeding.

Rule 8(b) does not define what is meant by "the same series of acts or transactions." Courts commonly require evidence of some actual relationship among the acts to constitute a series, such as evidence of a common scheme or plan. Because the primary rationale for the joinder rules is efficiency, courts tend to allow a charge naming multiple defendants when there is substantially overlapping evidence that allows for the same proof at trial. *United States v. Frost*, 125 F.3d 346 (6th Cir. 1997). Courts do not require that all of the evidence be admissible against each defendant, but there must be at least some core of evidence that can be used against all of them, even if some items might be excludable if there were separate trials.

Courts often find that a conspiracy charge is sufficient to establish that the defendants engaged in the same series of acts or transactions to allow for their joinder. The same approach is taken when there is a charge involving a criminal enterprise, such as under RICO, 18 U.S.C. § 1961 et seq., or Violent Crimes in Aid of Racketeering, 18 U.S.C. § 1959, which require proof of a continuing course of conduct by the members that are related to the criminal purpose of the organization. The conspiracy or enterprise charge means that any substantive offenses that were the object of the conspiracy or perpetrated by the organization may properly be joined in the same case. Only some of the defendants may be charged with particular substantive offenses, such as when one member joins a conspiracy after it has commenced. Joinder of the co-conspirators does not require that each defendant join the agreement at the same time so long as all of the substantive counts arise out of the same conspiracy. It is even possible that a series of conspiracies may be joined in one prosecution if they are part of a related series of acts.

Rule 8(b) provides that "[a]ll defendants need not be charged in each count," so defendants with different levels of culpability can be joined together in a single prosecution. All defendants must have participated in some manner in the series of acts from which the charges arose. But Rule 8(b) does not require that each defendant have participated to the same degree in each act. For example, joinder in a single trial has been allowed in cases with over twenty-five defendants involved in the importation and distribution of narcotics, with different levels of involvement ranging from organizer to street dealing. *E.g., United States v. Donnell,* 596 F.3d 913 (8th Cir. 2010). Prosecutors frequently charge a single conspiracy among the different defendants to aid in establishing joinder, but such a charge is not necessary. Even when a conspiracy charge is dismissed, however, courts may still permit joinder if the indictment or information sufficiently alleges a related series of crimes to support trying the defendants into a single proceeding. *Schaffer v. United States,* 362 U.S. 511 (1960).

A single trial with more than one defendant creates several risks for the accused, particularly for one whose culpability is significantly lower than a co-defendant's. A defendant in that situation will naturally be concerned that the jury will vote to convict based on "guilt by association," especially if other defendants are charged with more serious offenses. If there are a number of defendants, then a defendant accused of playing only a minor role in a large-scale criminal enterprise can reasonably fear that the jury will not look carefully at the evidence to determine individual guilt and will instead lump all the defendants together. Similarly, defendants may have antagonistic defenses, and trying them together could lessen the impact of a claim of innocence or reduced culpability if the jury fails to distinguish among them in assessing guilt.

Rule 14(a) authorizes severance if the defendant or government will suffer prejudice, but there is no definition of what constitutes prejudice in a particular case. Whether to grant a motion to sever or provide some other type of relief comes within the discretion of the trial judge, who balances the inconvenience and expense to the government of separate trials against the prejudice to the defendants from a joint trial. The burden is on the defendant to show that joinder, which otherwise meets the requirements of Rule 8(b), will result in significant prejudice in order to obtain a severance under Rule 14. Even if some harm from joinder could be shown because there are conflicting defenses between the defendants, the Supreme Court has pointed out that a trial court has available "less drastic measures, such as limiting instructions, [which] often will suffice to cure any risk of prejudice." *Zafiro v. United States,* 506 U.S. 534, 539 (1993).

Unless defendants can show that joinder will prejudice a specific trial right, or that the risk of jury confusion is so great as to make a guilty verdict unreliable, they are unlikely to prevail on a motion to sever based on conflicting defenses. In addition, courts often reject severance motions based on asserted differences in the culpability of the defendants, that co-defendants have a criminal record that can be introduced against them, that there is hostility or other conflicts among the defendants, or that a co-defendant is absent from the trial. On the other hand, if the evidence against one defendant is particularly complex, and not closely connected to the proof against another defendant, then a court will be more willing to sever the cases to reduce the potential for jury confusion.

E. MOTIONS IN LIMINE

Although both the prosecutor and defense counsel may file motions in limine in advance of trial to obtain rulings on the admissibility of evidence at trial, motions in limine are more frequently filed by defendants. Defendants frequently file these motions to prohibit the government from using privileged communications. In addition, defendants may file a motion in limine to challenge eye witness identifications. See Chapter 12. Defendants also rely on motions in limine to attempt to prevent the government from introducing otherwise admissible evidence under Federal Rule of Evidence 403 on the ground that any probative value is outweighed by the unfair prejudice to the defendant. Common defense motions include attempts to exclude evidence of prior criminal convictions or bad acts and to prevent the introduction of statements of co-defendants.

1. EVIDENTIARY PRIVILEGES

Defendants may file a motion to preclude the introduction of evidence based on an evidentiary privilege. Federal Rule of Evidence 501 provides:

> Except as otherwise required by the Constitution of the United States or provided by Act of Congress or in rules prescribed by the Supreme Court pursuant to statutory authority, the privilege of a witness, person, government, State, or political subdivision thereof shall be governed by the principles of the common law as they may be interpreted by the courts of the United States in light of reason and experience.

While testimonial privileges are generally disfavored, this Rule permits courts to recognize privileges when shielding the relationship serves a greater public good. Accordingly, the federal courts have recognized that privileges may exist between spouses, *Trammel v. United States,* 445 U.S. 40 (1980), between an attorney and client, *Upjohn Co. v. United States,* 449 U.S. 383 (1981), between doctors, including psychotherapists, and patients, *Jaffee v. Redmond,* 518 U.S. 1 (1993), between clergy members and congregants, sometimes called the priest-penitent privilege although it is not limited to Roman Catholic clergy, and other similar relationships.

These privileges are read narrowly. If the information has been disclosed to a third party, the defendant will be deemed to have waived the privilege and the government may use the communication. In addition, while the spousal privilege extends to confidential communications, it does not permit a defendant to suppress the testimony of a spouse regarding his or her criminal activity. Similarly, the crime-fraud exception to the attorney-client privilege precludes a defendant from asserting a privilege when the purpose of the communications with the lawyer was to commit a pending or future crime or fraud. When the government raises a claim that the crime-fraud exception applies, the court may conduct an in camera review of the testimony or documents to evaluate the government's attempt to pierce the shield of the privilege. *United States v. Zolin,* 491 U.S. 554 (1989). Decisions by the trial courts to abrogate the privilege are not immediately appealable under the collateral order doctrine. *Mohawk Industries v. Carpenter,* 558 U.S. 100 (2009).

2. CHARACTER EVIDENCE AND PRIOR CONVICTIONS OR BAD ACTS

Although character evidence is not generally admissible as proof of a substantive crime, the government is permitted to introduce evidence of prior bad acts and convictions in certain circumstances, such as impeaching a defendant who testifies. Because the government can seek to introduce evidence not only of prior convictions but of uncharged, alleged misconduct, and because of the potential impact on the jury of such evidence, defendants may wish to file a motion in limine to obtain a ruling in advance as to whether the government will be permitted to introduce bad acts evidence to the jury. A ruling on whether the prosecution can use the defendant's prior conduct or convictions as impeachment should the defendant testify helps the defense lawyer decide whether to advise the client to take the witness stand and testify.

The government must give the defense notice of its intent to introduce evidence of prior misconduct if the defense requests such a notice. The purpose of this notice requirement is to permit defense counsel to make motions in limine prior to trial and to permit the defendant evaluate the risks on going to trial. Because the government need only provide such notice on request, it makes sense for defense counsel to include a request for notice of intent to use any alleged prior misconduct in its discovery request under Federal Rule of Criminal Procedure 16. See Chapter 7. Once a request is made, it places a continuing obligation on the government to provide notice whenever it determines that it may use prior misconduct against the defendant. The notice the government provides need not be in writing and need only be a "general nature."

The federal rules distinguish between the use of character evidence or prior bad acts as proof of the substantive crime and as a means of impeachment. Federal Rule of Evidence 404(a) provides:

(a) Character Evidence.

(1) Prohibited Uses. Evidence of a person's character or character trait is not admissible to prove that on a particular occasion the person acted in accordance with the character or trait.

(2) Exceptions for a Defendant or Victim in a Criminal Case. The following exceptions apply in a criminal case:

(A) a defendant may offer evidence of the defendant's pertinent trait, and if the evidence is admitted, the prosecutor may offer evidence to rebut it;

(B) subject to the limitations in Rule 412, a defendant may offer evidence of an alleged victim's pertinent trait, and if the evidence is admitted, the prosecutor may:

(i) offer evidence to rebut it; and

(ii) Offer evidence of the defendant's same trait; and

(C) in a homicide case, the prosecutor may offer evidence of the alleged victim's trait of peacefulness to rebut evidence that the victim was the first aggressor.

(3) Exceptions for a Witness. Evidence of a witness's character may be admitted under Rules 607, 608, and 609.

The general rule is that character evidence may not be used by the prosecution in its chief to prove that the defendant committed the offense. However, because defendants are permitted to introduce evidence of their own good character, the government may introduce character evidence when the defendant is deemed to have put his or her character into issue. In addition, a defendant may introduce evidence of the character of the accused when relevant unless the case is one involving a sexual offense. Sexual offenses are governed by Federal Rules of Evidence 412 and 413.

Although the prosecution is prohibited from using a wrongful act to obtain a conviction based on the bad character of the defendant, the prosecution may use prior actions in several situations. Rule 404(b) provides:

(b) Crimes, Wrongs, or Other Acts.

(1) Prohibited Uses. Evidence of a crime, wrong, or other act is not admissible to prove a person's character in order to show that on a particular occasion the person acted in accordance with the character.

(2) Permitted Uses; Notice in a Criminal Case. This evidence may be admissible for another purpose, such as proving motive, opportunity, intent, preparation, plan, knowledge, identity, absence of mistake, or lack of accident. On request by a defendant in a criminal case, the prosecutor must:

> (A) provide reasonable notice of the general nature of any such evidence that the prosecutor intends to offer at trial; and
>
> (B) do so before trial—or during trial if the court, for good cause, excuses lack of pretrial notice.

Under this Rule, the prosecution may introduce evidence of prior misconduct or convictions when that evidence is "inextricably intertwined" with the elements of crime charged. This test most obviously is satisfied when the government is charging the defendant with an offense that requires proof of underlying crimes, such as a conspiracy charge. *See, e.g., United States v. Pace,* 981 F.2d 1123 (10th Cir. 1992). The Rule also permits the prosecution to introduce evidence of prior misconduct for purposes other than showing that the defendant has a "bad character." This evidence may include evidence of uncharged misconduct as well as prior convictions, as long as the prosecution satisfies the relevancy requirement of Federal Rule of Evidence 104 (b) and the probative value of the evidence outweighs the dangers of unfair prejudice. *Huddleston v. United States,* 485 U.S. 681 (1988).

3. UNFAIR PREJUDICE

Federal Rule of Evidence 403 provides that "[t]he court may exclude relevant evidence if its probative value is substantially outweighed by a danger of one or more of the following: unfair prejudice, confusing the issues, misleading the jury, undue delay, wasting time, or needlessly presenting cumulative evidence." When the defense can anticipate the use of prejudicial evidence, a challenge to the use of that evidence may clarify the risks of trial. The introduction of prior bad conduct obviously carries the risk of prejudice and can be challenged in a motion in limine, as discussed above. And, defense counsel may also anticipate the government's use of scientific evidence and challenge its use under *Daubert v. Merrell Dow Pharmaceuticals, Inc.,* 509 U.S. 579 (1993).

A trial court is not required to rule definitively on the admissibility of evidence simply because the defendant has asked for such a ruling in a motion in limine. An evaluation of the prejudicial impact of the evidence may depend on what has occurred at trial, so often trial courts defer a ruling. When courts postpone ruling on the motion, defense counsel must renew the Rule 403 objection when the evidence is proffered to preserve the issue for appeal.

CHAPTER 11

MOTIONS TO SUPPRESS EVIDENCE FOR VIOLATIONS OF THE FOURTH AMENDMENT

■ ■ ■

Federal Rule of Criminal Procedure 12(b)(3)(C) requires a defendant to file a motion to suppress evidence before trial when seeking to suppress evidence on an alleged Fourth Amendment violation. The Fourth Amendment provides:

> The right of the people to be secure in their persons, houses, papers, and effects, against unreasonable searches and seizures, shall not be violated, and no Warrants shall issue, but upon probable cause, supported by Oath or affirmation, and particularly describing the place to be searched, and the persons or things to be seized.

The Fourth Amendment thus prohibits the government from obtaining evidence through an unreasonable search or seizure. The Amendment also anticipates that the government can search for evidence and seize items and people if the government obtains a warrant based on probable cause.

Fourth Amendment law draws a distinction between actions pursuant to a warrant and warrantless searches and seizures. When the evidence has been obtained pursuant to a warrant, the courts presume that the conduct was constitutional and thus, it is the defendant's burden to demonstrate that the evidence must be suppressed. When a search or seizure occurred without a warrant, by contrast, the government bears the burden of justifying the official's conduct. Even where there is a violation of the Fourth Amendment, however, the Court has restricted the availability of relief for the defendant by limiting who can raise Fourth Amendment claims, by doctrines such as attenuation and inevitable discovery, and by the good faith exception to the exclusionary rule.

A. SEARCHES PURSUANT TO A WARRANT

As a general rule, the government must obtain a warrant before conducting a search. Federal Rule of Criminal Procedure 41 sets forth the procedure for issuing, executing, and returning the warrant and any evidence seized pursuant to that warrant. Searches and seizures executed pursuant to a warrant are presumed valid, and challenges to the government's actions are limited to whether there was probable cause for the issuance of the warrant and whether the search was within the scope of the warrant. Moreover, the government may use any evidence that was obtained in good faith reliance on the warrant, even if the warrant was not supported by probable cause or the search technically violated Rule 41's requirements.

1. PROBABLE CAUSE

The Fourth Amendment requires the government to demonstrate to a magistrate judge or other judicial officer that there is "probable cause" justifying a search warrant. The government must show that there is probable cause to believe both that the item the government is looking for will be found in the proposed search and that there is a federal crime involved. "Probable cause" is more than a "reasonable suspicion," but less than a "certainty." Whether there is probable cause in a given situation depends on the totality of the circumstances. *Illinois v. Gates*, 462 U.S. 213 (1983).

This totality of the circumstances test requires an evaluation of whether the facts available to an officer would warrant "a person of reasonable caution" to conclude that a either a crime had been committed (for an arrest warrant) or there was evidence of a crime in the area (for a search warrant). *Carroll v. United States*, 267 U.S. 132, 162 (1925). In making this evaluation, courts are not to apply a particular checklist, but rather consider a "more flexible, all-things-considered approach." *Florida v. Harris*, 133 S. Ct. 1050, 1055 (2013). Thus, for example, when evaluating information supplied by an informant, a "deficiency [in one indicia of reliability] may be compensated for, in determining the overall reliability of a tip, by a strong showing as to . . . other indicia of reliability." *Illinois v. Gates*, 462 U.S. at 233. Moreover, there is probable cause even if law enforcement acts on a mistaken understanding of the facts or the reach of substantive law, as long as the mistake is an objectively reasonable one. *Heien v. North Carolina*, 135 S. Ct. 530 (2014).

In reviewing whether probable cause existed for the warrant, the court may only consider the evidence that was before the magistrate judge at the time the warrant was issued. *Aguilar v. Texas*, 378 U.S. 108 (1964). Moreover, because of the strong preference for warrants, courts reviewing a warrant are not to exercise their own independent judgement on whether probable cause existed to support the warrant. Instead, the Supreme Court has instructed that the magistrate judge's probable cause determination should be sustained if there is a "substantial basis" for the magistrate's decision. *Illinois v. Gates,* 462 U.S. at 213. Finally, even if the warrant is subsequently determined to be invalid, the evidence will not be suppressed if the police had an "objectively reasonable belief that their conduct did not violate the Fourth Amendment." *United States v. Leon,* 468 U.S. 897, 919 (1984). This so-called good faith exception is further discussed below.

When the defendant claims there were false statements in an affidavit or oral testimony to a judge to obtain a warrant, the court undertakes a two-fold inquiry. First, because the probable cause standard permits mistakes, it must be shown that the officer made the statements with knowledge of their falsity or at least with a reckless disregard for the truth. Second, even when this standard is satisfied, a court will uphold the warrant if the affidavit or testimony, stripped of the false statements, was sufficient to establish probable cause. *Franks v. Delaware*, 438 U.S. 154 (1978).

2. SCOPE OF THE WARRANT

The Fourth Amendment requires that the search warrant be particular as to the place to be searched and the things to be seized. *Groh v. Rameriz*, 540 U.S. 551 (2004). The officer is limited by the scope of the warrant in the search. This limitation, however, does not apply if the officer is where he has a right to be and observes an item in plain view that is evidence of a crime. *Arizona v. Hicks*, 480 U.S. 321 (1987).

When executing a search warrant, police officers may detain occupants of the premises while conducting a search. *Michigan v. Summers*, 452 U.S. 692 (1981). In addition, the officers may place the occupants in handcuffs for the duration of the search, at least when there are safety concerns justifying the use of restraints. *Muehler v. Mena,* 544 U.S. 93 (2005). However, the police may not detain individuals who are beyond the vicinity of the premises being searched. *Bailey v. United States,* 133 S. Ct. 1031 (2013).

3. RULE 41 REQUIREMENTS

Federal Rule of Criminal Procedure Rule 41 sets forth the process for obtaining and executing a warrant. Rule 41(b) provides that only a federal law enforcement official or a government attorney may request a warrant, and this request must be presented to a neutral and detached official. Under Rule 41(d), a request for a warrant must be accompanied by either an affidavit or sworn testimony that sets for the grounds for probable cause. Rule 41(d) also permits officials to apply for search warrants via telephone conversations and electronically.

Rule 41(c)(1)–(4) describe the type of persons and property that may be the subject of a warrant. Rule 41(b)(1)–(4) provide the authority for magistrate judges to issue these warrants. Warrants seeking electronically stored information are authorized by Rule 41(e)(2)(B). This subsection permits the government to seize the entire storage medium and review it at a later time to determine what information falls within the scope of the warrant.

Search warrants are generally required to be executed during the daytime, although a search may continue into the night if it is begun during the day. And, a government agent may be authorized in the search warrant to execute it at night when good cause is shown. The officer executing the search warrant must enter on the warrant the exact time and date that the warrant specifies.

> **Practice Note:** A search or seizure pursuant to a warrant is presumptively constitutional. It is therefore the defendant's burden to show that the warrant was defective or that the search exceeded the scope of the warrant. Even if the defendant makes such a showing, however, the government will be permitted to use the evidence if the government can show that an exception to the warrant requirement applies or that the officers reasonably believed that their conduct was permissible.

The officer conducting the search is required to create an inventory of all items seized. Rule 41(f)(1)(B). A copy of this inventory must be provided to the magistrate judge designated in the warrant. Rule 41(f)(1)(D). The magistrate judge then files this inventory with the clerk of the court. Rule 41(i).

B. WARRANTLESS SEARCHES AND SEIZURES

When the government has obtained the evidence without a warrant, the courts engage in a two-step process. First, the defendant must show that the government's conduct rose to the level of a search or seizure within the meaning of the Fourth Amendment. Second, if it is obvious that a search or seizure occurred or the defendant shows that one did, the government must show that the conduct fell within an exception to the warrant requirement.

1. SEARCH OR SEIZURE REQUIREMENT

Before a court will reach the question of whether the government's actions were unreasonable under the Fourth Amendment, the defendant must show that: (1) the evidence was seized by a government official and (2) there was a search or seizure within the meaning of the Fourth Amendment. The first prong is easily established as long as a governmental official is involved in the seizure of the evidence. The Supreme Court has held that action by a government employee, who is not a law enforcement official, may satisfy the governmental action requirement. *New Jersey v. T.L.O.,* 469 U.S. 325 (1985). The Amendment does not apply, however, when a private party obtains the evidence and provides the government with the information. *United States v. Jacobsen*, 466 U.S. 109 (1984).

> **Practice Note:** The determination as to whether there is a search or seizure is heavily fact-bound. Both prosecutors and defense attorneys should focus on facts of the Supreme Court cases, as well as the cases in their jurisdiction, and analogize the facts of their case to cases in which the courts have either rejected or found that there was a reasonable expectation of privacy on the citizen's part.

The question of whether a search occurred is more complex. A search may be found where there is an invasion of an constitutionally protected space—an area in which there was a reasonable expectation of privacy. Alternatively, a defendant can establish that there was search if the government used sense-enhancing technology that is not widely available to obtain information from a constitutionally-protected space or the government physically occupied a constitutionally-protected space to obtain information.

a. Searches

For many years, it was understood that the question of whether there was a search should be resolved under the so-called *Katz* test, derived from Justice Harlan's concurrence in *Katz v. United States*, 389 US 347 (1967). Under the *Katz* test, a search occurs when (1) the defendant had an expectation of privacy (a subjective test) and (2) that expectation is one that society is willing to recognize as reasonable (an objective test). This two-test is frequently collapsed into a test as to whether the defendant had a reasonable expectation of privacy that was violated by the conduct of the government official.

The Court provides the highest degree of protection to invasions of a home. *Kirk v. Louisiana*, 536 U.S. 635 (2002); *Payton v. New York*, 445 U.S. 573 (1980). This protection applies to the "curtilage," the areas surrounding the home, and the courts apply a functional test to determine whether the area is within the curtilage. *United States v. Dunn*, 480 U.S. 294 (1987). When the area is not a part of the curtilage, it is considered an "open field," to which no reasonable expectation of privacy attaches, and this land, and any structures on that land, may be examined by the officers. *Dow Chemical Co. v. United States*, 476 U.S. 227 (1986); *California v. Ciraolo*, 476 U.S. 207 (1986). Moreover, the plain view doctrine means that no search occurs when the police observe activities within the curtilage of the house from outside that area.

As a general rule, if the defendant has disclosed the information to a third party, there is no expectation of privacy, and, therefore, no search has occurred. Defendants do not have a reasonable expectation of privacy in items they throw in trashcans, in preventing third parties from reporting on things the defendants willingly disclose to them, or in telephone numbers dialed and collected by telephone companies. *California v. Greenwood*, 486 U.S. 35 (1988). Defendants also have no reasonable expectation of privacy with respect to things that are in the plain view of the public, including anything that can be perceived by smell. The Court extended this plain perception doctrine to the use of canine sniffs in *Illinois v. Caballes*, 543 U.S. 405 (2005), at least where the use of the narcotics-sniffing dog does not extend the duration of a lawful stop. *Rodriguez v. United States,* 135 S. Ct. 1609 (2015).

Although police may rely on their senses under the plain view doctrine, the use of sophisticated technology may elevate the activity to the level of a search. *Kyllo v. United States*, 533 U.S. 27 (2001). In *Kyllo,* the Court held that the use of sense-enhancing technology that was not widely available to the public (a thermal imaging device) to obtain information about activities inside the home constituted a search.

Finally, a search for purposes of the Fourth Amendment occurs when the government gains information by physically occupying or intruding on a constitutionally protected space. Attaching a Global Positioning System ("GPS") to an automobile and using the GPS to track the movement of a suspect over a period of time constituted a search within the meaning of the Fourth Amendment. *United States v. Jones,* 132 S. Ct. 945 (2012). Similarly, the government's use of a drug-sniffing dog on the porch of a home to investigate a tip that marijuana was being grown inside was a search for Fourth Amendment purposes. *Florida v. Jardines,* 133 S. Ct. 1409 (2013). In both cases, the government physically intruded on the defendant's effects or home—constitutionally protected areas under the Fourth Amendment—to obtain evidence.

b. Seizures

A person is seized within the meaning of the Fourth Amendment when the actions of the government official would lead a reasonable person to conclude that he or she was not free to go. *Terry v. Ohio*, 392 U.S. 1 (1968). An item is seized when there is meaningful interference with an individual's control of that item. *United States v. Jacobsen,* 466 U.S. 109 (1984). Whether the government is required to justify the seizure under a probable cause standard or under the lesser standard of reasonable suspicion depends upon whether the seizure amounts to a custodial arrest or is merely a stop.

2. EXCEPTIONS TO THE WARRANT REQUIREMENT

The Court has frequently announced that warrantless searches "are *per se* unreasonable . . . subject only to a few specifically established and well-delineated exceptions." *City of Los Angeles v. Patel*, 135 S. Ct. 2443,

2452 (2015). At the same time, the Court has recognized that the "the ultimate touchstone of the Fourth Amendment is reasonableness." *Riley v. California,* 134 S. Ct. 2473, 2482 (2014). Thus, many searches are now conducted without a warrant based on one of the recognized exceptions to the warrant requirement. In warrantless searches or seizures, the government bears the burden of showing that one of the exceptions is satisfied. This showing involves a two-part analysis. First, the government must show that the situation falls within one of the enumerated exceptions. Second, the government must meet whatever burden is imposed upon it under the particular exception to justify its conduct. Some of the exceptions require the government to show that the officials had probable cause for the search or seizure. Other exceptions lower the burden on the government to a "reasonable suspicion" or eliminate the burden of any justification for the search beyond the existence of the exception.

a. Search Incident to Arrest

When police officers validly arrest a person, they may search the person and the area within the individual's immediate control. *Chimel v. California,* 395 U.S. 752 (1969). The Supreme Court has explained that this exception "enables officers to safeguard evidence, and, most critically, to ensure their safety during 'the extended exposure which follows the taking of a suspect into custody and transporting him to the police station.'" *Virginia v. Moore,* 553 U.S. 164, 177 (2008) (quoting *United States v. Robinson,* 414 U.S. 218, 234–35 (1973)). This exception has several limits. First, the exception requires a valid arrest. If the arrest was invalid because the officers lacked probable cause, the search incident to arrest exception cannot be relied on by the government. *Virginia v. Moore,* 553 U.S. at 176.

Second, the police are limited as to the extent of the search permitted under this exception, both in terms of the place where the arrest occurs and the search of the person. Although officers may seize items that are in plain view of the room in which a defendant is arrested, they may not search the entire premises where an arrest takes place. *Chimel v. California,* 395 U.S. 752 (1969). The police may, however, open a closed drawer if that drawer is within the immediate reach of the person arrested. *New York v. Belton,* 453 U.S. 454 (1981). And, the police may look in closets and other spaces adjoining the place of arrest from which someone could launch an attack on police. *Maryland v. Buie,* 494 U.S. 325 (1990).

In addition, the police may search the person arrested and may generally seize and search objects found on the person. *United States v. Robinson,* 414 U.S. 218 (1973). Relying on this basic rule, the Court in *Robinson* upheld a search of a cigarette wrapper found in the pocket of an individual arrested. The Court, however, recently held that the police may not search data on cell phones as part of a search incident to arrest because of the vast amount of personal information that cell phones hold. *Riley v. California,* 134 S. Ct. 2473 (2014).

Third, there is a temporal limit to the search incident to arrest exception. If the "search is remote in time or place from the arrest," and there are no other exigencies involved, the government may not justify the search under the search incident to arrest exception, at least where items in which there is a legitimate expectation of privacy, such as a locked piece of luggage, are involved. *United States v. Chadwick,* 433 U.S. 1, 15 (1977).

Finally, the permission to search the body of the person arrested may not include intrusive body searches. *Cupp v. Murphy,* 412 U.S. 291 (1973). The Supreme Court, however, has held that correctional officers may conduct invasive body searches of all incoming inmates, even those who were arrested for traffic infractions, as long as the search is conducted pursuant to standard policy. *Florence v. Bd. of Chosen Freeholders of the County of Burlington,* 132 S. Ct. 1510 (2012). Moreover, the police may use a swab to obtain a DNA sample from individuals who are arrested and brought into custody. *Maryland v. King,* 133 S. Ct. 1958 (2013).

b. Protective Sweep

Police may conduct a search without a warrant as a "protective sweep." The Supreme Court has defined a "protective sweep" as "a quick and limited search of the premises, incident to an arrest and conducted to protect the safety of police officers or others. It is narrowly confined to a cursory visual inspection of those places in which a person might by hiding." *Maryland v. Buie,* 494 U.S. 325, 327 (1990).

The federal courts of appeals disagree as to whether this type of search requires an arrest or simply requires that the police are lawfully present. At a minimum, this exception means that when police are acting pursuant to an arrest with probable cause, they may search the space from which an attack on them could be launched without any justification and may search beyond that area if they have a reasonable suspicion of danger.

c. Exigent Circumstances

Police may enter a home without a warrant when they have a reasonable belief that there are exigent circumstances justifying entry into the home. *Kirk v. Louisiana,* 536 U.S. 635 (2002). The Supreme Court has identified the following three situations as constituting exigent circumstances that permit warrantless entries into a home: (1) the police are in hot pursuit of a fleeing suspect; (2) there are reasons to believe that there is a danger to the lives of the police or others; or (3) there are reasons to believe that a suspect will destroy evidence. *Kentucky v. King*, 563 U.S. 452, 461–62 (2011). In *King*, the Court held that it did not matter if police conduct created the exigent circumstances as long the police conduct did not violate the Fourth Amendment.

d. Plain View/Perception

Police are permitted to seize items without a warrant if the police have a right to be where they are and have probable cause to conclude that the items are evidence of a crime. *Horton v. California*, 496 U.S. 128 (1990). This exception permits police to seize items perceive as contraband through sight, smell, or touch as long as they are lawfully in a position to perceive the object seized. *Washington v. Chrisman*, 455 U.S. 1 (1982). However, police are limited to seizure of items whose character is immediately apparent. They may not inspect an item or move it to determine that it is contraband. *Arizona v. Hicks*, 480 U.S. 321 (1987).

e. Vehicle Searches

Motor vehicles have a particular set of rules. In dealing with motor vehicles, it is important to distinguish the automobile exception from searches under the search-incident-to-arrest exception. Under the automobile exception, police may search automobiles and other vehicles without a warrant as long as they have probable cause for the search (that is, probable cause that the car contains evidence of criminal activity). *Carroll v. United States*, 267 U.S. 132 (1925). Containers within the cars may be searched if the government can show that there was probable cause to believe that the containers searched contained the items sought. *California v. Acevedo*, 500 U.S. 565 (1991). This rule applies whether the police are examining the owner's containers or belongings of a passenger in the car. *Wyoming v. Houghton*, 526 U.S. 295, 300 (1999).

Under the search-incident-to-arrest exception, the authority to search the car is more limited. When a person in a vehicle is arrested, the police may (1) search the passenger compartment of the car if the arrestee is unsecured and within reaching distance of the compartment at the time of the search or (2) if the arrestee is secured, search the car for evidence related to the offense of the arrest. *Arizona v. Gant*, 556 U.S. 332 (2009).

f. Inventory or Booking Exception

If a person is lawfully arrested, the police may search that individual's personal effects at the stationhouse as long as the search was pursuant to "routine administrative procedure" and was conducted in good faith. *Illinois v. Lafayette*, 462 U.S 640, 643 (1983). The government does not have to show probable cause to justify these searches. *Colorado v. Bertine*, 479 U.S. 367 (1987). This is because these searches serve to "protect an owner's property while it is in the custody of the police, to insure against claims or lost, stolen, or vandalized property, and to guard the police from danger." *Id.* at 373. Thus, as long as the individual was validly arrested, the government may justify a search under the inventory exception if the officers were following standardized procedures and acted in good faith.

When the police have lawfully impounded a car, the police may conduct a routine inventory search of the car and seize any incriminating evidence. The police may open locked trunks and open closed containers in conducting these searches. No probable cause is required for these searches; however, the search must be conducted pursuant to standardized criteria. *Colorado v. Bertine*, 479 U.S. 367 (1987). Moreover, if the original impoundment was invalid, the results of the inventory search must be suppressed. *Dyke v. Taylor Implement Mfg. Co.*, 391 U.S. 216 (1968).

g. "Stop and Frisk"

There are three categories of police-citizen encounters. There are arrests and searches incident to arrests (which require probable cause for the seizure); stop and frisks (which require less than probable cause and allow less of a search); and encounters that do not amount to a seizure. In *Terry v. Ohio*, 392 U.S. 1 (1968), the Supreme Court held that the police can "stop and frisk" people without a warrant and with less proof than probable cause. Both the "stop" and the "frisk" elements of this ruling have their own set of rules.

i. Terry *stops*

There are generally three issues with respect to "*Terry* stops": (1) whether the "stop" constituted a "seizure"; (2) whether the police had a sufficient basis for the seizure; and (3) whether the actions were sufficiently limited that the conduct did not amount to an arrest (which does require probable cause). A stop goes beyond an encounter and becomes a seizure when a reasonable person would not feel free to walk away. *United States v. Mendenhall*, 446 U.S. 544 (1980). The Court has concluded that police officers do not transform questioning into a seizure when they board a bus, question passengers, and ask for permission to search luggage. *United States v. Drayton*, 536 US 194 (2002). In addition, when police order someone to stop or use another non-physical restraint, there is no seizure until the individual submits to the police authority. *California v. Hodari D.*, 499 U.S. 621 (1991). By contrast, a seizure occurs whenever the police stop a private vehicle to question its occupants. *United States v. Cortez*, 449 U.S. 411 (1981).

Once the stop has risen to the level of a seizure, a police officer is required to have more than a "hunch" that the individual was engaged in illegal activity to justify stopping the individual. *Terry v. Ohio*, 392 U.S. at 22. Rather, the government must show some particularized and objective basis for believing that the individual was, is, or is about to be, engaged in criminal activity. *United States v. Cortez,* 449 U.S. 411 (1981). As is the case with probable cause, the reasonable suspicion standard is a totality of the circumstances standard that looks at the information possessed and its reliability. *Alabama v. White,* 496 U.S. 325, 21–22. However, the Supreme Court has made clear that the level of suspicion required to satisfy this standard is "obviously less demanding than for probable cause." *United States v. Sokolow,* 490 U.S. 1, 7 (1989). And while an anonymous tip standing alone does not satisfy the reasonable suspicion standard, the Court recently held that there was reasonable suspicion to stop a truck for possible drunk driver based on an anonymous 9-1-1 call reporting that a truck had run the caller off the road, the caller supplied the make, color and license plate of the vehicle, and the police confirmed the caller's claims about the truck's location. *Naverette v. California,* 134 S. Ct. 1683 (2014).

Finally, the police conduct must be limited to a stop and not rise to the level of an arrest. In general, the seizure of the individual must be limited to the time necessary to confirm or dispel the police officer's suspicions. *United States v. Sharpe,* 470 U.S. 675 (1985). If the duration and other factors of the detention render the detention "indistinguishable from a traditional arrest," the government will not be able to justify the seizure under the reasonable suspicion standard but will have to show probable cause. *Dunaway v. New York,* 442 U.S. 200, 212 (1979). In addition, in the context of a traffic stop, the police may not extend the detention of the indiviual beyond the time necessary to decide whether to issue a ticket and to conduct "ordinary inquiries" such as checking the driver's license and registration. *Rodriguez v. United States,* 135 S. Ct. 1609, 1615 (2015).

ii. Terry *frisks*

Terry authorized police officers to conduct "frisks" in connection with the stops. These frisks are essentially a pat down for weapons after a legitimate stop. If the stop is invalid, the subsequent frisk will also be invalidated. Even if the stop was valid, however, the frisk is only permissible if the officer had a reasonable belief that the suspect is armed and dangerous. *Arizona v. Johnson,* 555 U.S. 323 (2009).

h. Administrative and Special Needs

There are some settings apart from the criminal context in which the Court has concluded that the Fourth Amendment does not require that the government have probable cause to conduct a search. These situations generally involve regulated industries or other situations that counsel in favor of a more relaxed standard. Thus, for example, administrative inspections of highly regulated industries are permitted without a warrant. *Marshall v. Barlow's, Inc.,* 436 U.S. 307 (1978). In addition, while the government is required to obtain a warrant for housing safety inspections and other sorts of regulatory inspections of businesses that are not highly regulated, these administrative warrants do not have to be supported with probable cause; rather, the Court balances the public interest in the inspection against the intrusion suffered by the owner of the property or business. *Camera v. Municipal Court,* 387 U.S. 523 (1967). However, owners must have the opportunity to have a neutral decisionmaker review the warrant or subpoena before suffering penalties for refusing to comply. *City of Los Angeles v. Patel,* 135 S. Ct. 2443 (2015).

Some settings allow screenings and searches that would not ordinarily be permissible by law enforcement absent probable cause, reasonable suspicion, or a warrant. For example, airport screenings of passengers and their belongings are permissible. *United States v. Biswell,* 406 U.S. 311 (1972). And, police officers are permitted to set up fixed highway checkpoints for combating drunk driving, but not for interdicting narcotic trafficking. *City of Indianapolis v. Edmond,* 531 U.S. 333 (2000). Finally, people may be searched at the border without probable cause or a warrant. *United States v. Ramsey,* 431 U.S. 606 (1977). Instead, at the border, the government may conduct non-routine searches and detentions upon a showing of reasonable suspicion. *United States v. Montoya de Hernandez,* 473 U.S. 531 (1985).

Schools are also special environments. Students may be searched by school officials if they have a reasonable suspicion that the student has contraband, but that search must be reasonably related to the objectives of the search and may not be excessively intrusive. *Safford Unified Sch. Dist. No. 1 v. Redding,* 557 U.S. 364 (2009). School officials are also permitted to conduct random, suspicionless drug testing of students involved in extracurricular activities. *Bd. of Educ. of Ind. School District No. 92 of Pottawatomie County v. Earls,* 536 U.S. 822 (2002).

3. CONSENT TO SEARCH

A search without either a warrant or probable cause is permissible if there is voluntary consent to a search. The burden is on the government to show that consent was given. In order to constitute a voluntary consent, however, the Court does not apply the "waiver test" requiring the "intentional relinquishment or abandonment of a known right or privilege" that was enunciated in *Johnson v. Zerbst,* 304 U.S. 458 (1938). Instead, "voluntary consent" in the context of the Fourth Amendment is defined as consent that "was in fact voluntarily given, and not the result of duress or coercion, express or implied." *Schneckloth v. Bustamonte,* 412 U.S. 218, 248–49 (1973). Moreover, consent may be given by any co-occupant of the property or any individual whom the police reasonably believe has the authority to consent. *Illinois v. Rodriguez,* 497 U.S. 177, 188–89 (1990). Although the police cannot rely on the consent of a co-occupant when the defendant is physically present and objects to the police request to enter or search the premises, *Georgia v. Randolf*, 547 U.S. 103 (2006), the defendant's objection does not prevent the police from returning to the property and obtaining consent from a co-occupant once the defendant has left, or been removed from, the property. *Fernandez v. California*, 134 S. Ct. 1126 (2014).

C. LIMITS ON CLAIMS FOR FOURTH AMENDMENT VIOLATIONS

Defendants may file a motion to suppress evidence seized in violation of the Fourth Amendment. Under the exclusionary rule, the courts will suppress evidence seized unconstitutionally, as well as all "fruits" of the illegal conduct. *Wong Sun v. United States*, 371 U.S. 471 (1963). The exclusionary rule, however, may only be invoked by persons who have a certain relationship to the violation—a relationship that is frequently referred to by the courts as standing. In addition, the exclusionary rule does not apply to (1) the "fruits" of a search that are too attenuated from the illegality; (2) to "knock and announce" violations of the Fourth Amendment, *Hudson v. Michigan*, 547 U.S. 586 (2006); and (3) when the officials acted in good faith reliance on a warrant that is later invalidated or reasonably relied on incorrect information. Finally, a violation of Rule 41 procedures, as opposed to a violation of constitutional requirements, is not cause for suppressing the evidence.

1. WHO MAY FILE MOTIONS TO SUPPRESS

Defendants moving to suppress evidence under the Fourth Amendment must show a violation of their own Fourth Amendment rights. There is no vicarious liability. A defendant must show that the police violated his or her reasonable expectation of privacy. *Rakas v. Illinois*, 439 U.S. 128 (1978). This means that evidence that must be suppressed as to one defendant may be used against a different defendant who is unable to show that his or her rights were violated. Whether the defendant is able to show a reasonable expectation of privacy is a fact-bound inquiry. *Minnesota v. Olson*, 495 U.S. 91 (1990); *Minnesota v. Carter*, 525 U.S. 83 (1998).

2. FRUIT OF AN ILLEGAL SEARCH

The exclusionary rule bars the government from using not only the evidence that it seized illegally but also other evidence it obtained using that initial evidence, or the "fruit of the poisonous tree." Thus, when an illegal search leads to the discovery of other evidence, that other evidence will be suppressed.

This "fruits" doctrine is subject to several limitations. First, although the exclusionary rule applies to more than "physical, tangible materials,"

Wong Sun v. United States, 371 U.S. 471, 486 (1963), the Supreme Court has announced that "the exclusionary rule should be invoked with much greater reluctance where the claim is based on a causal relationship between a constitutional violation and the discovery of a live witness than when a similar claim is advanced to support suppression of an inanimate object." *United States v. Ceccolini*, 435 U.S. 268, 280 (1978). Second, even if the evidence could be viewed as a "fruit" of a prior illegal search, the government will be able to use the evidence if it obtained the evidence from an "independent source," *Silverthorne Lumber Co. v. United States*, 251 U.S. 385, 392 (1920), or if discovery of the evidence was "inevitable," *Nix v. Williams*, 467 U.S. 431, 444 (1984). Finally, the evidence will not be considered the impermissible fruit of an illegal search where the discovery of the evidence was "so attenuated as to dissipate the taint." *Nadone v. United States,* 308 U.S. 338, 342 (1939), or when the police violate the knock-and-announce requirement before entry. *Hudson v. Michigan*, 547 U.S. 586 (2006). Thus, even if the government is not able to satisfy its burden of showing that an exception to the warrant requirement applies, the evidence still may be admissible if the government can show an exception to the exclusionary rule applies.

3. THE GOOD-FAITH EXCEPTION

Perhaps the most significant limitation on the exclusionary rule is the good faith exception. In *United States v. Leon,* 468 U.S. 897 (1984), the Supreme Court held that when police execute a search pursuant to a warrant that is later invalidated, the evidence should not be suppressed when the police's reliance on the warrant was "objectively reasonable." This exception to the exclusionary rule applies as long as the police did not mislead the magistrate in obtaining the warrant, the warrant was facially valid, and the police did not unreasonably exceed the bounds of the warrant when executing it.

This good faith exception has been extended to apply to situations in which the police arrested someone based on a statute later declared unconstitutional, *Illinois v. Krull,* 480 U.S. 340 (1987), where police relied on information from court clerical personnel that happens to be wrong, *Arizona v. Evans,* 514 U.S. 1 (1995), where police rely on erroneous information from another police employee that was a result of a negligent bookkeeping error, *Herring v. United States,* 555 U.S. 135 (2009), and where police rely on binding precedent that is overturned while the defendant's case is pending. *Davis v. United States,* 131 S. Ct. 2419 (2011). In both *Herring* and *Davis,* the Court used quite expansive language in describing the good faith exception to the exclusionary rule, explaining that the exclusionary rule was a rule of "last resort" and should only be applied in situations involving "deliberate, reckless, or grossly negligent conduct, or in some circumstances recurring or systemic negligence." *Herring,* 555 U.S. at 144; *Davis,* 131 S. Ct. at 2427–28. All of the good faith exception cases deal with police reliance on an actor with no involvement in the criminal investigation. The Court has not addressed whether the exception should apply when the mistake was made by someone involved in the investigation or stop and that mistake has been found to violate the Fourth Amendment.

CHAPTER 12

MOTIONS TO SUPPRESS STATEMENTS AND EYEWITNESS IDENTIFICATIONS

■ ■ ■

Like motions to suppress evidence under the Fourth Amendment, Federal Rule of Criminal Procedure 12 requires that motions to suppress defendants' statements or identification of the defendants by eyewitnesses be made prior to trial. The Fifth and Sixth Amendments limit how the government can obtain a statement from a defendant that may be used at trial. The Fifth Amendment provides that "no person . . . shall be compelled in any criminal case to be a witness against himself." The Sixth Amendment provides that "the accused shall enjoy the right . . . to have the Assistance of Counsel for his defence." Criminal defendants may file a motion to suppress their statements on the ground that the government violated their rights under either, or both, of these Amendments.

Criminal defendants may also challenge the procedures used to obtain an eyewitness identification under either the Due Process Clause or the Sixth Amendment. A due process claim requires a showing that the procedure used was unnecessarily suggestive, while a Sixth Amendment claim rests on a showing that the right to counsel had attached and the identification occurred in a line-up without the presence of counsel. Under both claims, to preclude an in-court identification, the defendant will have to show that the violation so impacted the witness's memory that an in-court identification cannot be permitted.

A. FIFTH AMENDMENT *MIRANDA* REQUIREMENTS

The Fifth Amendment requires that any statement that the government elicits from the defendant be given voluntarily. In *Miranda v. Arizona,* 384 U.S. 436 (1966), the Court adopted a prophylactic test to determine whether any statements were voluntary. Under *Miranda,* if the police provide the required warnings, any statement given by the defendant is considered to be voluntary. The *Miranda* warnings include informing the defendant "[1] that he has the right to remain silent, [2] that anything he says be used against him in a court of law, [3] that he has the right to the presence of an attorney, and [4] that if he cannot afford an attorney one will be appointed for him prior to any questioning is he so desires." *Id.* at 479.

Miranda requires these warnings whenever there is a "custodial interrogation." The courts have defined both these terms. In addition, the Court has provided further guidance on the language that is sufficient to provide the warnings and to show an invocation of these rights. Once these warnings are given, the police may not question a defendant without counsel unless the defendant waives the rights to silence and counsel.

1. CUSTODY

The police are only required to provide a suspect with the *Miranda* warnings if the individual is in custody. *Dickerson v. United States,* 530 U.S. 428 (2000). Whether an individual is in custody for purposes of *Miranda* is an objective test that focuses on "first, what were the circumstances surrounding the interrogation; and second, given those circumstances, would a reasonable person have felt he or she was at liberty to terminate the interrogation and leave." *J.D.B. v. North Carolina,* 564 U.S. 261 (2011) (quoting *Thompson v. Keohane,* 516 U.S. 99, 112 (1995)).

The Court employs an objective test to determine whether a suspect is in custody. The subjective beliefs of either the officers or the suspect are irrelevant to this inquiry. *Berkermer v. McCarty,* 468 U.S. 420 (1984). This objective test, however, does not mean that no case-specific facts can be considered in determining whether a reasonable person would have believed that she could terminate the interrogation and leave. Rather, the Court has held that the courts should consider the fact that a juvenile was questioned in evaluating what a reasonable person would have believed, as long as the age was known to the officer at the time of the interview or would have been "objectively apparent to any reasonable officer." *J.D.B.* 564.

Although the custody requirement for *Miranda* sounds similar to the Fourth Amendment test for whether there is a seizure of an individual, the courts treat the two tests differently. There can be a seizure for purposes of the Fourth Amendment without triggering the "custody" requirement of *Miranda. Berkemer v. McCarty,* 468 U.S. 318 (1994). For example, in *Berkemer,* the police questioned the defendant during a routine traffic stop. This stop was undoubtedly a "seizure" under the Fourth Amendment. The Court, however, concluded that the defendant was not in custody for purposes of *Miranda*. The Court reasoned that in contrast to the stationhouse interrogations that raise *Miranda* concerns, routine traffic stops involve public questioning and are generally brief and temporary.

The location of the interrogation has some bearing on whether the individual is in custody. Questioning at the stationhouse is more likely to be considered custodial. But, an individual who voluntarily goes to a police station and leaves without resistance cannot claim that he was in custody. *Oregon v. Mathiason,* 429 U.S. 492 (1977). Moreover, even when a suspect is questioned outside the stationhouse, courts may conclude that the suspect may be in custody if the circumstances show that the person was not free to leave. *Orozco v. Texas,* 394 U.S. 324 (1969). For example, in *Orozco,* the Court held that individual was in custody when he was awakened at 4:00 a.m. in his bedroom and questioned by four police officers.

2. INTERROGATION

Miranda is only implicated if the police "interrogated" the defendant. Whether an interrogation took place is an objective test that focuses on whether the police officer should have known that his conduct was "reasonably likely to elicit an incriminating response." *Rhode Island v. Innis,* 446 U.S. 291 (1980). As with the custody requirement, the suspect's beliefs are irrelevant. Rather, what matters is whether the police engaged in questioning of the suspect or its functional equivalent. For example, in *Innis,* two police officers engaged in a conversation while transporting the suspect in which they expressed concern that the missing shotgun could be found by a young student at a nearby school for handicapped children. The Court concluded that this conversation was not the functional equivalent of questioning because there was no indication that the police were aware of any particular susceptibility of the suspect that would render it likely that the conversation would elicit an incriminating response. Moreover, courts require more than a possibility that an incriminating response will be elicited to conclude that official "interrogated" the defendant. *Arizona v. Mauro,* 481 U.S. 520 (1987). Finally, there is no interrogation for purposes of *Miranda* if the officer appears to be conducting only on-the-scene questioning.

3. CONTENT OF THE WARNINGS

Miranda requires that, prior to any questioning, a suspect be told "[1] that he has the right to remain silent, [2] that anything he says be used against him in a court of law, [3] that he has the right to the presence of an attorney, and [4] that if he cannot afford an attorney one will be appointed for him prior to any questioning is he so desires." *Miranda,* 384 U.S. at 479. The Court, however, has rejected requiring any particular phrasing of these warnings be used. *Florida v. Powell,* 559 U.S. 50 (2010). Rather, the test is whether "the warnings reasonably convey to [a suspect] his rights as required by *Miranda.*" *Id.* at 76. And, on a number of occasions, the Court has found that this test is satisfied, notwithstanding the fact that the officers did not use the precise language outlined in *Miranda. Id.*; *Duckworth v. Eagan*, 492 U.S. 195 (1989); *California v. Prysock*, 453 U.S. 355 (1981) (*per curiam*).

4. INVOCATION AND WAIVER OF MIRANDA RIGHTS

Once the government shows that the warnings were given and understood by the defendant, the defendant has the burden of showing that he unambiguously invoked his right to silence or counsel in order to have the statements he made suppressed. Police officers are not required to either stop the questioning or clarify whether the defendant is invoking her *Miranda* rights when the defendant makes a statement that can be viewed as ambiguous or equivocal. *Davis v. United States*, 512 U.S. 452 (1994). Remaining silent for 2 hours and 45 minutes of police questioning is not an invocation of the right to remain silent. *Berguis v. Thompkins*, 560 U.S. 370 (2010).

Moreover, statements made will not be suppressed if the defendant is deemed to have waived his *Miranda* rights. The government bears the burden of showing by a preponderance of the evidence that the defendant waived the rights to remain silent and to counsel. *Colorado v. Connelly*, 479 U.S. 157 (1986). This does not mean, however, that the government must show that the defendant expressly waived those rights before the questioning began. Rather, the government can establish a waiver for purposes of *Miranda* when a defendant responds in a custodial interrogation if the government demonstrates that (1) the *Miranda* warnings were given; (2) the defendant understood those rights; and (3) the defendant made an uncoerced statement. *Berghuis v. Thompkins*, 560 U.S. at 386-87.

When a defendant unambiguously invokes the right to counsel, the police may not renew a custodial interrogation until counsel has been provided or the defendant initiates contact. *Edwards v. Arizona*, 451 U.S. 477 (1981). The police may not renew an interrogation once the defendant invokes the right to counsel simply by providing the Miranda warning again to the defendant, even if the defendant is approached by different officers. However, this limitation on questioning by the government does not apply when there is at least a fourteen-day break in custody. *Maryland v. Shatzer*, 559 U.S. 98 (2010).

Different rules apply when a defendant invokes her right to silence. As with the right to counsel, when a defendant invokes the right to silence, the police must cease the questioning. But, unlike the right to counsel invocation, a different officer may question the defendant if the defendant is given the *Miranda* rights again and given the opportunity to exercise the right to remain silent, at least when the second police officer questions the defendant about an unrelated crime. Thus, in cases involving the invocation of the right to silence, what is required is that the police "scrupulously honor" the suspect's rights. *Michigan v. Mosely,* 432 U.S. 96 (1975).

5. FRUIT OF THE POISONOUS TREE

The fruit of the poisonous tree doctrine is less applicable in the *Miranda* context than it is in the Fourth Amendment context. The government may use physical evidence that is obtained from a confession elicited in violation of *Miranda. United States v. Patane,* 542 U.S. 630 (2004). In addition, an initial failure to provide the required warnings will not taint a later statement given after receipt of the warnings, as long as the later statements were voluntarily given. *Oregon v. Olstead,* 470 U.S. 298 (1985). On the other hand, when the police adopt a protocol for giving no warnings until a confession is obtained and then giving the warnings and leading the suspect through the same confession, *Miranda* bars the use of those latter statements. *Missouri v. Seibert,* 542 U.S. 600 (2004).

6. EXCEPTIONS TO *MIRANDA*

The Court has recognized two express exceptions to *Miranda:* (1) routine booking practices and (2) public safety. The government may use answers to police questions normally asked during a booking against the defendant, even though no *Miranda* warnings were given. *Pennsylvania v. Muniz,* 496 U.S. 582 (1990). In addition, when there are circumstances indicating a danger to the public, the government may use answers to questions given to protect public safety, even though the defendant was not provided the required warnings. *New York v. Quarles,* 467 U.S. 649 (1984).

Moreover, *Miranda* only applies when the defendant knows he is talking with a police officer. Thus, unlike the Sixth Amendment right to counsel discussed below, *Miranda* does not apply when the defendant is talking to an undercover officer or private individual. *Illinois v. Perkins,* 496 U.S. 292 (1990).

Miranda is also not applicable when the communication is not "testimonial." *Pennsylvania v. Muniz,* 496 U.S. 582 (1990). A "testimonial response" is one in which the suspect's communication "relate[s] a factual assertion or disclose[s] information." *Doe v. United States,* 487 U.S. 201, 210 (1988). For example, in *Muniz,* the Court concluded that *Miranda* did not bar the use of a videotape that showed a drunk driving suspect slurring his words because it was not communicative. However, *Miranda* did bar introduction of his answer to a question about the date of his sixth birthday because it was incriminating not only due to the manner of the delivery but in the content of the response as well. Similarly, *Miranda* warnings are not required when defendants are asked to submit handwriting samples, state certain words in a line-up, or submit to blood alcohol tests.

Finally, the government cannot use a statement obtained in violation of *Miranda* in its case-in-chief against the defendant making it, nor may prosecutors introduce evidence of a defendant's invocation of the right to remain silent in either the case-in-chief or as a means of impeachment. *Greer v. Miller,* 483 U.S. 756 (1987); *Doyle v. Ohio,* 462 U.S. 610 (1976). However, the government can use a statement obtained in violation of *Miranda* to impeach the defendant if she chooses to testify. *Harris v. New York,* 401 U.S. 222 (1971). The prosecution may also point out a defendant's silence in response to some questions, at least where the person did not invoke the privilege against self-incrimination and was not in custody at the time of the questioning. *Salinas v. Texas,* 133 S. Ct. 2174 (2013).

B. THE SIXTH AMENDMENT REQUIREMENTS

Once formal adversary proceedings begin, the Sixth Amendment prohibits the government from eliciting incriminating statements from a person charged with a crime about that offense unless the defendant knowingly, voluntarily, and intelligently waives the Sixth Amendment right. In contrast to *Miranda,* which involves only questioning by police, the Sixth Amendment applies to conversations with undercover police and other persons acting at the government's behest. The reach of the Sixth Amendment is limited because it is offense specific and the defendant may waive the right to counsel. In addition, although the government cannot use the statement or its fruit in its case-in-chief, the prosecution can use the statement for impeachment if the defendant elects to testify. *Kansas v. Ventris,* 556 U.S. 586 (2009).

1. DELIBERATELY ELICITING INFORMATION

Once judicial proceedings are initiated against a defendant, and the defendant invokes the right to counsel, the government may not deliberately elicit a statement from the defendant without counsel present. *Massiah v. United States,* 377 U.S. 201 (1964). This prohibition includes actions by police to surreptitiously elicit information from the defendant as well as interrogations by police officers. *Brewer v. Williams,* 430 U.S. 387 (1977). The prohibition also extends to the government using a third party to circumvent the right to counsel and obtain information. *Maine v. Moulton,* 474 U.S. 159 (1985).

The government, however, may use statements obtained "by luck and happenstance." Thus, the government may use statements it obtained by placing an informant in a jail cell with a defendant when the informant was instructed by the police to simply listen. *Kuhlman v. Wilson,* 477 U.S. 436 (1986). By contrast, when the informant actively participated in the conversation, the government may not use the statements obtained even if the informant was told by law enforcement agents that she should not engage in conversation. *United States v. Henry*, 447 U.S. 264 (1980).

2. OFFENSE-SPECIFIC LIMITATION

The Sixth Amendment right to counsel only applies to the offense that the defendant is charged with. The government may interrogate a defendant or surreptitiously obtain information from the defendant about a different offense, even if it is related to the charged offense. *Maine v. Moulton*, 474 U.S. 159 (1985). The test for whether the right to counsel bars further action by the government is the same as the test for whether double jeopardy attaches: whether the second offense contains all of the elements of the charged offense. If the elements are not the same, then the government may interrogate, either expressly or covertly through a third party, a defendant without counsel present. *Texas v. Cobb*, 532 U.S. 162 (2001).

3. WAIVER

Once a defendant invokes his or her Sixth Amendment right to counsel, the police may not attempt to initiate any interrogation of that defendant without counsel present. But, the government may use statements obtained without counsel present if the defendant waives the right to counsel. *Patterson v. Illinois*, 487 U.S. 285 (1988). Even after a defendant has asserted her right to counsel in a judicial proceeding, the government may subsequently approach and interrogate the defendant if the defendant knowingly and voluntarily waives the right to have counsel present. Thus, even after a defendant asserts the right to counsel at arraignment or other preliminary proceeding, a defendant who receives and understands the *Miranda* warnings can agree to waive the right to have counsel present. This waiver is valid for both Sixth Amendment purposes as well as for the Fifth Amendment. *Montejo v. Louisiana*, 556 U.S. 778 (2009).

4. FRUIT OF THE POISONOUS TREE

The fruit of the poisonous tree doctrine applies to any statements obtained in violation of the Sixth Amendment right to counsel. Thus, to use evidence that is traceable to that statement in its case-in-chief, the government must show that it had an independent source for that evidence, that discovery of the evidence was inevitable, or that the evidence was too attenuated from the statement to be traceable to it. *Nix v. Williams*, 467 U.S. 431 (1984). The government may, however, use such evidence, and any statements obtained in violation of *Massiah*, to impeach a defendant as long as those statements were voluntarily obtained. *Kansas v. Ventris*, 556 U.S. 586 (2009).

C. EYEWITNESS IDENTIFICATIONS

A defendant may move to suppress eyewitness identifications on two grounds: (1) the identification process employed by the police violated the Due Process Clause, or (2) the identification violated the Sixth Amendment because it occurred post-indictment outside the presence of counsel. When either of these rights are violated, courts may suppress the witness's out-of-court identification of the suspect, any fruits of the identification, and at times, the in-court identification of the defendant by the witness.

1. DUE PROCESS REQUIREMENTS

The fundamental fairness protected by the Due Process Clause requires the suppression of any out-of-court identification when, given the totality of the circumstances, the procedures used by the police were so unnecessarily suggestive that they created a substantial likelihood of misidentification. *Neil v. Biggers,* 409 U.S. 188 (1972). A procedure is likely to run afoul of due process requirements if the police intentionally or inadvertently indicate to the witness that the suspect is the person who committed the crime. Police may not parade a suspect in front of an eyewitness for an identification, at least in the absence of some urgent reason for employing the procedure. Similarly, police must use non-suggestive techniques in both line-ups and photographic arrays. Police must make reasonable attempts to harmonize the appearances of the individuals displayed and refrain from suggesting to the witness that a perpetrator is present in the array.

Even when police used an unnecessarily suggestive process to obtain the identification, the government may be able to use the out-of court identification or ask the witness to identify the perpetrator in court. In deciding whether the government may use the identification, courts examine whether the eyewitness had a reliable, independent basis for the identification. To make this determination, courts look at a number of factors including: the opportunity of the witness to view the suspect; the degree of attention paid by the witness to the suspect; the accuracy of the witness's prior description of the suspect; the amount of time the witness observed the suspect; and the length of time between the crime and the identification. A court weighs these factors against the possible corrupting effect of the suggestive technique in deciding whether to admit the out-of-court identification. *Manson v. Brathwaite,* 432 U.S. 98 (1977). Courts consider these same factors in determining whether the suggestive technique so tainted the identification that the eyewitness should be barred from identifying the defendant as the perpetrator in the courtroom.

Finally, due process claims are limited to those situations in which the government arranged the suggestive circumstances. When there was no impropriety by law enforcement officials, the defendant does not have a due process right to have the identification excluded. *Perry v. New Hampshire,* 132 S. Ct. 716 (2012).

2. THE SIXTH AMENDMENT RIGHT TO COUNSEL

Once adversarial proceedings have begun against a defendant, that defendant has the right to counsel under the Sixth Amendment at any out-of-court identification. *United States v. Wade,* 388 U.S. 218 (1967). Formal adversarial proceedings are begun whenever a complaint is filed or an indictment or information is issued. When an out-of-court identification is conducted without counsel after criminal proceedings have begun, both the out-of-court identification and any in-court identification will be suppressed unless the government can show by clear and convincing evidence that the witness's identification in the courtroom was a result of the witness's independent observations at the scene of the crime rather than the identification conducted without counsel. In evaluating whether the government has met this burden, courts consider the same sorts of factors as they do under the due process analysis.

CHAPTER 13

PRETRIAL MOTIONS, MEMORANDA OF LAW, EVIDENTIARY HEARINGS, AND ORAL ARGUMENTS

■ ■ ■

This Chapter discusses the basic requirements for drafting motions and memoranda of law supporting those motions, preparing for and conducting evidentiary hearings as well as for oral arguments. It provides sample motions and memoranda of law, as well as basic checklists and recommendations for drafting a motion and accompanying memoranda of law in support of a position being advanced to the trial court. In addition, it provides general considerations for conducting both an evidentiary hearing and oral arguments before a federal district court.

A couple of initial comments are in order. First, because most arguments to trial courts are based on whether a particular set of facts meet an established standard, such as probable cause, it is critical for counsel to go beyond the Supreme Court cases found in this book and research the cases in the jurisdiction in which the case is being argued. Counsel should spend time analyzing the cases in the jurisdiction and be able to analogize and distinguish those cases. Second, it is important that counsel spend time before the evidentiary hearing conducting this research so that counsel is clear what facts need to be elicited during the evidentiary hearing. Finally, counsel should ensure that any motions or memoranda are free of errors and comply not only with the Federal Rules but any local district court rules and specific rules of the judge. Mistakes in documents filed with the court can be a significant distraction, may cause the judge to mistrust the argument offered by the party, and may even result in a rejection of the filing.

Throughout this Chapter, the hypothetical used to provide examples is that the defendant challenges a "pat down" search by a police officer that resulted the discovery of a gun with a scratched off serial number in violation of 18 U.S.C. § 922(k), which prohibits possession of a firearm in which the serial number is "removed, obliterated, or altered." The defendant contends that the stop was invalid under *Terry v. Ohio*, 392 U.S. 1 (1968), which requires the government to show that the police officer had both a reasonable suspicion of criminal behavior to initiate the stop and a reasonable concern for personal safety to initiate the pat-down search. The defendant is claiming that the officer did not have articulable facts that could reach the level of reasonable suspicion. As discussed above in Chapter 11, although the defendant will make the motion to suppress the evidence, the prosecution will in fact bear the burden of proof because there was no warrant.

A. PRETRIAL MOTIONS

Any request to the trial court to dismiss charges or suppress evidence should be made in the form of a motion. When a motion involves more than a simple issue, the parties may ask for, or the court may order, briefing on the issue(s) before the court renders a decision on the motion. Whenever filing a motion or a memorandum of law, the attorney must made sure that the filing complies with three sets of rules: (1) Federal Rule of Criminal Procedure 12; (2) the rules of the local United States District Court; and (3) the individual requirements of the district judge or magistrate judge who will be deciding the motion. For example, many local rules also require a statement as to whether the motion is opposed or unopposed, and some judges may add their own additional requirements.[3] Compliance with all of the rules and expectations of the court in which the case is being heard is essential.

1. STRUCTURE OF MOTION

As a general rule, a motion to a court contains at least the following:

- Caption of the Case
- Title
- Statement of Grounds for Relief
- Request for Relief
- Signature Block
- Proposed Order
- Certificate of Service

A sample motion can be found at the end of this Chapter.

a. Caption and Title

The caption should include: the district court, the parties, the case number, and the name of the judge to whom the case is assigned. The title should reflect the party filing the motion and the requested relief. For example, rather than saying "Motion to Suppress Evidence," a

---

[3] For example, a judge from the United States District Court for the Eastern District of Michigan requires the following: "Courtesy copies of all motions must be submitted to the court with exhibits clearly labeled. The labels must extend to the right side of the paper. An index of the exhibits must be included." Practice Guidelines of Judge Marianne O. Battani, https://www.mied.uscourts.gov/index.cfm?pageFunction=chambers&judgeid=1 (accessed July 3, 2015).

defense motion to preclude the testimony of the defendant's physician is better titled "Defendant's Motion to Suppress Testimony of Defendant's Physician" or "Motion to Suppress Testimony Based on Physician-Patient Privilege."

b. Grounds for Relief

The body of the motion should set forth the basic claim of the movant, the legal standard, and the factual basis for the claim. Each claim or factual assertion should be a separately numbered paragraph. When the motion is accompanied with a memorandum of law, the motion itself may not contain the legal argument or multiple citations to authority. Instead, the motion may simply refer to the accompanying memorandum of law, or it could highlight the basic law and the most important facts and serve as a summary of the moving party's argument.

When the issue is fairly simple, a motion may be sufficient for the court to rule. In these circumstances, the motion would contain the legal argument. In organizing this legal argument, it is helpful to follow this basic structure: position, basic legal standard or rule, explanation of rule, and application to the facts of the case (in short, the basic IRAC or CREAC formulae taught in most law schools). In following this structure, it is helpful to make each part of the argument a separate paragraph. If there are several parts to the legal standard or several reasons why the standard is (or is not) met, each reason will probably merit its own paragraph.

c. Request for Relief

The motion should end with a specific statement of the relief requested. There should be no doubt in the judge's mind as to the precise nature of the relief sought. Consider whether there are alternative requests to be made. For example, as the sample at the end of this Chapter shows, when asking that the gun be suppressed because the *Terry* standard was not complied with, defense counsel asks in the alternative for an evidentiary hearing to be held on the motion.

d. Signature Block, Proposed Order and Certificate of Service

The signature block should include the names of the attorneys who have worked on or have responsibility for the matter, as well as the information required by the local court rules—usually the addresses, telephone numbers, e-mail addresses, and bar numbers of the attorneys.

A proposed order should be provided on a separate page, with caption and title, that the judge can sign to grant the relief sought.

All motions must be served on the opposing counsel and must contain a certificate of service reflecting that this service was made. The form of the certificate of service should comply with local rules and formats.

B. DRAFTING MEMORANDA OF LAW

When the issues raised by a motion are more complex, counsel may decide (or the court may order) that providing a brief or memorandum of law is required. In addition, counsel may ask the court for permission to file briefs after an evidentiary hearing. When submitting a brief, counsel also prepares a motion with a proposed order and a certificate of service for both the motion and the memorandum of law. Once again, it is important to check the local rules of the trial court in which the case is pending. Some districts permit the motion and memorandum to be in one single document, some districts would like two separate documents, and some, while permitting a single document, require the memorandum to begin on a new page.

1. STRUCTURE OF A MEMORANDUM OF LAW

Assuming the memorandum of law is filed separately from the motion, the components of a memorandum of law are similar to those of a motion and generally include:

- Caption of the Case
- Title
- Introduction
- Statement of Facts
- Argument
- Conclusion
- Signature Block
- Certificate of Service and Certificate of Compliance (if required by local rules)

Samples of parts of both a defendant's brief and a government reply brief are included at the end of this Chapter.

a. Caption and Title

These should mirror the caption and title of the motion (aside from indicating that the document is the memorandum of law supporting or opposing the motion).

b. Introduction

The introduction is the first opportunity to persuade the court. It should provide the court with a clear statement of what is being requested and why the judge should rule as requested. As a general rule, the focus in the introduction should be on the critical facts that support the result sought.

The introduction should provide the court with the following information: the identity of the parties and posture of the case; the relief requested; and the basic reason supporting the relief, including the important facts and key legal claim(s). Citations should be kept to a minimum in this section. At most, the controlling Supreme Court case(s) may be identified. But, there should not be detail about these decisions. Rather, in the introduction, the focus should be on the application of the legal standard to the case before the court.

c. Statement of Facts

The goal of the statement of facts is to provide the court with the basic information necessary to understand the issue and to persuade the judge that the facts favor granting the relief sought. Because most disputes at the trial level turn on the facts as opposed to the law, it is important to focus the judge's attention on those facts that would lead to the result sought.

As a general rule, the facts should be presented in chronological order. Where, however, there is conflicting testimony or evidence, the story might be told topically or by witness. What matters is that the story is told in a manner in which the court can easily understand. Favorable facts can be emphasized by using active voice, and those less favorable may be deemphasized—*but not ignored*—by use of the passive voice. Word choice, particularly choice of verbs, is especially important. The phrase "the defendant was escorted by two police officers" evokes a different image from "the defendant walked with two police officers."

The focus should be on facts, not legal conclusions. For example: "Although the speed limit was 25 miles per hour, John was going 50 miles per hour," paints a clearer picture than "John was speeding and driving recklessly." In addition, editorializing or excessive adjectives should be avoided. Overstatements and flowery language detract from the quality of the work product. Twisting facts so that they are unrecognizable or incredulous detracts from an advocate's credibility and provides an opponent with easy ways to discredit arguments.

Finally, counsel should provide the court with citations to the record, so that the judge (or law clerk) can easily find the information referenced. If counsel is relying on the agent's 302 report for a particular fact, the report should be clearly identified for the court, e.g. Agent Smith's 302 report dated April 3, 2015. Similarly, if the fact was developed during the evidentiary hearing, that should be made clear to the court with a cite to the transcript. Moreover, it can be helpful for the court (and is required by some judges) for counsel to attach as appendices any documents being relied upon.

d. Argument

The goal of the argument section is to persuade the court that the applicable legal standard justifies the outcome sought by the party. The argument section should begin with a roadmap paragraph that tells the court what the legal issue is, how that issue should be resolved, and what the individual arguments are in support of that conclusion.

> **Practice Note:** Rule 3.3 of the Model Rules of Professional Responsibility imposes a duty of candor on attorneys, and every state has a version of this duty in its professional rules. This duty of candor applies to both statements of fact and the law. Counsel should never provide the opposing side with a credible basis for contending that this ethical obligation was violated.

After the introductory paragraph, each argument should begin with a persuasive point heading. Structure each argument by writing: (1) a statement of the thesis—why relief is appropriate; (2) an accurate statement of the legal standard governing the issue; (3) an explanation of how that legal standard works (if necessary); (4) an application of that legal standard to the facts; and (5) a conclusion that connects the individual argument to the requested relief.

At the trial level, the primary focus of the argument section is usually on the application of the facts to the governing legal standards. In drafting the discussion of the legal standard, care should be taken to describe the rule accurately, yet also in a way that is most persuasive for the position being advocated. For example, in the sample defense brief at the end of the chapter, the explanation of the requirements for a *Terry* stop focuses on the need for articulable and particularized facts to satisfy the reasonable suspicion standard. On the other hand, the government reply brief reminds the court that the standard for reasonable suspicion is less than that required for probable cause and that deference is given to the experience of police officers in evaluating the circumstances.

Once the legal standard is explained, the brief should provide an understanding of how the courts in the governing jurisdiction have applied these standards. In order to provide the court with this information, counsel will want to explain the critical facts in the cases on which counsel is relying and why those facts did (or did not) meet the legal standard. In discussing particular cases, it is important to start with an explanation of why the case is relevant, as opposed to diving right into the facts of the case or the case's holding.

Once the cases are explained, a persuasive brief will provide an explanation of how those facts are like (or not like) the facts in the case before the court. It is not sufficient to talk in generalities. Counsel should provide specific cites to specific parts of the record (either from the evidentiary hearing or in the documents) that support the position of the party and draw specific analogies to facts from cases on which counsel is relying. In addition, in drawing the analogies for the court, it is helpful if the factual comparisons follow the same order that the facts were discussed in the case illustrations.

The discussion should anticipate and address likely counter-arguments by the opposing party. Every state has a provision similar to Model Rule of Professional Conduct 3.3(a)(2), which states that an attorney shall not "knowingly fail to disclose to the tribunal legal authority in the controlling jurisdiction known to the lawyer to be directly adverse to the position of the client and not disclosed by opposing counsel. . . ." Thus, counsel must acknowledge and distinguish any controlling contrary legal authority. In one Seventh Circuit decision, *Gonzalez-Servin v. Ford Motor Company*, 662 F.3d 931 (7th Cir. 2011), Judge Richard Posner included photographs in the opinion of an ostrich and what appears to be an attorney with their heads in the sand as a reminder to counsel to cite relevant authority. Do not put a judge in the position of recalling (or using) that image.

Finally, when writing a reply brief, counsel should explain to the court exactly where there is disagreement with the moving party. If the disagreement is over a misunderstanding of the law, explicitly state so. By contrast, if the contention is that the moving party misapplied the law or misapprehended the facts, make that clear to the court. In the example at the end of this Chapter, the government contends both that the defense brief misapplied the law and ignored some of the facts developed at the evidentiary hearing. The government makes clear that it is raising these two distinct arguments in the introduction as well as the discussion section of the brief. In addition, the government challenges the defense's claim that certain cases support a ruling in the defendant's favor. The critical thing is to be responsive when writing a reply brief and to explain what is wrong with the defendant's position, or conversely, why the response is the preferable ruling. This approach can be challenging when the initial brief is less than clear. In that case, the reply brief may also have to bring some order or clarity to the issue before the court.

e. Conclusion

This should be a one or two sentence statement of what relief is being requested.

f. Signature Block, Certificate of Service and Certificate of Compliance

Some courts require a Certificate of Compliance, stating that the filing complies with the local rules. In addition, all memoranda should conclude with a signature block and a certificate of service.

2. BRIEF WRITING TIPS

The point of a memorandum of law is to convince the judge that the request for relief should (or should not) be granted based on the governing law and the facts of the case. This of course may seem obvious. But, it is important to keep this basic goal in mind when drafting a brief. Counsel will likely be more familiar with the particulars of a case than is the judge. It is therefore important to provide the court with sufficient explanations to support the requested relief, both in terms of the law governing the issue and the facts of the case before the court.

a. Before Writing a Memorandum of Law

As noted above, counsel should review the local rules and an individual judge's guidelines before writing a brief so that the memorandum of law complies with the required format. It is also helpful to draft the stock parts of the motion and memorandum before beginning the substantive drafting. Having the required certificates and proposed order completed before beginning drafting ensures that nothing is forgotten in the haste of getting a memorandum filed with the court.

It is also helpful to review both the evidence that has been developed and the relevant cases before writing the brief. This review will likely reveal facts that had not seemed important at first glance and will help to develop the argument.

Finally, an outline of the basic points makes drafting much easier as the order of the argument will be planned before actually attempting to write. Of course, during the drafting process, the order will need to be evaluated and perhaps revised. But, having a plan before starting the drafting process certainly helps conquer writer's block and the agony of staring at a blank computer screen.

b. During the Drafting Process

It is important to quiet the inner critic during the drafting process. Very few advocates are able to produce a well-organized and tightly-written legal argument in a first draft. Accepting that revisions will be made allows the legal writer to move on and get a first draft written. One way to do this is to write notes to one's self in the draft of issues or concerns that need to be looked at, researched or further expanded.[4]

In addition, although the final memorandum will have a specific order—introduction, statement of facts, argument, and conclusion—there is no requirement that the drafting process follow that order. In fact, it is usually easiest to write the introduction and statement of facts after the argument has been written. Similarly, it may make more sense to write the roadmap paragraph for the argument section after the argument is written, or simply write a skeletal roadmap paragraph in the initial draft that can be refined once the argument section is complete.

Within the argument section, remember that persuasive legal writing should begin with the conclusion that you are arguing for and then explain the law and apply it to the facts. In the explanation of the law, avoid long historical discussions of case law. Instead, provide the court only with the details of particular cases when those details help the court understand your ultimate conclusion. In any case discussion, moreover, you should begin with an explanation of the principle for which the case is being used before reviewing any details about the case. You should explain the critical facts of any case you are discussing and relate those facts to the reasoning and holding of the court.

When you turn to the application of the law to the facts of the case before the court, you need to draw explicit connections or contrasts between the facts of the prior cases you have relied on and the facts of your case. And, you need to explain to the court why the comparison matters. It is not sufficient to say the facts are the same—the judge must understand what facts are the same and why that similarity should result in the result counsel is urging. Moreover, the order of the discussion should mirror the order of the discussion in your case illustrations.

If the argument contains several subarguments, counsel should explain to the court the connection between the arguments. For example, in the sample brief, the defendant is arguing both that the initial stop was invalid and that the search exceeded the boundaries set by *Terry v. Ohio*. The brief is careful to explicitly draw the connection between the two arguments, explaining "Even if the initial search were valid, the evidence should be suppressed because the officers exceeded the scope of the search permitted during a *Terry* stop." Do not make the court connect the arguments.

---

[4] Mary Beth Beazley and Monte Smith call this process of using private memos or notes to "quiet your inner demon and prevent writer's block." Mary Beth Beazley & Monte Smith, *Legal Writing for Legal Readers* 115 (2014). They suggest that writers allow themselves to create imperfect first drafts and drop footnotes or comments to preserve concerns that arise during the writing process, but to not allow those concerns to derail the process of getting the draft written. *Id.*

Finally, it should go without saying, but accuracy in a statement of facts or in an explication of law is essential. It is required by the professional rules governing attorney conduct. Moreover, nothing hurts the credibility of an argument more than an inaccurate recitation of a case or the facts. This also means that counsel should make sure that any case that is being relied on remains good law in the jurisdiction.

c. Editing the Memorandum of Law

Because it is rare that a motion or brief will be ready for filing after an initial drafting, it is important to leave time for both editing and proof reading the memorandum. Editing requires counsel to evaluate the substance of the argument, while proofreading focuses on issues of grammar, citation, and typographical errors. It is important to separate these two processes as much as possible; most of us cannot successfully do both tasks at the same time.

In the editing process, it is important to tackle big issues before smaller concerns. The following is a suggested order of evaluation during the editing process.

1. **Complying with the rules**. Have you complied with the rules regarding length? If not, understand that you will be making decisions as to where to delete arguments, issues, or verbiage, or deciding that you need to ask the court for permission to file a longer brief. Trial courts are busy, and unless you have an exceptional reason for the longer brief, you should comply with the page or word limit by editing your brief.

2. **Briefly outline your arguments**. Does the order make sense? All other things being equal, successful advocacy generally suggests placing the strongest argument first. However, when the courts always follow a particular order in evaluating a claim, then it is likely best to follow that order if arguments are being made on all of the points. If the order does not make sense, revise it.

3. **Review each argument**. Have you provided the court with a conclusion for each argument and a connection to the following argument or the argument above? If not, revise.

4. **Simplify and shorten**. It is difficult to read long arguments, long paragraphs, and long sentences. Moreover, the reader may get confused or lost with lengthy explanations that do not have signposts along the way. Thus, break arguments apart into distinct sections that do not run more than three to four pages. Break longer paragraphs into shorter paragraphs if possible—a reader

loses attention when paragraphs are longer than two-thirds of a page. And break long sentences (generally more than three lines) into shorter ones, unless the longer sentence is necessary to capture your meaning.

5. **Review each point heading**. Does it succinctly state the conclusion of your argument? If not, revise it.

6. **Review each topic sentence**. Does the main idea of each paragraph appear in the topic section locations? If a reader skims the document and reads only the first sentence, can the reader understand the argument? One way to test this is to copy the first sentences into a separate document and read that document. If the order of those topic sentences does not make sense or if you are missing a key point in your argument, revise your topic sentences.

7. **Review each paragraph**. Does each sentence begin with the ending point of the last sentence and end with the new point? This order of familiar to new drafting allows the reader to understand your argument easily. Moreover, reviewing a draft for this will allow you as a writer to see where there may be points that were in your head, but not explicitly made to the court. If there are problems, revise.

d. Proofreading the Memorandum of Law

Once you have made your substantive edits, only then should you proofread your brief. The best way to proofread is to print out a clean version and work on it in hard copy rather than attempting to proof read on the computer screen. The following is a suggested order for proofreading.

1. **Check your subjects and verbs in each sentence**. Are your subjects and verbs close together? Do the subject and verb agree? Make sure you do not have a single comma between the subject and verb.

2. **Check pronouns**. The use of pronouns—he, she, it, this, they—can be confusing to the reader. Make sure that there are clear references to the nouns.

3. **Eliminate overstatements** like "clearly," "merely," and "obviously". They tend to be either trivial terms or overstatements and thus, they can distract the court. Replace with a more descriptive verb.

4. **Review citations**. Ensure they are accurate and comply the citation rules and practices of your jurisdiction.

5. **Check Spelling and Grammar.** Make sure to use a computer program that highlights issues, but do not rely exclusively on such a program. The programs do not pick up when you have inadvertently typed "to" instead of "two" or "trail" instead of "trial."

6. **Check your headings** after you have made all of the proofreading changes. They should not be at the bottom of a page Adjust if necessary.

C. CONDUCTING AN EVIDENTIARY HEARING

If a Rule 12 motion contains sufficient allegations to entitle the defendant to suppression of the evidence, the district court may hold an evidentiary hearing to resolve any disputed factual issues. In these hearings, the prosecution bears the burden of demonstrating that the disputed evidence is admissible. Under Rule 12(h), the government must disclose any statements of its witnesses that qualify as Jencks material under Rule 26.2. The defense may call witnesses, including the defendant, to refute the government's version of events.

> **Practice Note:** Under Rule 3.4(b) of the Model Rules of Professional Conduct, advocates cannot do anything to encourage a witness to change his or her truthful testimony. In addition, counsel should not offer evidence that she knows or "reasonably believes" is false. Rule 3.3(a)(4). The duty of candor to the court extends to advocates discouraging witnesses from lying and to correct any false testimony they discover has been given. Rule 3.3(a)(2), (4).

The defendant's testimony at an evidentiary hearing cannot be used at trial as part of the prosecution's case-in-chief. *Simmons v. United States*, 390 U.S. 377, 394 (1968). However, if the defendant testifies at trial, the testimony given during the evidentiary hearing can be used in cross-examination for impeachment purposes. As the Supreme Court noted, "every criminal defendant is privileged to testify in his own defense, or to refuse to do so. But that privilege cannot be construed to include the right to commit perjury." *Harris v. New York*, 401 U.S. 222, 225 (1971). In addition, the rules of evidence do not apply to evidentiary hearings, and hearsay is admissible. *United States v. Matlock*, 415 U.S. 164, 173 (1974). That does not mean counsel should always be silent when the opponent is questioning a witness; counsel should object to leading questions, or those that go beyond the scope of the issues before the court, doing so judiciously.

1. PREPARING FOR AN EVIDENTIARY HEARING

At an evidentiary hearing seeking to suppress evidence because of an alleged constitutional violation, defendants typically claim that state actors violated their Fourth, Fifth, or Sixth Amendment rights. Thus, the prosecution presents the testimony of officers or agents to explain what occurred. After the prosecution calls its witnesses, the defense may call witnesses to refute the government's version of events.

In preparing for the hearing, the prosecution should, if possible, both review the officer's notes or reports and interview the officer. Similarly, defense counsel should carefully review any notes or reports filed by investigators, as well as interview the defendant and any other witnesses who could have facts relevant to the evidentiary hearing. It is critical to develop a timeline or flowchart that allows counsel to see quickly what happened, where there are ambiguities and inconsistencies in the record, and the source of those inconsistencies or ambiguities in the record. This timeline or flowchart will allow counsel to listen carefully to any direct examination and develop targeted questions for a cross examination.

If counsel plans to ask a witness about a particular document, and show that document to the witness, counsel should have clean copies of the document for opposing counsel, the witness, and the judge. Counsel should offer the document to the judge before questioning the witness about it. In addition, although the rules of evidence do not apply, counsel should recognize that they are in a courtroom and ask permission before approaching either a witness or the judge.

For the sake of simplicity, this Chapter explains the direct examination from the point of view of the prosecutor and the cross-examination from the point of view of the defense counsel. The techniques explained, of course, are the same regardless of the position of the advocate.

2. THE DIRECT EXAMINATION

Direct examination questions should be planned in advance to present the testimony in the light most likely to obtain the legal ruling sought. While rules of evidence concerning the use of leading questions on direct, laying a proper foundation, and hearsay may be somewhat relaxed at a suppression hearing, the presentation is more likely to be effective if all the typical formalities are followed. In fact, providing a foundation for the witness's testimony is likely to enhance the credibility of the witness.

It is critical that the government advocate consider how best to present the case that the officer's conduct was consistent with constitutional requirements. And, this requires counsel to consider the following: (1) the governing legal standards; (2) the factual content of the testimony and its relationship to the governing legal standards; (3) the organization and order of the direct examination; and (4) the form the questions take.[5]

---

[5] Steven Lubet, *Modern Trial Advocacy: Law School Edition* at 42–43 (NITA 3d ed. 2010).

a. The Substance of a Direct Examination

The goal of the government's direct examination is to show that the requirements of the Constitution were complied with. Before government counsel is able to develop the direct examination questions, counsel must have mastery of the substantive requirements of the law. For example, if the defendant is claiming that the evidence was seized in violation of the Fourth Amendment proscription on unreasonable searches, the prosecution must present evidence, depending on the facts of the case, that there was not a search, or that the search was within the scope of a warrant supported by probable cause, or that the warrantless search was within one of the exceptions to the warrant requirement.

Once the prosecutor is clear as to the substantive standards, counsel should make a list of all of the facts known and determine which are helpful for meeting the legal standard, which facts are less helpful (or harmful), and which facts are simply irrelevant. Of course, the prosecutor should also consider whether there are some undisclosed facts that, if true, would help the prosecutor's position, and see if those as-yet unknown facts can be elicited from a witness, preferably during an interview before actual testimony takes place.

At the end of this process, the prosecutor should have a list of facts that need to be elicited through the direct examination: the critical facts and the background facts that either help the court understand those critical facts or establish the credibility of the witness's testimony, such as the background of the officer testifying. The prosecutor should also be cognizant of any facts that may harm the government's position.

b. Structuring a Direct Examination

Once the prosecutor has determined the facts that should be elicited on the direct examination, she should plan the order in which those facts should be elicited. In determining this order, the prosecutor should consider the following: first, fact finders (in this case the judge) tend to pay the most attention to information given at the beginning and the end of a story; and, second, people want information provided in a way that connects what they have previously learned to what they are now learning.[6]

In the scenario involving the motion to suppress the gun found in a pat down, the prosecutor must show that there were articulable facts showing a reasonable suspicion of criminal behavior permitting the initiation of the stop and a reasonable concern for personal safety to initiate the pat-down search. Therefore, the prosecution would want to bring forth facts supporting both the officer's reasonable suspicion of criminal behavior and concern for personal safety as quickly as possible,

---

[6] Id. at 47–49.

without violating the second principle that people need to hear the connections between ideas. Compare the following two examinations:

Q: Why did you stop the defendant?

A: Because his actions led me to suspect that he was dealing drugs and was most likely armed.

Q: Why did you think he was acting like a drug dealer?

A: Well, it was around 10 p.m. and my partner and I saw him standing on the corner of Washington and Main Streets and in my experience as a police officer, that corner is where drug dealers hang out on. We watched him for about 5 to 10 minutes. During that time, I saw him talk briefly with several people and I thought he was acting in a way that indicated that he was either dealing drugs or serving as a look out for drug dealers. Both my partner and I just thought that his behavior was really suspicious and that he was likely carrying a gun.

Q. Why did you think he was armed?

A. I'm familiar with this area, and there has been a significant amount of drug dealing there as well as gun violence connected to drugs. When a person is alone on a street corner in that area after dark and meeting with others, there is a good chance that he's dealing drugs and that he's going to protect himself by carrying a gun.

Q. After observing the defendant on the street corner, what did you do?

A. My partner and I approached the defendant, and I asked him why he was hanging out on the corner. He walked towards us with one hand in his pocket and he said, "No reason." I quickly patted him down to protect myself. I felt something that seemed like a gun in his jacket pocket. I removed the object and discovered that it was a gun, and that the gun's serial numbers had been scratched out. I immediately placed him under arrest.

Here is questioning that takes a chronological approach to draw out the information from the witness:

Q. On the night of Tuesday, November 7, around 10 p.m., where were you?

A. I was sitting in my patrol car with my partner at the corner of Washington and Main Street.

Q. And what did you observe?

A. I saw the defendant walking back and forth between the corners of Washington and Main Streets.

Q. Why was that observation important?

A. In my experience as a police officer, those corners are places where drug dealers hang out on.

Q. Did you see anything else?

A. I saw the defendant talk briefly with several people and I thought he was either dealing drugs or serving as a look out for drug dealers.

Q. How long did you observe him for?

A. At least 5 minutes, probably closer to 10.

Q. Then what did you do?

A. I approached the defendant with my partner and I asked him why he was hanging out on the corner. He approached us with a hand in his jacket packet and said "no reason." I quickly patted him down and felt something that felt like a gun in his jacket pocket. I removed the object and discovered that it was a gun, and that the gun's serial numbers had been scratched out. I then arrested him for possession of a gun with obliterated serial numbers.

In both versions, the prosecution is attempting to establish that the police officer had a reasonable suspicion of criminal activity and fear for personal safety to allow a pat-down search. But, the latter version takes longer to get to the point, and it does not bring the basic position to the attention of the court before giving the details. Of course, the topical approach also has limits. There may be situations in which the government's position is best served by a more chronological approach, and in such cases, counsel would use the latter approach to structuring her questions.

When planning the organization of the direct examination, counsel should also avoid interrupting the main points with extraneous details and should consider whether it is in the government's interest to "front" or introduce any adverse facts. Bringing up adverse facts not only is consistent with counsel's duty of candor to the court, but it can also lessen the impact of those facts by placing them within the larger context of the prosecution's case. If adverse facts should be presented, those facts should be presented in the middle of the direct exam so that the questioning can start and end with the most persuasive and important points for the government. Always remember: people tend to focus on what they hear first and last.

c. The Form of Direct Examination Questions

Direct examination questions should be open-ended, short, and pointed. A direct examination is not about the attorney but about the witness. Thus, the questions should not be opportunities for oration or speech-making. Nor should they be confusing to either the court or the witness. Compound questions with multiple factual assertions are difficult for both the witness and the judge to understand.

The questions should also serve to emphasize the points that counsel is eliciting from the witness. In the first example above, the prosecution repeated the witness's testimony in the next question and thereby emphasized the critical points. In the latter example, the prosecutor did not do so and, thus, lost an opportunity at persuasion. Of course, this approach should not be taken the extreme. The questions should remain conversational.

Finally, the questioning should contain the equivalent of point headings that would be incorporated into a brief. For example, once the prosecutor had elicited the facts supporting the claim that the officer had a reasonable suspicion for the stop, the prosecutor would want to move explicitly to the next parts of *Terry:* the reasonable fear for safety and the limited scope of the pat-down search. Being able to do this requires the prosecutor to understand what must be shown and how those elements relate to one another.

3. THE CROSS-EXAMINATION

While conducting an effective direct examination is often relatively straight-forward, developing an effective cross-examination is more difficult and much more of an art. In a cross-examination, counsel is dealing with at best a neutral witness, and often someone who is hostile to counsel's position. In addition, on cross-examination, counsel always runs the risk of undermining the client's position by strengthening the opposition or allowing the witness to fill in gaps that had been left at the end of the direct examination. An effective cross-examination minimizes these risks and strengthens the client's case by detracting from the opponent's position or discrediting the witness.

A particular trap for counsel in a criminal case is expecting to achieve too much through a cross-examination, the so-called "Perry Mason" moment when the witness recants prior testimony and admits to the opposite. The witness has, in all likelihood, been prepared for the cross-examination by opposing counsel, and will have thought through the basic outlines of the testimony. Moreover, a government agent is likely to be an experienced witness who understands what defense counsel is trying to accomplish through a line of questioning. The cross-examiner should consider what can be emphasized from the direct testimony that is supportive of the client's case, and whether there are inconsistencies that can undermine a witness's credibility.

a. The Substance of a Cross-Examination

Like the direct examination, an effective cross-examination depends on an understanding of the law and the facts. Thus, counsel should begin with the same steps of analyzing the factual record in light of the substantive standards and determining what facts are critical, as was discussed above. However, unlike direct examination, counsel cannot prepare fixed questions in advance because, particularly in the absence of transcripts of prior testimony or witness interviews, cross-examination may depend largely on what the person actually states on direct examination. Counsel, therefore, should develop an outline for cross-examination with likely subjects for questioning and then annotate that outline during the direct examination to select the actual topics for the cross-examination. Counsel should understand the purpose for which the facts being elicited will be used in making the argument to the court and use that purpose in determining which topics and questions to pursue in the cross-examination.

In preparing to cross-examine a law enforcement official, counsel should pay careful attention to the reports that have been turned over by the prosecution and listen for any discrepancies between the direct examination and those reports. Counsel should also look for discrepancies between any hand-written contemporaneous notes and the official reports. Officers testify quite frequently and it is especially difficult to have them admit they were wrong. Defense counsel may, however, undermine an officer's credibility by pointing out to the judge that there are inconsistencies in the witness's accounts of the events. Having a timeline or flowchart prepared that points out those inconsistencies will help counsel listen carefully to the direct examination and determine where there are points that could be developed further on the cross-examination to undermine the testimony of the witness.

b. Structuring a Cross-Examination

In order to minimize the risks of cross-examination, the cross-examiner must remain in control. One way to do this is to limit the cross-examination in terms of the number of subjects covered and the number of questions asked. In the world of cross-examination, shorter is usually better.

Like the direct examination, a topical organization generally works best. Unlike direct examination, however, the cross-examination should not begin with overarching points; the witness is likely to disagree with those points. Thus, beginning the questioning with statements like "You ignored the scope of the warrant" or "My client believed he was in custody" are unlikely to elicit a helpful response. Instead, the questioning should focus on the details. Working in small, incremental steps is more likely to permit counsel to gather the information needed than is a broad statement that goes to the heart of the argument.

To maintain control of the examination, counsel must listen carefully to each answer. Witnesses may try to go beyond the scope of the questions asked, and it is counsel's responsibility to cabin the testimony to the question actually being asked. Similarly, a witness may give a non-responsive answer that does not actually address the question asked. Counsel must be aware when a witness is not being forthcoming with information. So it is up to the cross-examiner to ensure the witness answers the question asked. Witnesses will frequently equivocate if an answer will not help their position or will show an inconsistency with prior testimony or statements. Counsel can, and should, repeat her question when this occurs. This may heighten the adversarial nature of the cross-examination, so it is crucial that counsel remain calm and in control of the questioning. Appearing frustrated or making a snide remark about the unresponsiveness of the witness, especially someone in law enforcement, is unlikely to play well with the court.

Resist the urge to strike the winning blow by asking the ultimate question. Real evidentiary hearings do not play out like they do on television, and opposing witnesses will rarely agree with your conclusions. Do not tempt fate by asking the ultimate question; the only likely result is a vociferous denial by the witness and a loss of control of the entire argument. Instead, understand that the inferences from the details elicited from the witness can be argued to the court. The cross-examination should not give the witness the opportunity to disagree with those inferences or arguments. For example, it is difficult to imagine a police officer agreeing with defense counsel that she lacked a reasonable suspicion for stopping the defendant. However, if the testimony on direct examination indicates a shift in the officer's story from the one contained in the police report, defense counsel could attempt to have the officer elaborate on this new story and then argue to the court that the testimony should be discounted because it shows a marked departure from the original police report.

Finally, as a general rule, successful cross examinations resist asking questions for which the answer is unknown. One exception to the adage of never asking a question counsel doesn't know the answer to is when the answer, regardless of its substance, will be good for the case being presented. For instance, consider a defense counsel question to the officer such as, "You suspected my client of being a drug dealer from the moment you saw him, didn't you?" Regardless of the officer's answer, defense counsel is likely to find fertile ground:

Q. You suspected my client of being a drug dealer from the moment you saw him, didn't you?

A. No, of course not.

Q. But you testified, didn't you, that it was 10 p.m. at night, right?

A. Yes.

Q. And that this street corner, Washington and Main, was frequented by drug dealers?

A. Yes.

Q. And my client was walking back and forth talking with various people?

A. Right.

Q. But you didn't suspect him of being a drug dealer?

A. Well, um, I don't know what to say.

Consider this approach to examining the witness to draw out the information sought:

Q. You suspected my client of being a drug dealer from the moment you saw him, didn't you?

A. Yes, that's true.

Q. And that was based on the circumstances, right?

A. Yes.

Q. That it was 10 p.m. at night?

A. Yes.

Q. And that this street corner, Washington and Main, was frequented by drug dealers?

A. Yes.

Q. So your testimony is that you would have been suspicious of any person on that street corner that night?

A. Right.

Q. And just like my client, you would have frisked any person on that street corner that night, just for being there?

A. Well, um, I don't know what to say.

Both lines of questioning lead to a good result for defense counsel, regardless of whether the officer answers the initial question in the affirmative or negative. Either the officer seems less than credible by claiming he did not suspect the defendant from first sight based simply on the circumstances, or the officer admits that any individual who happened to pass by that evening would have subjected himself to a pat-down search for the perfectly legal act of walking along a particular street corner. In either event, the government's case for reasonable, particularized suspicion is damaged.

c. The Form of Cross-Examination Questions

Counsel can also remain in control of the examination through the form of the questions asked. Questions on cross-examination should be leading (*"The street lights were not working, is that right?"*). The focus should be on the story counsel wishes to tell. Thus, questions should be framed to include the answer and to elicit a simple "yes" or "no" from the witness. Counsel should avoid asking open-ended questions that begin with words such as "why."

The questions should be short. A direct question that seeks to elicit one fact is likely to minimize the risk of losing control. A longer question invites a longer answer from the witness, and longer answers generally mean an opportunity for the witness to make her case and therefore a loss of control by counsel. Moreover, questions should focus on discrete facts that do not indicate to the witness the ultimate purpose or point of the line of questioning until the witness has boxed herself in by her answers to the questions. Thus, it is generally not a good idea to confront a witness with an inconsistency until counsel develops as a factual basis for arguing an inconsistency. And, even then, counsel should be exceedingly careful to ask questions that call only for a yes or no answer. Confronting the witness (as opposed to using the inconsistency in a brief) gives the person the opportunity to explain that inconsistency to the court. Thus, for example, if there is a discrepancy between the agent's notes and the official report, defense counsel should consider asking questions designed to have the agent affirm the quality of her notes rather than asking directly for an explanation of the discrepancy.

Questions should not be fishing expeditions. The goal is to present the client's story through an adverse witness, not to engage in discovery of facts. A witness should never be asked open-ended questions on cross-examination or questions that invite the witness to explain herself. For example, defense counsel should not ask a police officer, "Why did you think this was a lawful search?" because the response will be a summary of the government's position. In addition, the age-old adage of never asking a question to which counsel does not know the answer is sound advice, although it is not always possible to know what the exact response will be. Of course, when the substance of the answer does not matter because counsel can make an argument either way (as was shown above), then counsel should not be afraid to pursue a possible fertile ground for argument.

D. PREPARING FOR ORAL ARGUMENT

Oral arguments are an opportunity for advocates to learn what the particular concerns of the court are and to answer them, or at least persuade the court that—notwithstanding those concerns—it should rule as counsel is suggesting. Courts decide many motions without oral argument, and thus, advocates are wise to anticipate that the court has particular questions if oral argument is scheduled in a case (especially if the court asks for argument after the briefs are filed). It is therefore critical that counsel approach an oral argument as a conversation with the court, as opposed to giving a speech.

To be prepared for this conversation, counsel should review the opponent's brief and the authority cited, as well as the authority cited in counsel's brief. In addition, counsel should review the record in the case. Because there may have been a time lapse between the time the motion was filed and the time of the oral argument, counsel should make sure that there have been no recent decisions that touch on the issues before the court.

Once this review is complete, counsel should then develop a clear statement of the issue, the legal standard, and the two or three reasons why the court should rule in her favor. And once able to state simply and clearly why the court should rule in her favor, counsel should develop a theme or "back pocket" that she can fall back on to explain why the court should in fact rule in her client's favor. This theme or back pocket should be one sentence, and it ideally is a point with which the opposing counsel cannot reasonably disagree.

It is important to think through the weaknesses of one's case in preparing for oral argument. It is easy for counsel to fall in love with his own argument and believe he should win. Yet, the court may have a different view of the law or the facts, and it is important to consider where any weaknesses may be. It is equally important to understand where concessions can be made without losing a motion, and where those concessions cannot be made.

After thinking through the above, the advocate for the moving party should prepare an introduction, including writing the introduction out if it helps counsel get started. The opening should begin (after introducing oneself) with the theme and a roadmap of the basic reasons that the court should rule in favor of counsel's client. While this introduction might be written out, it is important to memorize the introduction so that eye contact is made with the judge from the beginning. The rest of the argument should be outlined to stress the most critical points and authorities. It should not be completely written out because oral arguments are not orations. Moreover, counsel should practice moving between the points gracefully so that she can respond to questions and still make the points she would like to impress upon the court.

In contrast to the advocate for the moving party, the counsel for the responsive party should not generally prepare a scripted opening. Rather, the most effective responsive arguments have openings that are structured to address the points made by the court during the opening argument. Counsel should prepare to be responsive and to present her case to the court by creating an outline of the main points and her theme. Careful listening and notetaking during the oral argument of her opponent is essential here.

Finally, a word about the oral argument itself. It is important to recall that the purpose of the oral argument is to answer the court's concerns and that the time before the judge is likely to be limited. Therefore, it is vital to give the judge the opportunity to ask questions by looking directly at the bench and speaking slowly enough that the judge can intervene. As soon as a judge begins asking a question, the advocate should stop speaking. Moreover, the advocate needs to answer the question asked—regardless of where the advocate is in the argument. In answering the question, counsel should respond to it directly and then follow up with an explanation of the answer. In the end, counsel needs to be *flexible*. If counsel faces significant resistance on a particular point, it is best to move to a different issue rather than waste valuable time on something that the judge has already signaled she is rejecting.

SAMPLE MOTION WITH ARGUMENT

United States District Court
For the Eastern District Of Wayne

UNITED STATES OF AMERICA,
Plantiff

v.   Case No. _____

John Smith,   Honorable_____

Defendant

_____/

DEFENDANT'S MOTION TO SUPPRESS EVIDENCE,
OR IN THE ALTERNATIVE, FOR AN EVIDENTIARY HEARING

Defendant JOHN SMITH, by his attorneys George Michaels and Nancy Sims of the Federal Defender Office, moves this Court to suppress the evidence of a firearm seized from Mr. Smith on January 29, 2015. In the alternative, Defendant John Smith requests an evidentiary hearing on this motion. In support of this motion, the defendant states as follows:

1. On January 29, 2015, the defendant, John Smith, was unlawfully stopped and searched by the police.

2. The Fourth Amendment protects individuals against "unreasonable searches and seizures" by the government. U.S. Const. Amend. IV. This protection extends to brief investigatory stops of persons and vehicles that fall short of an arrest. *Terry v. Ohio,* 392 U.S. 1, 9 (1968). A person is seized for purposes of the Fourth Amendment when a police officer "by means of physical force or show of authority has in some way restrained [his] liberty." *Id.* at 19. When such a seizure occurs, the government must demonstrate a proper basis for the seizure, namely, that there was a "reasonable, articulable suspicion that the person has been, is, or is about to be engaged in criminal activity." *United States v. Place,* 462 U.S. 696, 702 (1983). Moreover, this suspicion "must be based on specific, objective facts." *United States v. Beauchamp,* 659 U.S. 560, 569 (6th Cir. 2011) (quoting *Brown v. Texas,* 443 U.S. 47, 51 (1979)).

3. Even if a stop is justified, a search is only reasonable when the government can show that there was "a reasonable suspicion that the person subjected to the frisk is armed and dangerous." *Arizona v. Johnson,* 555 U.S. 323, 327 (2009).

4. Mr. Smith was subject to a *Terry* seizure that was not justified when he was approached by two police officers on the corner of Washington and Main Streets. Mr. Smith complied with the request of police officers to approach them and he responded to their questions.

5. After seizing Mr. Smith, the police conducted a pat down and recovered a firearm from his person.

6. The police did not have reasonable suspicion to justify a *Terry* stop and frisk because there were no specific and objective facts that Mr. Smith had engaged in criminal activity. Nor was there a reasonable basis for the police to conclude that Mr. Smith was armed and dangerous.

7. Because there was no legal basis for the stop and seizure of Mr. Smith, the firearm seized from Mr. Smith and any other evidence obtained as a result of the seizure should be suppressed. *Wong Sun v. United States,* 371 U.S. 471, 487 (1963).

8. Counsel contacted Assistant United States Attorney Anna Freeman, who has declined to concur in this motion.[7]

9. Wherefore, Mr. Smith respectfully requests that this Court grant his motion to suppress the evidence seized and any statements or other evidence seized as a result of the unlawful search and seizure of Mr. Smith on January 29, 2015. In the alternative, Mr. Smith requests that this Court hold an evidentiary hearing and allow the parties to file supplemental briefs on this motion.

Respectfully submitted

FEDERAL DEFENDER OFFICE

s/George Michaels

Email:
Phone:

s/Nancy Sims

Email:
Phone:

Attorneys for Defendant John Smith

[address]

Date:

---

[7] Please note: Many trial courts require moving counsel to contact opposing counsel prior to filing a motion and to state the position of opposing counsel on the motion.

SAMPLE MOTION IF PLACING ALL ARGUMENT IN MEMORANDUM OF LAW

UNITED STATES DISTRICT COURT
FOR THE EASTERN DISTRICT OF WAYNE

UNITED STATES OF AMERICA,
Plantiff

v.   Case No. _____

John Smith,   Honorable_____

Defendant

_____/

<u>DEFENDANT'S MOTION TO SUPPRESS EVIDENCE, OR IN THE ALTERNATIVE, FOR AN EVIDENTIARY HEARING</u>

Defendant JOHN SMITH, by his attorneys George Michaels and Nancy Sims of the Federal Defender Office, moves this Court to suppress the evidence of a firearm seized from Ms. Smith on January 29, 2015. In the alternative, Defendant John Smith requests an evidentiary hearing on this motion. The support for this motion is provided in the accompanying memorandum of law. Counsel contacted Assistant United States Attorney Anna Freeman, who has declined to concur in this motion.

                              Respectfully submitted,

                              <u>s/George Michaels</u>

                              Email:
                              Phone:

                              <u>s/Nancy Sims</u>

                              Email:
                              Phone:

                              Attorneys for Defendant John Smith

                              [address]

Date:

SAMPLE PROPOSED ORDER

UNITED STATES DISTRICT COURT
FOR THE EASTERN DISTRICT OF WAYNE

UNITED STATES OF AMERICA,
Plantiff

v.   Case No. _____

John Smith,   Honorable_____

Defendant

_____/

ORDER

After reviewing the motion to suppress or for an evidentiary hearing submitted by the defendant John Smith, and the objections of the government to the motion to suppress, the motion for an evidentiary hearing on the defendant's motion to suppress evidence seized from him is GRANTED.

The hearing is scheduled for the following date: _____

Dated this _____ day of _____, _____.

By the Court: _____

Hon. _____

SAMPLE CERTIFICATE OF SERVICE

UNITED STATES DISTRICT COURT
FOR THE EASTERN DISTRICT OF WAYNE

UNITED STATES OF AMERICA,
Plantiff

v.   Case No. _____

John Smith,   Honorable_____

Defendant

_____/

CERTIFICATE OF SERVICE

  I hereby certify that on _____, I electronically filed the following document with the Clerk of Court using the ECF system which sill send notification of such following, and sent by electronic mail to Assistant United States Attorney Anna Freeman:

  Defendant's Motion to Suppress Evidence, or in the Alternative, for an Evidentiary Hearing.

            Respectfully submitted,

            <u>s/ Nancy Sims</u>

            Email:
            Phone:

            Attorney for Defendant John Smith

            [address]

SAMPLE MEMORANDUM OF LAW IN SUPPORT OF MOTION TO DISMISS FILED AFTER AN EVIDENTIARY HEARING

United States District Court
For the Eastern District Of Wayne

UNITED STATES OF AMERICA,
Plantiff

v.   Case No. _____

John Smith,   Honorable_____
Defendant
_____/

DEFENDANT'S BRIEF IN SUPPORT OF MOTION TO SUPPRESS EVIDENCE[8]

Defendant John Smith asks this Court to find that the stop and search of Mr. Smith on January 29, 2015, violated his Fourth Amendment rights and therefore to suppress the firearm seized as well as all evidence obtained by the Government as a consequence of the unlawful search and seizure. At the evidentiary hearing, Officer Jones admitted that he suspected that Mr. Smith was a drug dealer as soon as he saw Mr. Smith. The stop was thus based not on an objective and particularized indicia of criminal activity, as is required, but on Officer Jones' hunch that Mr. Smith was a drug dealer. Consequently, Mr. Smith's motion to suppress should be granted.

---

[8] This brief and the government's brief that follows are written for a district court under the jurisdiction of the United States Court of Appeals for the Sixth Circuit. The law is consistent in other circuits, but a brief should always focus on the law of the particular circuit in which the case is being heard (assuming the circuit has addressed the issue).

STATEMENT OF FACTS

[In this section, the writer should provide a chronological or topical discussion of the facts. The statement of facts should include citations to the record evidence and the transcript of the evidentiary hearing so that the judge can easily find the information needed to render a decision.]

ARGUMENT

Mr. Smith's Fourth Amendment rights were violated when he was stopped and searched on January 29, 2015. The Fourth Amendment protects individuals against "unreasonable searches and seizures" by the government. U.S. Const. Amend. IV. This protection extends to brief investigatory stops of persons and vehicles that fall short of an arrest. *Terry v. Ohio,* 392 U.S. 1, 9 (1968). When such a seizure occurs, the government must demonstrate a proper basis for the seizure, namely, that there was a "reasonable, articulable suspicion that the person has been, is, or is about to be engaged in criminal activity." *United States v. Place,* 462 U.S. 696, 702 (1983). Moreover, this suspicion "must be based on specific, objective facts." *United States v. Beauchamp,* 659 U.S. 560, 569 (6th Cir. 2011) (quoting *Brown v. Texas,* 443 U.S. 47, 51 (1979)). Even if a stop is justified, a search is only reasonable when the government can show that there was "a reasonable suspicion that the person subjected to the frisk is armed and dangerous." *Arizona v. Johnson,* 555 U.S. 323, 327 (2009).

Here, the government concedes there was a seizure under the Fourth Amendment and offered evidence at the evidentiary hearing in an attempt to justify the stop and search of Mr. Smith as consistent with the requirements of *Terry v. Ohio*. Because there was neither a specific objective basis for the stop nor a reasonable suspicion that Mr. Smith was armed and dangerous, Mr. Smith's Fourth Amendment rights were violated and the evidence must be suppressed.

I. The Police Lacked the Reasonable Suspicion Required for the Stop of Mr. Smith.

The government bears the burden of justifying a *Terry* stop by showing that there was some objective manifestation that the person stopped is, or is about to, engage in criminal activity. As the Supreme Court made clear in *Terry v. Ohio,* "[a]n officer must not act on an 'inchoate and unparticularized hunch." 392 U.S. at 27. Rather, a stop is permissible only if the officers have a "particularized and objective basis for suspecting the particular person stopped of criminal activity and were aware of specific and articulable facts which gave rise to reasonable suspicion." *United States v. Keith,* 559 F.3d 499, 503 (6th Cir. 2009). Here, this standard is not met.

In determining whether the government has met its burden of proof, the Sixth Circuit has instructed that ambiguity in conduct is not enough.

Rather, the government must show "the exact opposite of ambiguity: objective and particularized indicia of criminal activity." *United States v. Beauchamp,* 659 F.3d 560, 571 (6th Cir. 2011); *United States v. Davis,* 554 Fed. Appx. 485, 490 (6th Cir. 2014). In *Beauchamp,* the Sixth Circuit rejected the government's claim that a high-drug location, an early morning hour, talking to another person, and walking quickly away from an officer was sufficient to establish reasonable suspicion. *Id.* at 570–71. As the court explained, the first two facts could "apply to anyone who was in the [area] early that morning and therefore should not be given undue weight." *Id.* at 570. With respect to the defendant talking to another person, the court found that such a discussion simply "is not probative of criminal activity." *Id.* And, finally, the Sixth Circuit concluded that walking away from the officer was "susceptible to many different interpretations." *Id.* at 571. Therefore, the Court concluded that the defendant's conduct did not provide the type of objective and particularized indicia of criminal activity" required by the Fourth Amendment.

Similarly, in *Davis,* the Sixth Circuit upheld the district court's decision to suppress the evidence when the government attempted to justify the stop with innocuous and ambiguous facts. In *Davis,* the government pointed to the following facts: the officers saw the suspect at a gas station in a high crime area at midnight; the suspect walked toward the door of the gas station as the officers were approaching him; he made furtive hand motions in and out of his jacket pocket; and the officers saw a bulge that they believed was a gun in that pocket. 554 Fed. Appx. at 489. As the Court explained, this evidence consisted of innocuous facts and one ambiguous fact—"the bulge may have been a cell phone, wallet, or store purchases"—and therefore, there was not the "objective and particularized indicia of criminal activity" required under the reasonable suspicion standard. *Id.* at 491.

The testimony offered by the government at the evidentiary hearing similarly lacks an objective and particularized showing of criminal activity. There was no evidence that Mr. Smith was engaged in criminal activity. Officer Jones admitted at the hearing that he suspected Mr. Smith of being a drug dealer from "the moment" he saw him. [cite to Transcript of Hearing] Yet, it is precisely this type of hunch that the standard of reasonable suspicion was designed to protect against. As the Sixth Circuit found in both *Davis* and *Beauchamp,* the fact that an area is known for drug activity is not sufficient to justify the stop of a defendant. *Davis,* 554 Fed. Appx. at 489; *Beauchamp,* 659 F.3d at 570. But, that appears to be a principal reason why Mr. Smith was stopped. Moreover, as in *Beauchamp* and *Davis,* the other testimony offered by the police officers to support the stop—standing on a street corner and talking with a few people—were innocuous and did not show that a crime had taken or was about to take place. Thus, the Court should conclude that the stop was not supported by reasonable suspicion and suppress the evidence.

II. The Search of Mr. Smith Violated the Fourth Amendment.

Even if the initial search were valid, the evidence should be suppressed because the officers exceeded the scope of the search permitted during a *Terry* stop. [The memorandum of law would go on to address the search of Mr. Smith. It would conclude with the final components of the brief: Conclusion, Signature Block, Certificate of Service and Compliance (if required), and a Proposed Order.]

SAMPLE MEMORANDUM OF LAW IN OPPOSITION TO A MOTION TO DISMISS FILED AFTER AN EVIDENTIARY HEARING

United States District Court
For the Eastern District Of Wayne

UNITED STATES OF AMERICA,
Plantiff

v.

John Smith,

Defendant

_____/

Case No. _____

Honorable_____

GOVERNMENT'S RESPONSE TO DEFENDANT'S MOTION TO SUPPRESS

The Defendant's argument ignores both the law on reasonable searches and the facts adduced at the evidentiary hearing supporting the stop and frisk of the defendant. First, the Defendant asks this Court to look at each piece of evidence separately in evaluating whether there was reasonable suspicion for the stop. Yet, both the Supreme Court and the Sixth Circuit have made it clear that an evaluation of reasonable suspicion requires courts to consider all of the officer's observations under a totality of the circumstances analysis. Second, the Defendant asks this Court to focus on the Officer Jones's suspicions of the Defendant and ignores the officer's testimony that he observed the Defendant engaging in activity that confirmed his original suspicions before he approached the Defendant. Therefore, the Defendant's motion to suppress the firearm should be denied.

STATEMENT OF FACTS

[In this section, the writer should provide a chronological or topical discussion of the facts. The statement of facts should include citations to the record evidence and the transcript of the evidentiary hearing so that the judge can easily find the information needed to render a decision.]

ARGUMENT

The Fourth Amendment permits police officers to investigate suspicious activity by stopping individuals if the officers have a reasonable suspicion that the individuals are engaged in, or will engage in, criminal activity. *Terry v. Ohio,* 392 U.S. 1 (1968). Because police officers should not be expected to ignore the potential dangers associated with these brief detentions, officers are permitted to pat down suspects who are stopped if they have a reasonable suspicion that the suspects are armed and dangerous. *Arizona v. Johnson,* 555 U.S. 323, 327 (2009). Moreover, as the Supreme Court has explained, "Reasonable suspicion is a less demanding standard than probable cause not only in the sense that reasonable suspicion can be established with information that is different in quantity or content than that required to establish probable cause, but also in the sense that reasonable suspicion can arise from information that is less reliable than that required to show probable cause." *Alabama v. White,* 496 U.S. 325, 330 (1990). Because Officer Jones had reasonable suspicion for both the stop and pat down of the Defendant, the motion to suppress should be denied.

I. The Officers Had Reasonable Suspicion that Mr. Smith was Engaged in Criminal Activity.

In the Defendant's brief, he asks this Court to break apart the government's evidence and examine each piece to determine if the reasonable suspicion standard is met. This intense and individualized scrutiny, quite frankly, flies in the Supreme Court's admonition that *Terry* precludes this sort of "divide-and-conquer analysis." *United States v. Arvizu,* 534 U.S. 266, 274 (2002). Moreover, the Defendant ignores the fact that Officer Jones observed the Defendant for a period of them and saw activity that confirmed his suspicions. Because Officer Jones possessed reasonable suspicion for the stop, the Defendant's motion should be denied.

As the Sixth Circuit has explained, under the reasonable suspicion standard, "[t]he lawfulness of an investigatory stop is judged by the totality of the circumstances to 'determine whether the individual factors, taken as a whole, give rise to reasonable suspicion, even if each individual factor is entirely consistent with innocent behavior when examined separately.'" *United States v. Campbell,* 549 F.3d 364, 371 (6th Cir. 2008) (quoting *United States v. Perez,* 440 F.3d 363, 371 (6th Cir. 2006)). Moreover, this standard "allows officers to draw on their own experiences and specialized training to make inferences from and deductions about the cumulative information available to them that might well elude an untrained person." *Campbell,* 549 F.3d at 371 (quoting *United States v. Pearce,* 531 F.3d 374, 380 (6th Cir. 2008)). Finally, "while an 'individual's presence in an area of expected criminal activity, standing alone is not enough to support a reasonable, particularized suspicion that the person is committing a crime,' police 'officers are not required to ignore the relevant characteristics of a location in determining whether the circumstances are sufficiently suspicious to warrant further investigation.'" *Pearce,* 531 F.3d at 383 (quoting *Illinois v. Wardlaw,* 528 U.S. 119, 124 (2000)).

While the Defendant is correct in asserting that presence in a high-crime area alone is not sufficient to justify a stop, the Sixth Circuit has also recognized that the location of a high-crime area should be considered, especially "when 'the specific criminal history of the [area]' corresponds with 'the same crime for which the citizen was stopped.'" *United States v. Carter,* 558 Fed. Appx. 606, 610–11 (6th Cir. 2014) (quoting *United States v. Young,* 707 F.3d 598, 604 (6th Cir. 2012)). Thus, where the police officer observes conduct which indicates that the defendant is engaged in criminal activity in an area of expected criminal activity, the Sixth Circuit has repeatedly found that the reasonable suspicion standard was satisfied. For example, in *Campbell,* 549 F.3d at 371, the Court concluded that the cumulative observations of the officer, including a vehicle parked with lights out under a viaduct in a high crime area, coupled with the defendant's evasive answers and furtive posture, constituted a reasonable basis to stop the defendant. Similarly, in *United States v. Paulette,* 457 F.3d 601, 606 (6th Cir. 2006), the Court concluded that the reasonable suspicion standard was met when the defendant was in a high crime area, the officer saw the defendant engaged in activity consistent with drug dealing, and the defendant attempted to evade the police.

Here, the information taken as a whole that Officer Jones relied on for the stop meets the reasonable suspicion standard. As in *Carter,* where the Sixth Circuit recognized the relevance of the criminal history of the neighborhood when the history corresponds with the reason for stopping the defendant, here the Defendant was stopped on suspicion of engaging in drug activity in an area known for drug activity. Moreover, as in *Campbell* and *Paulette,* where the officers relied on the high crime context plus other corroborating information, here Officer Jones relied on more than the criminal history of the area. Officer Jones testified that he watched the Defendant for five to ten minutes. During this time period, the Defendant talked briefly with several people while staying on the corner. The officer testified that it was a combinations of these observations that made him suspicious that the Defendant was either dealing drugs or serving as a look out for a drug dealer. Thus, Officer Jones had articulable facts on which to base his stop and thus the reasonable suspicion standard was satisfied.

Moreover, the cases that the Defendant is relying on, *United States v. Beauchamp,* 659 F.3d 560, 571 (6th Cir. 2011), and *United States v. Davis,* 554 Fed. Appx. 485, 489 (6th Cir. 2014), can be distinguished from our case. In *Beauchamp,* the officer did not witness any activity from which he could infer criminal activity—the officer saw the defendant talking to one individual in a high crime area in the early morning hours. 659 F.3d at 570. In contrast, in our case, the officers observed the Defendant for five to ten minutes, and concluded that his behavior in talking to a number of people while standing on the street corner was "really suspicious." [Cite to evidentiary hearing transcript] Similarly, in *Davis,* 554 Fed. Appx. at 489, the police officers only observed the defendant walking toward a store, whereas in our case, Officer Jones and his partner observed the defendant for a length of time and relied on their "own experiences and specialized training to make inferences from and deductions about the cumulative information available to them that might well elude an untrained person." *Campbell,* 549 F.3d at 371. Given the totality of the circumstances, Officer Jones could investigate his suspicions further by approaching and briefly detaining the Defendant. Therefore, the Defendant's motion should be denied.

II. The Officers Had Reason to Believe the Defendant was Armed and Dangerous

[The memorandum of law would go on to address the search of Mr. Smith. It would conclude with the final components of the brief: Conclusion, Signature Block, Certificate of Service and Compliance (if required), and a Proposed Order.]

PART 4

PLEA AGREEMENT AND SENTENCING
■ ■ ■

CHAPTER 14

PLEA AGREEMENTS

■ ■ ■

Guilty pleas in the federal criminal justice system are governed by Federal Rule of Criminal Procedure 11. Guilty pleas may arise as the result of a negotiated agreement with the government or may be made "straight up" by a defendant without benefit of a plea agreement. The United States Sentencing Guidelines provide for a two- or three-level reduction in the offense level, depending on the severity of the underlying offense, in return for a defendant's "acceptance of responsibility," U.S.S.G. § 3E1.1, which in turn results in a lower recommended sentence. Because a guilty plea can result in the reduction of a sentence under the Guidelines, agreeing to resolve the case before trial can be in a defendant's best interest, even if the specific terms of an agreement cannot be negotiated satisfactorily with the government.

A guilty plea must be knowingly and intelligently made. The Supreme Court stated that "[a] guilty plea operates as a waiver of important rights, and is valid only if done voluntarily, knowingly, and intelligently. . . ." *Bradshaw v. Stumpf*, 545 U.S. 175, 183 (2005). Before accepting any guilty plea, a court is required to ensure that the defendant is making the plea voluntarily, and not as a result of force, threats or promises, other than those expressly contained in any written plea agreement. Fed. R. Crim. P. 11(b)(2). In addition, the court must ensure that a defendant is not under the influence of illegal drugs, alcohol or mind-altering medications at the time of the plea hearing.

Rule 11(b)(1) further requires that the district judge inform the defendant at the plea hearing of the constitutional rights and protections being waived as a result of the plea and of the basic requirements of sentencing. Courts usually engage in a lengthy plea colloquy at the outset of the plea hearing to satisfy this requirement. These mandatory recitations include:

- The right to a jury trial;
- The right to counsel, including appointed counsel;
- The right to confront adverse witnesses, to be protected from self-incrimination, to testify, to present evidence, and to compel the attendance of witnesses;

- The specific charges to which the defendant is pleading guilty, including any mandatory minimum sentence and the maximum possible penalty, including imprisonment, fine, term of supervised release, restitution, special assessment, and forfeiture;
- The court's obligation to calculate the Sentencing Guidelines range and to consider that range in imposing sentence;
- Any appellate or post-conviction waiver contained in the plea agreement; and
- The potential immigration consequences if the defendant is not a United States citizen.

To ensure that a defendant fully understands his or her other rights, and to establish a record for any challenge to the proceeding, some judges utilize a written plea questionnaire containing these same recitations. Courts may require a defendant to review this questionnaire with counsel and to sign it prior to the plea hearing.

Defense counsel frequently can make the greatest impact in plea negotiations *before* charges are filed by convincing the prosecutor to bring those that carry lesser statutory minimums or a sentencing guideline range at a lower level than might otherwise be charged. Even after charges are filed, prosecutors can agree to a reduced charge, although this is discouraged if there is evidence of a more substantial crime, absent good reasons for doing so. The United States Attorney's Manual § 9–27.300 provides that "a faithful and honest application of the Sentencing Guidelines is not incompatible with selecting charges or entering into plea agreements on the basis of an individualized assessment of the extent to which particular charges fit the specific circumstances of the case, are consistent with the purposes of the Federal criminal code, and maximize the impact of Federal resources on crime."

A. TYPES OF GUILTY PLEAS

Guilty pleas generally require a defendant to accept responsibility for the charged offenses. Rule 11 provides for two variations on the traditional acceptance of responsibility, although most courts will not accept such pleas without the consent of the government. First, a "conditional plea" allows a defendant to reserve the right to appeal an adverse determination of a specified pretrial motion, such as a motion to suppress. Fed. R. Crim. P. 11(a)(2). If the defendant prevails on appeal, the defendant has the right to withdraw the plea. Second, a *nolo contendere* plea allows the defendant to receive the benefit of a negotiated plea agreement without admitting guilt for the underlying offense or, in a variation known as an *Alford* plea, even maintaining innocence. In such a plea, the factual basis is described by the prosecutor, who recites the evidence obtained against the defendant. Because these pleas raise fundamental questions of fairness and justice, the government disfavors *nolo contendere* and *Alford* pleas. In fact, these types of pleas require approval from the Assistant Attorney General for the Criminal Division in Washington, D.C., and are used infrequently.

When the defendant and the government negotiate a written plea agreement, Rule 11 provides for two basic forms of agreement. A "B plea," named after Rule 11(c)(1)(B), sets forth a negotiated sentencing range agreed to by the parties, but that range is *not* binding on the trial court. Under such a plea, a defendant has no right to withdraw his plea should the court decide to sentence the defendant outside of the range set forth in the agreement. The majority of federal district court judges only allow plea agreements incorporating the conditions for a "B plea."

Unlike a "B plea," a "C plea"—made pursuant to Rule 11(c)(1)(C)—*binds* the court to the terms of the parties' agreement once the court accepts the plea. A minority of judges allow "C pleas." Under a "C plea," the district judge *must* either

- Sentence the defendant within the range agreed to by the parties;
- Allow the defendant to withdraw from the agreement if the sentence will exceed the agreed range; or
- Reject the agreement altogether.

Those courts allowing "C pleas" typically take a defendant's plea under advisement at the plea hearing. This permits the court to decide whether to accept or reject the plea at the time of sentencing, which usually occurs three to four months later. This interregnum allows the Probation Department to prepare a Presentence Investigation Report ("PSR"). The district judge then has an opportunity to review the PSR, along with any sentencing memoranda submitted by the parties, before deciding whether to sentence the defendant within the range agreed to in the plea agreement or to reject the plea. If the court were to accept the plea agreement at the time of the plea hearing under a "C" plea, the court would be bound by the parties' agreed range without the benefit of being able to consider these later-created materials.

B. CONTENTS OF PLEA AGREEMENTS

A plea agreement should include the parties' understanding with respect to the following terms:

- The counts of conviction and the disposition of any other charges;

- A factual basis, including any relevant conduct for purposes of computing the sentencing guidelines;
- The parties understanding of the appropriate sentencing guidelines range;
- The term of supervised release;
- The range for any fine;
- The amount of restitution;
- Whether the defendant will waive any right to appeal or seek post-conviction relief; and
- The circumstances under which each party can withdraw from the plea agreement and what subsequent use, if any, can be made of a defendant's withdrawn guilty plea.

Although the government and the defendant generally are able to reach agreement on all relevant terms, there is no requirement that they do so to enter into a negotiated plea. Rather, so long as the parties are willing to allow the court to resolve any disputed issues at sentencing, the parties must agree only on the counts of conviction and the disposition of other charges. Indeed, it is not uncommon for a plea agreement to contain competing sentencing ranges, different restitution amounts, and even disagreements as to the underlying factual basis for the plea.

When the government and the defendant do reach agreement on an anticipated Sentencing Guidelines range, the agreed range is premised on the parties' calculation of (1) the defendant's offense level, including relevant conduct and enhancements, and (2) the defendant's criminal history. It is not uncommon for the Probation Department's PSR to subsequently calculate a different sentencing range than the range agreed to by the parties. This difference may be because the PSR applied a different offense level, either including or discounting relevant sentencing enhancements. More often, the difference results from the Probation Department uncovering additional criminal history.

A plea agreement typically provides that in the event the defendant's criminal history proves greater than anticipated by the parties, the agreed sentencing range automatically will be adjusted upward and the defendant will have no right to withdraw from the agreement on that basis. But when factors other than criminal history drive an increased sentencing range, plea agreements usually do not provide for automatic adjustment. In such circumstances, if the court accepts the PSR's calculation, which it typically does, it faces a corrected sentencing range different than that agreed to by the litigants. In the case of a "C plea," this departure generally requires allowing the defendant an opportunity to withdraw from the plea agreement. In the case of a "B plea," of course, the court is free to sentence the defendant above the range agreed to by the parties and the defendant need not be permitted to withdraw the guilty plea.

A cooperation agreement is often a critical term in reaching a negotiated plea. The plea agreement may include this cooperation agreement. When there is some concern that the defendant's cooperation may create a safety risk, the cooperation agreement is put in a separate document. Under such circumstances, the guilty plea is taken in open court with the plea agreement filed with the court but the cooperation agreement is placed under seal.

A cooperation agreement requires a defendant to provide substantial assistance to the government, in exchange for the government bringing a motion for reduction in sentence pursuant to U.S.S.G. § 5K1.1 (at or prior to sentencing) or Federal Rule of Criminal Procedure 35 (after sentencing). Cooperation agreements are particularly valuable to defendants facing mandatory-minimum sentences because a court may only sentence a defendant below the statutory minimum if the government makes a motion under one of these provisions. In some cases, the cooperation agreement spells out the precise nature of the defendant's anticipated cooperation (*e.g.*, testimony at a co-defendant's trial) and the expected sentence reduction to be recommended by the government. More typically, a cooperation agreement leaves it to the government's *exclusive* discretion to determine whether the defendant has provided substantial assistance and, if so, the

> **Practice Note:** Most United States Attorney's offices maintain a grid, specific to each office, setting out a range of outcomes resulting from various types of cooperation. Because sentences vary widely depending on a host of factors, including the type of offense and a defendant's criminal history, these outcomes will usually be expressed as a percentage reduction from a particular sentence rather than a set number of months or years. For example, the most significant type of cooperation—a defendant's testimony at trial or before a grand jury—may warrant a 50 percent reduction in sentence. A more minimal level of cooperation, such as a truthful proffer leading to legitimate investigative leads, may warrant a 20 percent reduction. And conduct beyond these two examples, such as making a controlled buy of narcotics or participating in a monitored phone call, may justify a 30 to 40 percent reduction. In unique cases, the anticipated recommendation may be negotiable. But in all circumstances, it is important that both a prosecutor and defense attorney negotiating a plea with a cooperation provision know that office's standard practices to ensure that an appropriate sentencing recommendation is made.

value of that assistance in terms of a recommended sentence reduction. Ultimately, the court has the power to decide whether to grant a downward sentencing departure for a defendant's substantial assistance to the government. In all cases, a defendant's failure to provide truthful information or the commission of new criminal conduct will nullify a cooperation agreement.

C. WITHDRAWAL OF GUILTY PLEAS

Rule 11(d) governs a defendant's ability to withdraw a guilty plea after one is made. A defendant may withdraw a plea "for any reason or no reason" before the court accepts the plea. Fed. R. Crim. P. 11(d)(1). After a court accepts a plea, however, the defendant may only withdraw a plea if he can show "a fair and just reason." Fed. R. Crim. P. 11(d)(2)(B). In determining whether such a showing has been made, courts look to a variety of factors, including: (1) whether the defendant asserts his innocence; (2) the length of delay between the defendant's plea and the motion to withdraw; (3) the reason for such delay; (4) prejudice to the government; (5) the circumstances of the plea, including quality of representation; (6) defendant's background, including prior experience with the criminal justice system; and (7) the impact on judicial resources.

The most common reason for a defendant to move to withdraw his plea is a claim that the government has breached the plea agreement. This may happen, for example, when the defendant alleges that the government has recommended a sentence greater than the range agreed to by the parties. In such circumstances, the defendant may also move for specific performance of the agreement. Plea agreements are governed by the law of contracts, with any ambiguity construed against the government as the drafter of the contract. In rare cases, it is the government that alleges the defendant has breached the plea agreement. If the government proves this to be so, it can withdraw from the agreement and reinstate any charges dismissed as a result of the plea. *Ricketts v. Adamson*, 483 U.S. 1 (1987). Ultimately, it is up to the court to determine, by a preponderance of the evidence, whether any breach has occurred.

SAMPLE RULE 11 PLEA AGREEMENT

United States District Court
_____ District Of _____

UNITED STATES OF AMERICA,
Plantiff

v.   Case No. _____

D-_____,   Honorable_____

Defendant

_____/

RULE 11(c)(1)(B) PLEA AGREEMENT

The United States of America and _____ _____ ("defendant") hereby enter into the following Plea Agreement pursuant to Rule 11(c)(1)(B) of the Federal Rules of Criminal Procedure ("Fed. R. Crim. P."):

RIGHTS OF DEFENDANT

1. The defendant understands his rights:

   a. to be represented by an attorney;

   b. to be charged by Indictment;

   c. to plead not guilty to any criminal charge brought against him;

   d. to have a trial by jury, at which he would be presumed not guilty of the charge and the United States would have to prove every essential element of the charged offense beyond a reasonable doubt for him to be found guilty;

   e. to confront and cross-examine witnesses against him and to subpoena witnesses in his defense at trial;

   f. not to be compelled to incriminate himself;

   g. to appeal his conviction, if he is found guilty; and

   h. to appeal the imposition of sentence against him.

AGREEMENT TO PLEAD GUILTY AND WAIVE CERTAIN RIGHTS

2. The defendant knowingly and voluntarily waives the rights set out in Paragraph 1(b)–(h) above. The defendant is aware that 18 U.S.C. § 3742 affords a defendant the right to appeal the sentence imposed. Acknowledging all this, the defendant knowingly waives the right to appeal any sentence within the maximum provided in the statute(s) of conviction (or the manner in which that sentence was determined) on the grounds set forth in 18 U.S.C. § 3742 or on any ground whatever, in exchange for the concessions made by the United States in this plea agreement. The defendant also waives his right

to challenge his sentence or the manner in which it was determined in any collateral attack, including but not limited to a motion brought under 28 U.S.C. § 2255. This agreement does not affect the rights or obligations of the United States as set forth in 18 U.S.C. § 3742(b). Nothing in this paragraph, however, shall act as a bar to the defendant perfecting any legal remedies he may otherwise have on appeal or collateral attack respecting claims of ineffective assistance of counsel or prosecutorial misconduct. The defendant agrees that there is currently no known evidence of ineffective assistance of counsel or prosecutorial misconduct. Pursuant to Fed. R. Crim. P. 7(b), the defendant will waive indictment and plead guilty to Count __ of the Indictment filed on _____ __, 20__, in the United States District Court for the _____ District of _____. Count __ charges the defendant with violating Title __, United States Code, Section, [title of section]. At sentencing, the United States will move to dismiss with prejudice Counts [fill in numbers] contained in the Indictment filed on _____ __, 20__.

3. The defendant, pursuant to the terms of this Plea Agreement, will plead guilty to the criminal charge described in Paragraph 2 above and will make a factual admission of guilt to the Court in accordance with Fed. R. Crim. P. 11, as set forth in Paragraph 4 below.

FACTUAL BASIS FOR OFFENSE CHARGED

4. The defendant knowingly, voluntarily, and truthfully admits as fact the allegations contained in Count __ of the Indictment filed on _____ __, 20__, which are incorporated herein by reference.[9] The defendant agrees that those facts establish his guilt beyond a reasonable doubt. The defendant will also provide an allocution in support of his plea in open court.

POSSIBLE MAXIMUM SENTENCE

5. The defendant understands that the statutory maximum penalty which may be imposed against him upon conviction for a violation of __ U.S.C. § ____ is:

   a. a term of imprisonment of [maximum sentence] (__ U.S.C. § __);

   b. a fine in an amount equal to the greatest of [amount] (18 U.S.C. § 3571(b) and (d)); and

   c. a term of supervised release of __ year(s) following any term of imprisonment. If the defendant violates any condition of supervised release, the defendant could be required to serve the entire term of supervised release in prison (18 U.S.C.

---

[9] If a charge that is not included in the indictment will be the basis for the guilty plea, then the paragraph should read:

Pursuant to Fed. R. Crim. P. 7(b), the defendant will waive indictment and plead guilty at arraignment to a one-count Information to be filed in the United States District Court for the _____ District of _____. The Information will charge the defendant with one count of violating Title __, United States Code, Section ____, [title of section]. At sentencing, the United States will move to dismiss with prejudice the Indictment filed on _____ __, 20__.

CH. 14   PLEA AGREEMENTS   189

§ 3559(a)(6); 18 U.S.C. § 3583(b)(3) and (e)(3); and United States Sentencing Guidelines ("U.S.S.G.," "Sentencing Guidelines," or "Guidelines") § 5D1.2(a)(3)).

6. In addition, the defendant understands that:

a. pursuant to U.S.S.G. § 5E1.1 or 18 U.S.C. § 3663(a)(1)(A) or 3583(d), the Court may order him to pay restitution to the victims of the offense; and

b. pursuant to 18 U.S.C. § 3013(a)(1)(A)(iii), the Court is required to order the defendant to pay a $25.00 special assessment upon conviction for the charged crime.

SENTENCING GUIDELINES

7. The defendant understands that the Sentencing Guidelines are advisory, not mandatory, but that the Court must consider the Guidelines in effect on the day of sentencing, along with the other factors set forth in 18 U.S.C. § 3553(a), in determining and imposing sentence. The defendant understands that the Guidelines determinations will be made by the Court by a preponderance of the evidence standard. The defendant understands that although the Court is not ultimately bound to impose a sentence within the applicable Guidelines range, its sentence must be reasonable based upon consideration of all relevant sentencing factors set forth in 18 U.S.C. § 3553(a).

SENTENCING AGREEMENT

8. Pursuant to Fed. R. Crim. P. 11(c)(1)(B), the United States and the defendant agree the Court should sentence the defendant using the following Guidelines calculation ("recommended sentence"):

a. The November 1, 20__ edition of the Guidelines applies.

b. The controlling Guideline applicable to the count charged is U.S.S.G. § _____.

c. Pursuant to U.S.S.G. § _____, the base offense level is __. [If additional enhancements are applicable, note them here and provide the total offense level][10]

d. The United States does not oppose a [two- or three]-level reduction in the defendant's offense level, based upon the defendant's apparent prompt recognition and affirmative

---

[10] Insert the following if there is a disagreement regarding the application of one or more provisions of the Federal Sentencing Guidelines:

The parties disagree on the applicability of the following guideline(s): [list provisions]. The government recommends that the Court determine that defendant's guideline range is ___ months, as set forth on the attached worksheets. Defendant recommends that the Court determine that his guideline range is ___ months, as set forth on the attached worksheet addendum. The Court is not bound by either party's recommendation concerning the guideline range, and defendant understands that he will have no right to withdraw his guilty plea if the Court does not follow his recommendation.

acceptance of personal responsibility for his criminal conduct pursuant to U.S.S.G. § 3E1.1. The United States may oppose any adjustment for acceptance of responsibility if the defendant (a) fails to admit each and every item in the factual stipulation; (b) denies involvement in the offense; (c) gives conflicting statements about his involvement in the offense; (d) is untruthful with the Court, this Office, or the United States Probation Office; (e) obstructs or attempts to obstruct justice prior to sentencing; (f) engages in any criminal conduct between the date of this agreement and the date of sentencing; or (g) attempts to withdraw his plea of guilty. If a [two- or three]-level reduction for acceptance of responsibility is appropriate, defendant's adjusted offense level is ___.[11]

9. The parties agree that there exists no aggravating or mitigating circumstance of a kind, or to a degree, not adequately taken into consideration by the United States Sentencing Commission in formulating the Guidelines justifying a departure pursuant to U.S.S.G. § 5K2.0. The parties agree not to seek or support any sentence outside of the Guidelines range established in paragraph 8 nor any Guidelines adjustment for any reason that is not set forth in this Plea Agreement. The United States agrees to recommend that the defendant be sentenced within the Guidelines range established in paragraph 8, but not to recommend a specific sentence within that range. The parties agree that the agreed-upon Guidelines calculations set forth in paragraph 8 are reasonable.

10. The defendant understands that there is no agreement as to his criminal history or criminal history category, and that his criminal history or criminal history category could alter his adjusted offense level, if he is a career offender or if the instant offense was a part of a pattern of criminal conduct from which he derived a substantial portion of his income.

---

[11] If the prosecutor and the defendant enter into a cooperation agreement under which the government agrees to move for a downward departure below the recommended sentence, then insert the following paragraph:

If the United States determines that defendant has provided substantial assistance in any Federal Proceeding, and has otherwise fully complied with all of the terms of this Agreement, it will file a motion, pursuant to U.S.S.G. § 5K1.1, advising the sentencing judge of all relevant facts pertaining to that determination and requesting the Court to sentence defendant in light of the factors set forth in U.S.S.G. § 5K1.1(a)(1)–(5), and thus enabling the Court, in its discretion, to impose a sentence below the applicable Sentencing Guidelines ranges for incarceration and fine. The United States and defendant are free to recommend or argue for any specific sentence to the Court. Defendant acknowledges that the decision whether he has provided substantial assistance in any Federal Proceeding is within the sole discretion of the United States. It is understood that should the United States determine that defendant has not provided substantial assistance in any Federal Proceeding, such a determination will release the United States from any obligation to file a motion pursuant to U.S.S.G. § 5K1.1, but will not entitle defendant to withdraw his guilty pleas once they have been entered. Defendant further understands that whether or not the United States files its motions pursuant to U.S.S.G. § 5K1.1, the sentence to be imposed on him remains with the sole discretion of the sentencing judge.

11. The defendant understands that the Court will order him to pay a $25 special assessment pursuant to 18 U.S.C. § 3013(a)(1)(A)(iii) in addition to any fine imposed.

12. The United States and the defendant understand that the Court retains complete discretion to accept or reject the recommended sentence provided for in Paragraph 8 of this Plea Agreement. The defendant understands that, as provided in Fed. R. Crim. P. 11(c)(3)(B), if the Court does not impose a sentence consistent with the recommended sentence contained in this Agreement, he nevertheless has no right to withdraw his plea of guilty.

13. The defendant understands that he may be subject to administrative action by federal or state agencies other than the United States Department of Justice, based upon the conviction resulting from this Plea Agreement, and that this Plea Agreement in no way controls whatever action, if any, other agencies may take.

REPRESENTATION BY COUNSEL

14. The defendant has reviewed all legal and factual aspects of this case with his attorney and is fully satisfied with his attorney's legal representation. The defendant has thoroughly reviewed this Plea Agreement with his attorney and has received satisfactory explanations from his attorney concerning each paragraph of this Plea Agreement and alternatives available to the defendant other than entering into this Plea Agreement. After conferring with his attorney and considering all available alternatives, the defendant has made a knowing and voluntary decision to enter into this Plea Agreement.

VOLUNTARY PLEA

15. The defendant's decision to enter into this Plea Agreement and to tender a plea of guilty is freely and voluntarily made and is not the result of force, threats, assurances, promises, or representations other than the representations contained in this Plea Agreement. The United States has made no promises or representations to the defendant as to whether the Court will accept or reject the recommendations contained within this Plea Agreement.

ENTIRETY OF AGREEMENT

16. This Plea Agreement constitutes the entire agreement between the United States and the defendant concerning the disposition of the criminal charge in this case. This Plea Agreement cannot be modified except in writing, signed by the United States and the defendant.

17. The undersigned attorneys for the United States have been authorized by the United States Attorney for the [_____] District of _____ to enter this Plea Agreement on behalf of the United States.

18. A facsimile signature shall be deemed an original signature for the purpose of executing this Plea Agreement. Multiple signature pages are authorized for the purpose of executing this Plea Agreement.

NAME
United States Attorney

_____

NAME
Assistant United States Attorney

Date: _____, 20__

BY SIGNING BELOW, DEFENDANT ACKNOWLEDGES THAT HE HAS READ (OR BEEN READ) THIS ENTIRE DOCUMENT, UNDERSTANDS IT, AND AGREES TO ITS TERMS. HE ALSO ACKNOWLEDGES THAT HE IS SATISFIED WITH HIS ATTORNEY'S ADVICE AND REPRESENTATION. DEFENDANT AGREES THAT HE HAS HAD A FULL AND COMPLETE OPPORTUNITY TO CONFER WITH HIS LAWYER, AND HAS HAD ALL OF HIS QUESTIONS ANSWERED BY HIS LAWYER.

_____	_____
NAME	NAME
Attorney for Defendant	Defendant
Date: _____, 20__	

SAMPLE COOPERATION AGREEMENT

United States District Court
_____ District Of _____

UNITED STATES OF AMERICA,
Plantiff

v.

D-_____,

Defendant

_____/

Case No. _____

Honorable_____

COOPERATION AGREEMENT

Pursuant to paragraph ____ of the Rule 11 plea agreement entered into the parties this date, the parties agree as follows:

OPTION ONE (STANDARD): COOPERATION NOT COMPLETE; GOVERNMENT DECISION WHETHER AND WHEN TO FILE MOTION; AGREED UPON RECOMMENDATION

1. Cooperation. Defendant agrees to assist the United States Attorney's Office in the investigation and prosecution of others involved in criminal activities, as specified below.

A. Truthful Information and Testimony. Defendant will provide truthful and complete information concerning all facts of this case known to him. Defendant will provide full debriefings as requested to the U.S. Attorney, and federal, state, and local law enforcement agencies. Defendant will provide truthful testimony at all proceedings, criminal, civil, or administrative, as requested by the U.S. Attorney. Such testimony may include, but is not limited to, grand jury proceedings, trials, and pretrial and post-trial proceedings. Defendant agrees to be available for interviews in preparation of all testimony. Defendant further agrees to submit, upon request, to government-administered polygraph examinations to verify defendant's full and truthful cooperation. Defendant understands that this obligation to provide cooperation continues after sentencing and that failure to follow through constitutes a breach of this agreement.

B. Active Cooperation. The defendant shall provide the following active cooperation _____.

C. Nature of Cooperation. The defendant agrees to cooperate in good faith, meaning that the defendant will not only respond truthfully and completely to all questions asked, but will also volunteer all information that is reasonably related to the subjects discussed in the debriefing. In other words, the defendant may not omit facts about crimes, participants, or defendant's involvement, and then claim not to have breached this agreement because defendant was not specifically asked questions about those crimes, participants, or involvement. Defendant will notify the U.S. Attorney in advance if defendant intends to offer a statement or debriefing to other persons other than defendant's attorney. Defendant is not prevented in any way from providing truthful information helpful to the defense of any person. Any actions or statements inconsistent with continued cooperation under this agreement, including but not limited to criminal activity, or a statement indicating a refusal to testify, or any other conduct which in any way undermines the effectiveness of defendant's cooperation, constitutes a breach of this agreement.

D. Identification and Forfeiture of Property. Defendant agrees to identify all property known to defendant, in which defendant or any other person has a legal or equitable interest, that is or was the proceeds of, or acquired with the proceeds of, a drug or money laundering crime, or that was used in any manner to facilitate a drug or money laundering crime. Defendant also agrees to identify the extent of any person's or entity's (including defendant's) interest in any such property. Defendant agrees to forfeit to the United States, without contest, all personal and real property received as a result of drug trafficking or money laundering. Further, defendant agrees to transfer to the United States all other personal or real property, in which defendant has any equitable interest, obtained in whole or in part through the use of narcotics-related or money-laundering proceeds. Transfer of title, ownership, and interest will be completed prior to sentencing. If any other person or entity has any interest in such property, defendant will assist in obtaining a release of interest from any such other person or entity. Defendant will not transfer any interest in, or create any additional incumbrance on, any property listed for forfeiture.

2. Government's Authority Regarding Substantial Assistance

A. Substantial Assistance Determination. It is exclusively within the government's discretion to determine whether defendant has provided substantial assistance. Upon the government's determination that defendant's cooperation amounts to substantial assistance in the investigation or prosecution of others, the government will either seek a downward departure at sentencing under U.S.S.G. § 5K1.1, or a reduction of sentence pursuant to Fed. R. Crim. P. 35, as appropriate. If the government makes such a motion, the amount of the reduction, if any, will be determined by the Court.

B. Downward Departure. The parties agree that if the government makes such a motion at or before the time of sentencing, the government will recommend that the defendant be sentenced to a term of _____ months imprisonment. If the motion is made after sentencing (pursuant to Rule 35, Federal Rules of Criminal Procedure), the government will recommend the same departure as stated above. The Court may accept the government's recommendation and sentence defendant to a term of _____ months. Alternatively, the Court may reduce defendant's sentence but impose a sentence longer than _____ months, or the Court may refuse to reduce defendant's sentence at all. Defendant understands and agrees that the court's failure to reduce defendant's sentence, or its imposition of a sentence longer than _____ months shall not constitute a valid basis for defendant to withdraw from this agreement or to withdraw his plea of guilty.

(OPTIONAL)

The parties agree that, in the event the government makes a substantial assistance motion, defendant will not advocate that the Court impose a sentence which is less than that recommended by the government. The parties further agree that, in the event of a substantial assistance motion, if the defendant advocates a sentence which is less than that recommended by the government, the government may declare a breach of the agreement, and may seek all of the remedies set forth in Paragraph ___ of the Plea Agreement (regarding breach).

C. Use of Information Against Defendant. In exchange for defendant's agreement to cooperate with the government, as outlined above, the government agrees not to use new information that defendant provides (pursuant to this agreement) about defendant's own criminal conduct against defendant at sentencing in this case. Such information may be revealed to the court but may not be used against the defendant in determining defendant's sentence range, choosing a sentence within the range, or departing from the range. There shall be no such restrictions on the use of information: (1) previously known to law enforcement agencies; (2) revealed to law enforcement agencies by, or discoverable through, an independent source; (3) in a prosecution for perjury or giving a false statement; or (4) in the event there is a breach of this agreement.

OPTION TWO: COOPERATION COMPLETE OR GOV'T CONFIDENT DEFENDANT WILL FOLLOW THROUGH; COMMITMENT TO FILE MOTION; AGREED UPON REDUCTION.

1. Cooperation. Defendant agrees to assist the United States Attorney's Office in the investigation and prosecution of others involved in criminal activities, as specified below.

A. Truthful Information and Testimony. Defendant will provide truthful and complete information concerning all facts of this case known to him. Defendant will provide full debriefings as requested to the U.S. Attorney, and federal, state, and local law enforcement agencies. Defendant will provide truthful testimony at all proceedings, criminal, civil, or administrative, as requested by the U.S. Attorney. Such testimony may include, but is not limited to, grand jury proceedings, trials, and pretrial and post-trial proceedings. Defendant agrees to be available for interviews in preparation of all testimony. Defendant further agrees to submit, upon request, to government-administered polygraph examinations to verify defendant's full and truthful cooperation. Defendant understands that this obligation to provide cooperation continues after sentencing and that failure to follow through constitutes a breach of this agreement.

    B. Active Cooperation. The defendant shall provide the following active cooperation _____.

    C. Nature of Cooperation. The defendant agrees to cooperate in good faith, meaning that the defendant will not only respond truthfully and completely to all questions asked, but will also volunteer all information that is reasonably related to the subjects discussed in the debriefing. In other words, the defendant may not omit facts about crimes, participants, or defendant's involvement, and then claim not to have breached this agreement because defendant was not specifically asked questions about those crimes, participants, or involvement. Defendant will notify the U.S. Attorney in advance if defendant intends to offer a statement or debriefing to other persons other than defendant's attorney. Defendant is not prevented in any way from providing truthful information helpful to the defense of any person. Any actions or statements inconsistent with continued cooperation under this agreement, including but not limited to criminal activity, or a statement indicating a refusal to testify, or any other conduct which in any way undermines the effectiveness of defendant's cooperation, constitutes a breach of this agreement.

    D. Identification and Forfeiture of Property. Defendant agrees to identify all property known to defendant, in which defendant or any other person has a legal or equitable interest, that is or was the proceeds of, or acquired with the proceeds of, a drug or money laundering crime, or that was used in any manner to facilitate a drug or money laundering crime. Defendant also agrees to identify the extent of any person's or entity's (including defendant's) interest in any such property. Defendant agrees to forfeit to the United States, without contest, all personal and real property received as a result of drug trafficking or money laundering. Further, defendant agrees to transfer to the United States all other personal or real property, in which defendant has any equitable interest, obtained in whole or in part through the use of narcotics-related or money-laundering proceeds. Transfer of title, ownership, and interest will be completed prior to sentencing. If any other person or entity has any interest in such property, defendant will assist in obtaining a release of interest from any such other person or entity. Defendant will not transfer any interest in, or create any additional incumbrance on, any property listed for forfeiture.

    2. Government's Authority Regarding Substantial Assistance

    A. Substantial Assistance Determination. It is exclusively within the government's discretion to determine whether defendant has provided substantial assistance. Upon the government's determination that defendant's cooperation amounts to substantial assistance in the investigation or prosecution of others, the government will either seek a downward departure at sentencing under U.S.S.G. § 5K1.1, or a reduction of sentence pursuant to Fed. R. Crim. P. 35, as appropriate. If the government makes such a motion, the amount of the reduction, if any, will be determined by the Court.

B. Downward Departure. Based on the cooperation provided to date, the government shall file the motion referred to in Paragraph 2(A), and will recommend that the defendant be sentenced to a term of _____ months imprisonment. The Court may accept the government's recommendation and sentence defendant to a term of _____ months. Alternatively, the Court may reduce defendant's sentence but impose a sentence longer than _____ months, or the Court may refuse to reduce defendant's sentence at all. Defendant understands and agrees that the Court's failure to reduce defendant's sentence, or its imposition of a sentence longer than _____ months shall not constitute a valid basis for defendant to withdraw from this agreement or to withdraw his plea of guilty.

(OPTIONAL)

The parties agree that, in the event the government makes a substantial assistance motion, defendant will not advocate that the Court impose a sentence which is less than that recommended by the government. The parties further agree that, in the event of a substantial assistance motion, if the defendant advocates a sentence which is less than that recommended by the government, the government may declare a breach of the agreement, and may seek all of the remedies set forth in Paragraph ____ of the Plea Agreement (regarding breach).

C. Use of Information Against Defendant. In exchange for defendant's agreement to cooperate with the government, as outlined above, the government agrees not to use new information that defendant provides (pursuant to this agreement) about defendant's own criminal conduct against defendant at sentencing in this case. Such information may be revealed to the Court but may not be used against the defendant in determining defendant's sentence range, choosing a sentence within the range, or departing from the range. There shall be no such restrictions on the use of information: (1) previously known to law enforcement agencies; (2) revealed to law enforcement agencies by, or discoverable through, an independent source; (3) in a prosecution for perjury or giving a false statement; or (4) in the event there is a breach of this agreement.

NAME
United States Attorney

_____
Assistant United States Attorney
Date: _____, 20__

BY SIGNING BELOW, DEFENDANT ACKNOWLEDGES THAT HE/SHE HAS READ (OR BEEN READ) THIS ENTIRE DOCUMENT, UNDERSTANDS IT, AND AGREES TO ITS TERMS. HE/SHE ALSO ACKNOWLEDGES THAT HE/SHE IS SATISFIED WITH HIS/HER ATTORNEY'S ADVICE AND REPRESENTATION. DEFENDANT AGREES THAT HE/SHE HAS HAD A FULL AND COMPLETE

OPPORTUNITY TO CONFER WITH HIS/HER LAWYER, AND HAS HAD ALL OF HIS/HER QUESTIONS ANSWERED BY HIS/HER LAWYER.

_____   _____
Attorney for Defendant   Defendant

Chapter 15

Sentencing

■ ■ ■

After a defendant is convicted, whether at trial or pursuant to a plea, the federal court begins the determination of the appropriate punishment with the United States Sentencing Guidelines. The Guidelines provide a detailed map to a recommended sentence for most federal offenses. Under the Guidelines, it is not just the crime to which the defendant pleads or is convicted that determines the sentence. The judge can take into consideration other "relevant conduct" of the defendant, as well as the person's criminal history, background, and potential for future danger to the community, in setting the appropriate sentence.

The Guidelines are not mandatory. But judges must take them into consideration and explain the reasons for departure from the recommended sentence when choosing to impose a different punishment. Thus, both prosecutors and defense attorneys must determine the likely sentencing range under the Guidelines to negotiate a potential plea bargain, to decide to take the case to trial, and to argue for a particular sentence before the court. If the two sides do not agree on the appropriate application of the Guidelines in negotiating a plea, they can ask the judge to resolve the dispute at the sentencing hearing or at a presentencing hearing at which the court can receive evidence, receive testimony to make the appropriate Guidelines determination, and hear arguments from counsel.

A. SECTION 3553(a) FACTORS

Sentencing in the federal criminal justice system is governed by 18 U.S.C. § 3553(a). This statutory provision sets forth a series of defined factors that a district court must consider in imposing "a sentence sufficient, but not greater than necessary. . . ." These factors are:

(1) the nature and circumstances of the offense and the history and characteristics of the defendant;

(2) the need for the sentence imposed—

(A) to reflect the seriousness of the offense, to promote respect for the law, and to provide just punishment for the offense;

(B) to afford adequate deterrence to criminal conduct;

(C) to protect the public from further crimes of the defendant; and

(D) to provide the defendant with needed educational or vocational training, medical care, or other correctional treatment in the most effective manner;

(3) the kinds of sentences available;

(4) [the sentencing range determined by the United States Sentencing Guidelines];

(5) [consideration of pertinent policy statements issued by the Sentencing Commission];

(6) the need to avoid unwarranted sentence disparities among defendants with similar records who have been found guilty of similar conduct; and

(7) the need to provide restitution to any victims of the offense.

These § 3553(a) factors took on added importance in 2005, when the Supreme Court held in *United States v. Booker*, 543 U.S. 220 (2005), that the Sentencing Guidelines were advisory rather than mandatory. Although the Guidelines are advisory, district courts must begin sentencing proceedings by correctly calculating the applicable Guidelines range as "the starting point and the initial benchmark." *Gall v. United States*, 552 U.S. 38, 49 (2007). But, judges may not presume that the Guidelines range is reasonable. Rather, they are required to consider all of the § 3553(a) factors in arriving at a sentence and to make an individualized assessment based on the facts presented.

Gall held that a district court's sentence is reviewed on appeal for reasonableness, which has both a procedural and a substantive component. A sentence is procedurally unreasonable if the district court committed serious procedural error "such as failing to calculate (or improperly calculating) the Guidelines range, treating the Guidelines as mandatory, failing to consider the § 3553(a) factors, selecting a sentence based on clearly erroneous facts, or failing to adequately explain the chosen sentence—including an explanation for any deviation from the Guidelines range." *Gall*, 552 U.S. at 51. A sentence is substantively unreasonable if the district court selects the sentence arbitrarily, bases the sentence on impermissible factors, or gives an unreasonable amount of weight to any pertinent factor. An appellate court may apply a presumption of reasonableness in reviewing a within-Guidelines sentence but there is no presumption for a sentence falling outside of it. Moreover, when a trial court adopts a sentence that is a major departure from the Guidelines, the departure should be supported by a more significant justification than the justification for a minor departure.

B. THE SENTENCING GUIDELINES

A defendant's sentencing range is calculated by cross-referencing a defendant's "offense level" against the "criminal history" on the Sentencing Table. Offense levels range from 1 to 43, and criminal history categories range from I to VI. The Sentencing Table is broken down into four "zones." Zone A offenses are the least serious, with the lowest offense levels and criminal history categories. Zone A offenses carry recommended sentencing ranges of 0–6 months' imprisonment and the Guidelines stipulate that a probationary sentence generally is appropriate. U.S.S.G. § 5B1.1. Zone B offenses, with sentencing ranges between 4–14 months, and Zone C offenses, with ranges of 10–18 months, are more significant and may be satisfied through a combination of supervised release, community confinement, and imprisonment. U.S.S.G. § 5C1.1. Offenses coming within Zone D are the most serious and may involve a recommended sentence anywhere between 15 months and life imprisonment.

A defendant's offense level is calculated under Chapter Two of the Guidelines. Every federal criminal offense is indexed to at least one offense guideline section in Chapter Two. When more than one Guidelines section is cross-referenced to a particular offense, the court selects which section is most appropriate to the particular facts of the specific crime.

The Guidelines provide a base offense level for each crime. The base offense level is then adjusted upward or downward by a series of enhancements and reductions described both in specific offense characteristics set out in Chapter Two and in more generic adjustments found in Chapter Three. Specific offense adjustments may include the amount of money defrauded (U.S.S.G. § 2B1.1), the quantity of drugs distributed (U.S.S.G. § 2D1.1), the number of child pornographic images received (U.S.S.G. § 2G2.2), or the number of firearms possessed (U.S.S.G. § 2K2.1). Chapter Three adjustments include victim characteristics (U.S.S.G. Ch. 3A), the defendant's role in the offense (U.S.S.G. Ch. 3B), obstruction of justice (U.S.S.G. Ch. 3C), and the defendant's acceptance of responsibility. (U.S.S.G. § 3E1.1).

The credit afforded a defendant for acceptance of responsibility (such as pleading guilty) varies depending on the underlying offense level attributable to his criminal conduct. No more than a two-level reduction may be granted for an offense level of 15 or less. If the offense level is 16 or greater, it may be reduced by a third level, but only if the government certifies to the court that the defendant "timely notif[ied] authorities of his intention to enter a plea of guilty, thereby permitting the government to avoid preparing for trial and permitting the government and the court to allocate their resources efficiently." U.S.S.G. § 3E1.1(b). In some circumstances, the government can withhold the third-level reduction if the defendant fails to enter a guilty plea by a cut-off date set by the court or otherwise sufficiently in advance of trial.

Chapter Three also sets forth rules for "grouping" offense levels when a defendant is convicted on multiple counts. (U.S.S.G. Ch. 3D). When offenses are closely interrelated (*e.g.* a continuing course of conduct involving guns or drug trafficking), only the offense level for the most serious offense in that group is used, with quantities aggregated where appropriate. When offenses are independent of one another (*e.g.*, multiple instances of bank robbery) or unrelated (*e.g.*, one count of felon in possession of a firearm and one count of counterfeiting), Chapter Three instructs that the Guidelines calculation begin with the offense level for the most serious count, with the number and severity of additional counts enhancing the total offense level.

> **Practice Note:** The sentencing impact of small shifts in offense level and criminal history category are not proportional across the Sentencing Table. For relatively low-level offenses, a minor variance has little impact. For instance, a three-level increase in offense level from 12 to 15, assuming a criminal history category of I, will increase a defendant's sentencing range by less than a year, from 10-to-16 months to 18–24 months. Likewise, at an offense level of 13, an increase in criminal history category from IV to VI will result in an increase only from 24–30 months to 33–41 months. For more serious offenses, however, minor shifts can have a very substantial impact on the ultimate sentence. Thus, a three-level increase in offense level from 37 to 40, at a criminal history category of I, changes a defendant's advisory sentence from 210–262 months to 292–365 months. Likewise, a shift in criminal history category from IV to VI at offense level 38 results in a sentencing range of 360–life rather than 324–405.

Chapter Four of the Guidelines governs the calculation of a defendant's criminal history. Prior sentences served within the past 15 years are counted if they exceed 13 months in length. Sentences of 13 months or less, including non-custodial terms, are counted only if they were served within the past 10 years. The Guidelines also weigh longer sentences, like those greater than 13 months, more heavily than sentences lasting from 60 days to 13 months; sentences of 60 days to 13 months count more than sentences of less than 60 days. Additional criminal history points are added if the instant offense was committed while under a prior sentence.

Chapter Four also governs the treatment of career offenders, armed career criminals, and repeat sex offenders. "Career Offenders" are defined as those convicted of a crime of violence or drug trafficking offense, after having suffered two previous such convictions under either state or federal law. U.S.S.G. § 4B1.1. Career offenders are automatically slotted into the highest criminal history category, VI, and are assessed enhanced offense levels determined by the statutory maximum of the instant offense of conviction. "Armed Career Criminals" are those convicted of being felons-in-possession, pursuant to 18 U.S.C. § 924(e), after amassing three prior convictions for crimes of violence or drug trafficking offenses. In addition to a 15-year mandatory-minimum sentence, Armed Career Criminals face a minimum criminal history category of IV and a minimum offense level of 33. U.S.S.G. § 4B1.4. "Repeat and Dangerous Sex Offenders Against Minors" are those convicted of any child exploitation offense, excluding possession or trafficking in child pornography, after having sustained one previous such conviction. U.S.S.G. § 4B1.5. Such offenders face a minimum criminal history category of V and enhanced offense levels determined by the statutory maximum of the instant offense of conviction.

C. PRESENTENCE INVESTIGATION REPORT AND SENTENCING HEARING

For a criminal defendant, the sentencing process actually begins immediately or shortly after a guilty plea is entered or a finding of guilt is made following trial. Typically accompanied by counsel, the defendant is interviewed by a probation officer, who must conduct a presentence investigation and draft a Presentence Investigation Report ("PSR"). The PSR includes the history and characteristics of the defendant (including criminal history, drug and mental health issues, and family and financial circumstances), a description of the offense(s) involved and procedural history of the case, and the probation officer's calculation of the Sentencing Guidelines, as well as the amount of any restitution owed or fine to be imposed. Fed. R. Crim. P. 32(d). The PSR may also include the probation officer's sentencing recommendation to the court, although this recommendation typically is contained in a confidential addendum that is not shared with the parties. Fed. R. Crim. P. 32(e)(3). The PSR is not a public document and is available only to the prosecutor, the defense, and the sentencing judge.

The PSR must be provided to the parties at least 35 days prior to sentencing. Fed. R. Crim. P. 32(e)(2). Objections to the PSR's contents, by either the government or the defendant, must be made 14 days after receipt or are waived. Fed. R. Crim. P. 32(f)(1). Where such objections are minor or uncontested, they are resolved unilaterally by the probation officer. Fed. R. Crim. P. 32(f)(3). The court decides more substantial objections at the sentencing hearing. Fed. R. Crim. P. 32(i)(2). The court must resolve any disputes concerning the contents of the PSR at sentencing or in a presentencing proceeding at which the court can receive additional evidence and testimony, unless the court ignores any disputed portions of the PSR on the ground that it will not impact the court's sentence. Fed. R. Crim. P. 32(i)(3)(b).

At the sentencing hearing, after confirming that the defendant has reviewed the PSR and resolving any objections, the court must afford both the defendant and his attorney an opportunity to speak. Fed. R. Crim. P. 32(i)(4)(A)(i), (ii). In addition, the government and any victim present at the sentencing hearing must be allowed to address the court. Fed. R. Crim. P. 32(i)(4)(A)(iii), (B). After imposing sentence, the court is required to advise the defendant of his right to appeal. Fed. R. Crim. P. 32(j).

D. PROBATION AND SUPERVISED RELEASE VIOLATIONS

When a probationary sentence is imposed in lieu of a custodial term, and where a term of supervised release follows a custodial sentence, the release is accompanied by a series of conditions. Mandatory conditions include: (1) not committing any new criminal activity; (2) making any required payments towards restitution, fine, or special assessment; (3) avoiding illegal use of controlled substances; (4) surrendering a DNA sample; and (5) for various sex-related offenses, registering as a sex offender. 18 U.S.C. §§ 3563(a), 3583(d). The most common discretionary conditions include: (1) maintaining suitable employment; (2) refraining from use of alcohol; (3) not possessing or using firearms; (4) undergoing medical or psychiatric treatment; (5) residing at a community corrections center (*i.e.*, a halfway house); and (6) reporting as directed to a probation officer.

The court has discretion over the length of a probationary sentence. For a felony offense, probationary sentences may range from 1 to 5 years. 18 U.S.C. § 3561(c)(1). With respect to supervised release, the maximum term is determined by the underlying felony, with the maximum term increasing as the severity of the crime increases. For example, for a class E felony (those punishable by up to 5 years imprisonment), the maximum term of supervised release is one year. 18 U.S.C. § 3583(b). By contrast, for Class C (punishable by up to 10 years imprisonment) and Class D felonies (punishable by less than 25 years imprisonment), the maximum term of supervised release is 3 years. And, for Class A (punishable by up to life imprisonment) and Class B felonies (punishable by 25 years or more imprisonment), the maximum term of supervised release is five years. Finally, for certain child exploitation and terrorism offenses, the maximum term of supervised release is life. 18 U.S.C. §§ 3583(j), (k).

If the defendant violates conditions of supervision at any time prior to the end of the term, the court may either revoke probation/supervised release or continue the release, either with or without extending the term or modifying the conditions imposed. 18 U.S.C. §§ 3565(a), 3583(e).

Revocation is theoretically mandatory where the violation involves possession of controlled substances or firearms, although it is not uncommon for courts to ignore this requirement and it is rare for the government to appeal in this circumstance. 18 U.S.C. §§ 3565(b), 3583(g). When the court chooses to extend the supervision, it may do so up to the statutory maximum. 18 U.S.C. §§ 3565(a), 3583(e).

A defendant charged with a probation or supervised release violation is entitled to a hearing pursuant to Federal Rule of Criminal Procedure 32.1. This entitlement includes an initial appearance, detention hearing, and preliminary hearing to establish probable cause before a magistrate judge, and a substantive violation hearing before the district judge. The defendant is entitled to counsel at all stages of the violation proceeding. At the substantive hearing, the defendant must be provided: (1) written notice of the alleged violation; (2) disclosure of the evidence against him; (3) an opportunity to appear, present evidence, and question any adverse witness; and (4) an opportunity to make a statement and present any information in mitigation.

In the typical violation hearing, there is little dispute about the underlying conduct, which is well-documented by the defendant's probation officer. In fact, the defendant usually admits the underlying violation. Consequently, the hearing normally concerns the appropriate punishment. An exception to this general rule occurs when the probation violation consists of new federal or state criminal charges being lodged against the defendant. Under such circumstances, the defendant cannot admit the underlying conduct without creating a record in which he admits guilt that can be used in the parallel criminal case. The government, therefore, is required to prove the violation by a preponderance of the evidence. 18 U.S.C. § 3583(e). Since neither the rules of evidence nor the Confrontation Clause apply to violation hearings, some judges allow the probation violation to be proven through the hearsay testimony of defendant's probation officer, while others require direct evidence of the violation.

FORMS:

U.S. Sentencing Guidelines Worksheets:

http://www.ussc.gov/sites/default/files/pdf/training/online-learning-center/supporting-materials/Worksheets_for_Individuals.pdf

INDEX

References are to Pages

ARRAIGNMENT, 62–63

ARREST
Warrant, 3–5
Warrantless, 3

BAIL
Amount, 38
Appeal, 39
Conditions, 38–39

CHARGES (SEE INDICTMENT)

COMPLAINT
Requirements, 3–4, 6
Sample, 8–18

COUNSEL
Appointment, 20–22
Compensation, 22
Criminal Justice Act, 21–23
Discretionary Appointment, 23
Eyewitness Identification, 140–41
Fifth Amendment Right, 133–37
Initial Appearance, 20
Sixth Amendment Right, 138–39

DEFENSES (NOTICE OF)
Alibi, 87
Competency, 88
Insanity, 88
Notice, 87

DETENTION, PRETRIAL
Evidence, 37
Hearing, 35–36
Presumptions, 36
Pretrial Services Report, 38
Standard, 36–37
Temporary, 35

DISCOVERY
Brady
    Disclosure, 80
    Exculpatory, 81
    Material, 82
    Suppression, 81–82
Depositions, 78
Jencks Act (Rule 26.2)
    "Statement", 84
    Timing, 83
    Use, 85
Motion, 88
Reciprocal, 77
Requirements, 76–78

Rule 16, 76–78
Sample Defense Discovery Notice, 89
Sample Standing Order, 93
Subpoena, 79–80
Timing, 77–78
Witness Immunity, 85–87

ETHICAL RULES
Model Rule 3.3, 148, 149
Model Rule 3.4, 54
Model Rule 3.8, 7

EVIDENCE
Exclusionary Rule, 5, 47, 129–30
"Fruit of the Poisonous Tree", 129, 137, 139
Suppression, 5, 85, 99, 100, 117, 126, 129,
    130, 133, 136, 140, 144, 154

EVIDENTIARY HEARING
Conducting a Hearing, 154
Cross-Examination, 159–63
Direct Examination, 155–59
Preparation, 154

GRAND JURY
Indictment, 55–56
Rights, 49, 50–51
Subpoena, 49–50, 52–54

IDENTIFICATIONS
Due Process, 140
Sixth Amendment, 141
Timing, 140

IMMUNITY, 85–87

INDICTMENT
Amendment, 60
Bill of Particulars, 105–06
Duplicity, 57
Elements, 59
Grand Jury, 55–56
Joinder
    Defendants, 107–09
    Offenses, 110–113
Jurisdiction, 103–04
Multiplicity, 57
Notice, 58
Requirements, 103–05
Samples, 64–72
Validity, 56
Venue, 104

INITIAL APPEARANCE, 19–20

MOTIONS
Character, 114–15
In Limine, 113–16
Memorandum (Form), 166–67
Motion (Form), 168
Prejudice, 116
Prior Convictions, 114
Privileges, 113
Sample Certificate of Service, 170
Sample Proposed Order, 169
Suppression
    Good Faith, 130
    Identification, 140
    Miranda, 136–37
    Search, 117–19
    Sixth Amendment, 138–39
    Standing, 129
    Warrants, 119

PLEA AGREEMENT
Content, 183–84
Cooperation, 185
Sample Cooperation Agreement, 193–98
Sample Plea Agreement, 187–92
Types, 182
Withdrawal, 186

PRELIMINARY HEARING
Benefits, 45–46
Bindover, 46–47
Evidence, 43–44
Proof, 43
Testimony, 44
Timing, 43
Waiver, 44

PROBABLE CAUSE
Arrest, 4–5
Warrant, 118

PROSECUTORS
Discretion, 6
Ethical Obligations, 7
Organization, 6

SEARCH
Burden of Proof, 172–73
Consent, 128
Standing, 129
Warrant, 117–19
Exceptions, 122–27

SENTENCING
Factors, 199–200
Guidelines
    Adjustments, 201
    Base Offense, 201
    Calculation, 201–02
    Cooperation, 185, 201
    Table, 202
Hearing, 203–04
Presentence Report, 203
Probation Violation, 204
Supervised Release, 204

SPEEDY TRIAL ACT
Delays, 29–31
Requirements, 27–28
Sample Motion, 132–33

STATEMENTS
Miranda
    Custody, 134
    Interrogation, 135
    Invocation, 136
    "Fruit of the Poisonous Tree", 137
    Right to Counsel, 135
    Waiver, 136
Sixth Amendment
    Deliberately Elicit, 138
    "Fruit of the Poisonous Tree", 139
    Waiver, 139

TRIAL
Pretrial Conference,
Sample Pretrial Order, 93–95
Speedy Trial Act, 27–30

WARRANT
Arrest, 5
Exceptions
    Administrative, 127
    Exigent Circumstances, 124
    Incident to Arrest, 123
    Inventory, 125
    Plain View, 125
    Protective Sweep, 124
    "Stop And Frisk", 126
    Vehicle, 125
Execution, 5, 117
Probable Cause, 4–5, 118
Requirements,
Search, 118–19